M. U.

must
date
rev'

ECONOMIC GROWTH IN THE WEST

A TWENTIETH CENTURY FUND STUDY

ECONOMIC GROWTH
IN THE WEST

*Comparative Experience in Europe
and North America*

ANGUS MADDISON

THE TWENTIETH CENTURY FUND, New York

GEORGE ALLEN & UNWIN LTD, London

1964

TWENTIETH CENTURY FUND

The Fund is a non-profit, philanthropic foundation conducting research and public education on economic and social problems. It was founded in 1919 and endowed by Edward A. Filene. The Fund's income, administered as a public trust by a Board of Trustees, is devoted to its own research and educational activities. The Trustees choose subjects for research studies and vote the appropriation to cover the expenses of each project. The Trustees, however, assume no responsibility for the facts and opinions contained in research reports.

FIRST PUBLISHED IN 1964

PRINTED IN GREAT BRITAIN
in 10 on 11 pt. Times Roman type
BY SIMSON SHAND LTD
LONDON, HERTFORD AND HARLOW

FOREWORD

In studies of *America's Needs and Resources* and *Europe's Needs and Resources*, both under the direction of J. Frederic Dewhurst, the Twentieth Century Fund concerned itself with the problems and prospects of economic advance on the two sides of the North Atlantic. The present complementary work by Angus Maddison, briefer and more specialized but in its way as ambitious, is an effort to place in historical perspective the recent growth record of the major industrial countries of the Western world. Confronted by dramatic expansion of the continental European economy and a much slower rate of growth in the United Kingdom, the United States and Canada, we need to understand the reasons for the differences, and how far they have been influenced by policy rather than by adventitious factors. It is this which Mr. Maddison attempts to do, always with a mind to desirable lines of policy.

Mr. Maddison brings to this study wide experience with economic analysis and forecasting. Since 1953 he has been on the staff of the Organisation for European Economic Co-operation (now the Organisation for Economic Cooperation and Development), of which he became head of the Economics Division in 1958 and Director in the Development Department in 1963. The Twentieth Century Fund was fortunate that its interests and Mr. Maddison's coincided. He had been pursuing the present study for two years when the Fund undertook its sponsorship, enabling him to take leave from the O.E.C.D. in order to complete the research and writing.

AUGUST HECKSCHER, Director
The Twentieth Century Fund

41 East 70th Street, New York, N.Y.
August 1963

ACKNOWLEDGMENTS

I am greatly indebted to the Twentieth Century Fund for making it possible for me to take leave of absence from the O.E.C.D. to write this study. I am indebted also for the cooperation of the Fund staff. August Heckscher, Director of the Fund, and Thomas R. Carskadon and Ben Moore, Associate Directors, gave active encouragement and advice. Isador Lubin, Economic Consultant, made helpful comments on the whole manuscript. Elizabeth Blackert and Ruth Rocker prepared the manuscript for the printer and persuaded me to rewrite the more obscure passages.

Among the many individuals whom I consulted, I would like to thank in particular Odd Aukrust, Graham Bannock, Gilbert Bloch, Christopher Dow, C. H. Feinstein, Charles Ford, Louis Goreux, John and Anne-Marie Hackett, Professor Walther Hoffmann, Friedrich Kahnert, John W. Kendrick, Rolf Krengel, Jim McGibbon, Olaf Saetersdal, Professor H. A. Turner and Professor M. C. Urquhart. I am especially grateful to Wilfred Beckerman, J. Frederic Dewhurst and Milton Gilbert, with whom I have been discussing the issues covered in this book for many years.

I would also like to thank Luigi Ceriani for allowing me to reproduce some of the statistical material which I originally published in the *Quarterly Review* of the Banca Nazionale del Lavoro.

My biggest debt is to the O.E.C.D. where I have worked for more than ten years on the economic policy problems of the countries covered in this book.

ANGUS MADDISON

Paris, August 1963

CONTENTS

TABLES

INTRODUCTION

The purpose of this study is to compare the economic growth of the advanced industrial countries of Western Europe and North America over the past century in order to put their post-war performance into perspective. In continental Europe the economic achievements of the 1950s were unprecedented; by contrast with the continent, the economies of North America and the United Kingdom seemed to stand still. The facts about growth rates are set out in Chapter I. In the rest of the book our aim is to discover whether these developments of the 1950s represented a new trend or a passing phase of recovery, to see why some countries did better than others, to examine the role which economic policy played and to see whether we can distill a strategy for high growth in the future.

The twelve countries examined (see Table I–1) account for about half of world income, 60 per cent of world trade and industrial production, and a third of agricultural output. As they constitute only 15 per cent of the world's population, they are the world's richest countries. Few countries outside this group have comparable levels of income—perhaps only Australia and New Zealand. On average, our group of countries had a *per capita* income of $2,000 (at U.S. relative prices) in 1960 compared with an average for the rest of the world of about $300.

Apart from their importance in the world economy, the comparative development of these countries is worth examining because they have a basically similar economic system. All in their various ways are free enterprise or neo-capitalist economies, with most production activity in private hands. Although the government participates in the production process to some degree, public enterprises are in most cases run in the same way as private corporations, and the pattern of output is determined by entrepreneurs and consumers. The state modifies rather than determines the flow of income. The economy is a managed market economy.

These countries are closely linked by trade, and in the past decade have liberalized their commercial policies to enhance this interdependence. They are increasingly interdependent financially. They all have convertible currencies and only vestigial exchange controls. They include all the world's major capital exporters and the flow of capital between them is a rapidly growing portion of total international capital movements. Because of these trade and payments links, geographic propinquity, business and intellectual contacts, these countries built up in common and are constantly developing a modern industrial technology. Most of the ideas and practical know-how of modern industry have emanated from these countries; only in the past two or three decades have substantial contributions been made elsewhere—in Japan and the U.S.S.R.

Most of these countries are bound in close political association. In treating them as a group we are contributing to the study of their competitive co-existence with the Sino-Soviet group where production and resource allocation are decided entirely by the state. As we have not undertaken a comparative analysis of the performance of the Sino-Soviet economies, we can throw only incidental light on this question. Our main concern is to see what recipes for faster growth may be derived from within the economic system and policy methods of the West. The analysis is limited in some respects, as it is concentrated on the range of growth experience within our group; we have not enquired too deeply into the means by which the faster-growing countries could have improved their performance, as might be done in a study of co-existence. Nevertheless, it seems legitimate to assume that the scope for better performance in the Western industrial world is greatest in the slower-growing countries. It also seems likely that significant acceleration of Western growth must mainly rely upon acceleration in the slowest-growing countries—the United States and the United Kingdom—as they produce more than half the total Western output. It is not obvious that the Sino-Soviet group is doing better than the faster-growing countries covered here, though they are growing faster than the free-enterprise group as a whole. It is more of a weakness that this study omits Japan, which is operating within the same economic system and has been growing at a faster rate than any country in Europe. However, Japanese income levels are still below the range included in our group of countries, and large parts of the economy lead a separate or 'dual' existence, unaffected by the general momentum of growth and more akin to the situation in underdeveloped countries.

It is perhaps invidious to neglect the problems of the world's poorer countries and to devote a book to the problems of how the rich countries can get richer, at a time when so much literature and effort is devoted to narrowing the gap between the two. Yet the development of the richer countries deserves more analysis than it has received. It is surprising that the successes of post-war capitalism have aroused fewer studies than did its pre-war failures, or its post-war failures—such as inflation and payments problems. This is perhaps because so much of economic literature is in English and the post-war achievements of the English-speaking economies have not been so impressive.[1] Not only is rapid growth essential to the

---

[1] The recent tendency for Marxist economists to re-assess the prospects for capitalism is, however, significant. They have apparently abandoned the idea of the imminent collapse of capitalism in adopting the theory of competitive co-existence, but their confidence that the Soviet bloc can grow more quickly than

advancing welfare of the rich countries, but it is essential for the progress of the world economy that the rich countries get richer. They will thus be enabled to export more capital and provide better markets to the less privileged. And the process of pushing forward the frontiers of technology, even though it may not help to raise the relative position of the less developed, adds to the welfare of everybody in absolute terms.

The problem of explaining economic growth is of so broad a character that adequate analysis or testing of hypotheses requires comparisons between countries. We are fortunate to have twelve countries which have similar social and economic institutions and policy objectives but enough diversity of experience, size, temperament, history and politics to ensure that among them they have tried out most of the feasible policy weapons in some way or other. It is also helpful that the close economic cooperation between these countries in O.E.E.C. and O.E.C.D. has produced a fund of comparative statistics which makes possible a serious quantitative study of the growth record.

Several parts of the analysis, particularly on policy matters, concentrate on the problems of the largest countries. This is partly because of limits of time and space, but also because the fate of the others depends to a major extent on the large ones. They are not as specialized as the smaller countries, and hence their difficulties are less likely to be specific or structural than might be the case in Norway heavily dependent on shipping, or Denmark on bacon and eggs. The problems of attaining external balance are more difficult in the big countries, because of their size, than in smaller countries. It is less easy to deal with their liquidity needs or for them to change their exchange rates, and in many ways they seem to have greater political difficulty in making policy adjustments than do the smaller countries.

It cannot be claimed that the present analysis of the forces determining growth is of general applicability. The explanations of accelerated growth or the policy lessons derived here for developed countries may not be applicable to less-developed ones. The industrial countries all have a well-established entrepreneurial tradition, a diversity of skills, an articulated economic, institutional and financial structure, and a capacity for adaptation which make it feasible to analyze their problems in a macro-economic fashion, and to assume that general economic policy weapons are reasonably

the West is based largely on observation of U.S. performance. The formal acceptance of the possibility that with the aid of appropriate government policy capitalism can withstand major deflationary shocks is contained in the signature of the 1962 U.N. report on the economic consequences of disarmament by the Soviet economist V. Y. Aboltin.

B

adequate to keep the economy moving. This type of analysis must be used with much greater caution in less-developed countries where problems of structural adjustment are greater and general policy weapons less effective. Although our approach is almost wholly macro-economic, it nevertheless attempts to explain how the macro-economic factors made their impact felt on the motivations and decisions of entrepreneurs, which are a key element determining the momentum of this type of economy.

The argument does not allow much scope for misallocation of resources, or for differences in technical dynamism and management efficiency as explanatory variables for the difference in performance between fast- and slow-growing countries. Some of the analysis is devoted to structural changes, but we did not find them to be of sufficient importance to enter into the kind of industrial detail which figures so largely in Svennilson's classic study of the anatomy of inter-war stagnation.[1] There are, of course, inefficient practices and anti-growth policies in all countries due to efforts by pressure groups to protect inefficient sectors such as agriculture. These may affect growth to different degrees, but they have been practiced in both fast- and slow-growing countries.

This study did not arise from any desire to theorize about growth, but out of a practical interest in forecasting what the future development of the Western industrial economies would be. Our basic concern is to explain why accelerated growth occurred in mature economies that had been relatively stagnant for several decades in order to see whether the forces making for acceleration are likely to continue. The theoretical underpinning is rather simple.

A necessary condition for the full exploitation of the growth potential is a high and steadily expanding level of aggregate demand uninterrupted by major domestic or external deflationary forces. If this condition is fulfilled, entrepreneurs will have optimistic profit and market expectations. Because of the reduction in their macro-economic risks, they will maintain a higher rate of investment than they would in a position of slack capacity use, recurrent falls in activity, and downward price movements. A condition of high and stable demand was secured in post-war Europe by an active fiscal and monetary policy. There is every reason to believe that the successful experience of Europe in managing demand (analyzed in Chapter IV) represents a permanent sophistication in the technique of managing a capitalist economy with fairly general policy instruments. Further refinements would help, but the basic equipment of fiscal and monetary policy has been rather fully used in Europe. Unfortunately this is not true of the United States. There, policy was apathetic, and

---

[1] Ingvar Svennilson, *Growth and Stagnation in the European Economy*, E.C.E., Geneva, 1954.

resources went unused, even though the need to manage demand was greater than in Europe because the U.S. economy had less pent-up demand and entrepreneurs faced greater uncertainties, being nearer to the fringe of knowledge of technology and of future consumer tastes. The United States has thus a good deal to learn from Europe in the art of economic management. It particularly needs to develop an active fiscal policy.

The role of government in economic growth is not simply to maintain demand. Governments can also help foster the supply potential of the economy in several ways. They can take measures to increase the proportion of resources devoted to investment, they can improve skills and knowledge by education and research and give publicity to best-practice technologies, and they can provide perspective and guidance by making long-term forecasts. They can foster competition and improve allocation of resources by removing barriers to trade. In several of these respects a great deal was done by European governments in the 1950s. It is also true that some things were not done, particularly in the United Kingdom, which must be done in future to ensure a continuance of high growth rates.

The relative efficiency of policy cannot be judged simply by comparing the growth rates achieved in different countries. The physical growth potential of these countries varies and Chapter II attempts to explain the various major elements affecting this potential in order to clarify the analysis of the impact of policy.

Some of the growth of the 1950s was due to once-for-all factors such as the increased utilization of the labor force, the elimination of disguised unemployment accumulated in the previous decades of stagnation, and the reopening of the economies to the full benefits of international specialization. These once-for-all elements were larger in some economies than others and the rates of growth of the 1950s were exceptional to this extent. This does not mean that growth rates will now revert to those experienced in previous decades. All the European economies had made less than full use of their potential in the past because governments failed to provide a high and stable level of demand. Now that governments are doing this, the risks of investment have been reduced, and a momentum has been generated which is likely to maintain European growth at rates much higher than the long-run historical experience.

The major reason for assuming that the European economy has this increased supply potential, at least for several decades to come, is that the productivity level in Europe is only half that in the United States, and most of this productivity gap is due to missed investment opportunities. The European countries are working below the fringe of best-practice technology. They can push their rate of investment to a higher level than the United States without running into diminishing returns. They benefit from the fact that they will be harnessing techniques and factor combinations which to a wide degree are already known. The United States, having borne these pioneering burdens in the field of technology, has more restricted opportunities for productivity growth. Not that there are natural equilibrating forces which ensure that the United States as the most affluent country will have a slower productivity growth than Europe. This has obviously not been true historically. A fast growth of population, absence of war risks, and to some degree a superiority of natural resources led the United States to higher rates of investment and growth for decades, and led to a widening of the productivity lead it had already established in 1870. We are simply arguing that countries which have missed their chances can recoup something of the gap if they make sufficient effort. Europe is now making the effort, and is harnessing the equilibrating potential offered by known technology and high investment.

Chapter III gives a rather complex explanation of why the return on investment has differed between countries, demonstrates the interaction of investment and technical progress and attempts to show the relation between the return on investment for the economy and the rates of return actually experienced by entrepreneurs. This was done in some detail because we consider high investment to have been the major instrument by which the economies of Europe exploited their growth potential. We have been particularly concerned to provide rational explanations for the apparently erratic variation in capital-output ratios between countries, in order to counteract the type of argument which attributes acceleration of growth to waves of innovation, differences in entrepreneurial ability, or other accidental and uncontrollable factors. This discussion was necessary to justify our general emphasis on the explainable elements in growth and on the role of policy.

Some of the major problems of economic growth arise from the interdependence of economies. An open economic system provides both opportunities and challenges to growth. The flow of goods and capital allows specialization on the part of the lowest-cost producers, gives the consumer a much wider range of choice, and stimulates the growth and spread of technology. The flow of capital tends to equalize income levels if it moves in an equilibrating direction. On the other hand, external trade creates additional uncertainty and instability about part of one's market, foreign capital movements can be disturbing and the need to balance one's payments can be in conflict with the needs of domestic policy. The problems of international equilibrium are treated at some length because they were the major obstacle to growth in the 1950s in the United Kingdom. They have also become a major problem for the United States and reinforce the need for the United States to activate its economic policy effort.

These problems are examined in Chapter V. On the whole the external factors affecting growth were favorable in the 1950s. The fact that all European countries were simultaneously following expansionary demand policies and liberalizing their trade meant that export opportunities were good. External opportunities helped foster demand and productivity. The bulk of capital flows were governmental and stimulating to growth. Relations between countries were largely those of mutual trust. However, fluctuations in both exports and imports were a major source of demand instability, there were substantial destabilizing capital movements and there were persistent problems of attaining payments balance in the major countries. The lack of success in the payments field was the major obstacle to accelerated growth in the United Kingdom, as it led to domestic policies which created instability and harmed investment incentives.

In recent discussions of international payments problems heavy emphasis has been placed on the shortage of liquidity, but this was not a major problem of the 1950s for most countries except the United Kingdom. The real problem was the inadequacy of policy weapons to achieve the right degree of competitiveness. The chief drawback in international liquidity arrangements is that they lacked any degree of automaticity after the European Payments Union ended. In a system with free trade and fixed exchange rates there are very few special-purpose policy weapons which can affect the foreign balance substantially. Import controls and changes in exchange rates are too disturbing to the present payments system to be used except in extreme circumstances. A change in the payments system towards floating exchange rates could also be very dangerous for economic growth. Countries have had to surrender many of the policy weapons which fifteen to twenty years ago would have been regarded as the most powerful in their full-employment armory. It is because of a failure to develop an incomes policy as a substitute for those begger-your-neighbour correctives that the slow-growing countries have not done better.

In such a system the major burden of adjustment must be achieved by management of the price level, for the foreign balance is very sensitive to the relative price level. Management of the price level has proved extremely difficult because it involves government in the process of income determination, a problem most governments fought shy of in the 1950s. It was tried with success in the Netherlands and was independently achieved by the social wisdom of the Swedish and Norwegian employers and workers. In the early 1960s, however, most governments moved towards such a policy, and there was even some feeling that the obligations were symmetric as between surplus and deficit countries. It remains to be seen how successful this move will be. It is not a new field for governments, for all have an influence on income distribution through tax policy, but to affect the income stream directly by influencing employers', workers' and farmers' organizations requires great political skill. A satisfactory solution will involve greater participation of the major economic interest groups in the formulation of economic policy.

Another major problem of international equilibrium is the management of international capital movements. Such movements can be large and disturbing in the short-term and a longer-term problem may also arise if the United States economy continues to grow slowly while Europe grows fast. The United States would tend to assume the position that the United Kingdom occupied in the years 1870–1913. The United Kingdom then found its domestic prospects for profitable investment limited, and put a growing proportion of its savings abroad, as much as 8 per cent of gross national product by 1913. Given the level of U.S. government spending abroad it is unlikely that the United States would ever be able to finance a private capital outflow on this scale even if it were prepared to accept the implied deceleration in domestic growth. On both long- and short-term grounds, therefore, governments need to strengthen the special-purpose policy weapons which can modify the flow of international capital.

Thus the basic problems of an economic growth policy in the industrial West are not technical but political and institutional. The principal elements of such a policy are four: (a) a willingness of government to manage the level of overall demand so that resources are fully utilized and recessions avoided; (b) the maintenance of a competitive price level which requires both the management of demand and a measure of agreement on the fundamental aims of policy by workers, employers and the other major interest groups; (c) the stimulation of the growth potential by fostering savings and investment, improvement of education and research, effective management of state-owned enterprises, stimulation of efficient resource allocation through international trade and competition, and the provision of some explicit quantitative perspective of the economy's potential in a form which will stimulate entrepreneurs, investors and consumers to reach it; (d) a continuance of cooperative international arrangements and abstaining from the use of policy weapons which are harmful to one's neighbours.

Most of these problems except the first involve the resolution of conflicting group interests. The style adopted and the precise policies followed will vary with the country's institutions and the party in office. The limiting factors on growth will also vary with the level of development and with the country's past history; not all countries can achieve the same growth rates. However, there will probably be something wrong with policy if productivity grows less than 3 per cent a year in European countries, or 2·5 per cent in the United States. The same will be true if unemployment goes above 2 per cent by European definitions or is much above 3 per cent by U.S. definitions. If these levels are not attained the blame cannot all be laid at the door of individual national governments. Our economies are interdependent to a degree that makes growth a joint responsibility.

CHAPTER I

THE RECORD OF WESTERN GROWTH

In continental Europe the decade of the 1950s was brilliant, with growth of output and consumption, productivity, investment and employment surpassing any recorded historical experience, and the rhythm of development virtually uninterrupted by recession. In France and Switzerland there was also a large acceleration in population growth. In North America and the United Kingdom, the 1950s were no worse or better than many periods in the past, but in view of the continental experience, it seemed like stagnation. The evidence of this chapter indicates that this acceleration of growth in Europe has been much more than a passing phase of recovery, although recovery elements were certainly present. The later chapters will analyze the reasons for this acceleration of the growth trend and try to assess the role which economic policy has played. This chapter and most of the statistical appendices are concerned with the more prosaic task of establishing the facts on comparative growth rates.

Fortunately, many of the economic problems of our group of countries can now be quantified, with some confidence that we are comparing like with like. We are no longer dealing with the statistical crumbs collected by pioneer investigators like Colin Clark in the heroic days of comparative quantitative analysis of growth. Most of our countries have developed a heavy artillery of national accounts in the past decade, and national income statisticians, having become a closely-linked and well-travelled international fraternity, have standardized many of their techniques. An important by-product of post-war cooperation in O.E.E.C. and O.E.C.D. has been the creation of comparable statistics on matters relating to economic policy. This is not true to nearly the same extent for the countries outside our group. For underdeveloped countries, data have become available in large quantity thanks to the efforts of the U.N., but much of it is not comparable. Similarly, with the Sino-Soviet countries, the statisticians belong to a different fraternity, and the relevant figures are often not published or even calculated, so that comparative statistical enquiry for those countries is a kind of detective work, or a by-product of military intelligence. This situation is changing, but at the moment the most promising field for any quantitative testing of hypotheses about the causes of rapid growth is certainly in the countries covered here. There is now a big enough volume of reasonably comparable material to justify essays in broad quantitative analysis such as this. As a compensation for this temerity, the sources are set out in as great a detail as possible to facilitate the task of critics, and to make way for further improvements.

The importance of this quantitative approach to economic policy can hardly be doubted. Such quantification is often the only basis for making a rational choice between policies, and in many cases reveals the nature of the problem itself. Without the kind of data used here, it is doubtful if there would be much concern about the slow pace of growth in the United Kingdom or the United States at all.

The Growth of Output

Gross domestic product has been chosen as the measure of output because it is a more embracing concept than the other main measures available and thus reflects better the output of the whole community. This economy-wide measure fully reflects the impact of changes in economic structure, including the changing role of government in the economy. Industrial production would give too optimistic a picture of growth in societies which have been steadily increasing their degree of industrialization. It is also necessary in the analysis of economic growth to examine other significant variables which are often only available for the whole economy—such as the labor force, the rate of investment or the capital stock.

We also benefit in our choice of output measure from a good deal of research and discussion which has led the statistical authorities of our group of countries to adopt common definitions of national accounting totals. For the 1950s, the estimates are derived from currently collected official data which are almost identical in concept between countries, and are based on fairly similar techniques for calculating volume indices. More systematic thought and effort has been put into the derivation of these total economy aggregates than for any narrower measure. This is also true of the estimates which we have used for the period 1870–1950. These historical estimates draw upon considerable research on both income and commodity flows. Often they were made by people who are, or have been, responsible for the more recent official estimates. In some cases the historical figures are themselves official publications. Thanks to the efforts of Simon Kuznets and the International Association for Research in Income and Wealth, historical series have been prepared which are reasonably comparable in concept and technique of deflation. This is not to suggest that the long-term measures are as comparable as those for the 1950s, or that they cannot be further improved to ensure greater comparability; this study itself attempts to improve on previous estimates in some cases. It is simply suggested that long-term comparisons can now be made with a fair degree of confidence,[1] though the figures for Belgium, France and Switzerland are probably much weaker than those for the other countries.

In the appendices, figures are given wherever possible for individual years as a convenience to readers who may wish to refer to different periods or to use them in combination with other figures. Too much significance should not be attached to year-to-year movements. In general, the comparisons are for a long enough span to avoid purely cyclical influences. The figures on rates of growth refer in all cases to compound rates between the years cited and not to fitted trends.

The figures start from 1870 and run to 1960 or 1961, the latest year for which there were data at the time of writing. As they cover a span of about ninety years, 1913 seems a convenient mid-point to be used as a base year throughout this study. All the figures are adjusted to eliminate the effect of frontier changes, which in many cases would have significantly obscured underlying trends. The year 1870 was chosen as a starting point because it follows the unification of Germany and Italy and the American Civil War, and marks the beginning of a long period during which production was not interrupted by major upheavals. Beyond that date, in any case, the figures deteriorate sharply. Between 1870 and 1913 there were no large wars, the system of international payments operated fairly smoothly, experience of recession was frequent, but there was nothing like the collapse of the 1930s. The Great Depression of 1873–79 made its biggest impact on prices, and only in the United Kingdom did it have effects on output comparable with that of the 1930s. During the four decades preceding the first world war the (unweighted) average rate of growth of our twelve countries was 2·7 per cent. The United States was well above all other countries at 4·3 per cent (see Table

---

[1] This is also the conclusion of D. C. Paige, F. T. Blackaby and S. Freund, who analyzed the statistical problems in detail in 'Economic Growth: The Last Hundred Years', *National Institute Economic Review*, London, July 1961. This study uses many of the same sources for output and employment, as it makes extensive use of my article 'Economic Growth in Western Europe 1870–1957' from *Banca Nazionale del Lavoro Quarterly Review*, March 1959. John W. Kendrick, *Productivity Trends in the United States*, National Bureau of Economic Research, Princeton University Press, Princeton, 1961, has provided the most refined and explicit existing presentation of the statistical problems which arise for a single country. Kendrick's preferred concept of output is private product, i.e. excluding government. Kendrick excludes government partly because of the difficulty of measuring output in the government sector except in terms of input. But in practice these measurement difficulties also apply to parts of the commodity-producing sector where output flows are sometimes so heterogeneous that they have to be measured indirectly.

I–1). Denmark, Sweden and Canada also did substantially better than average. Italy and France were the laggards.

TABLE I–1

ANNUAL RATE OF GROWTH OF TOTAL OUTPUT

	1870–1913	1913–50	1950–60	1956–61
Belgium	2·7	1·0	2·9	2·5
Denmark	3·2	2·1	3·3	5·0
France	1·6	0·7	4·4	4·2
Germany	2·9a	1·2	7·6	5·9
Italy	1·4	1·3	5·9	6·7
Netherlands	2·2b	2·1	4·9	3·9
Norway	2·2a	2·7	3·5	3·4
Sweden	3·0	2·2	3·3	4·0
Switzerland	2·4c	2·0	5·1	5·2
United Kingdom	2·2	1·7	2·6	2·1
Canada	3·8	2·8	3·9	1·8
United States	4·3a	2·9	3·2	2·3
Average	2·7	1·9	4·2	3·9

a 1871–1913.
b 1900–13.
c 1890–1913.

Source: See Appendix A. These figures are compound rates, and refer to constant territory.

From 1913 to 1950 the pace of growth slackened under the impact of two world wars, a major depression and the collapse of world trade and payments. In all countries except Norway, output grew more slowly than it had in the preceding period. But here again, the United States and Canada did substantially better than almost all European countries. The average growth rate was 1·9 per cent, but the United States achieved 2·9 per cent.

Since 1950 all the European countries have grown faster than in the two earlier periods cited, and in most cases growth has been faster than over any previous period of equal length. The average for the twelve countries for 1950 to 1960 was 4·2 per cent. By contrast with the past, the United States lagged seriously behind the average at 3·2 per cent. Only the United Kingdom and Belgium grew more slowly than the United States.

As this acceleration in growth followed a period of retardation, it is natural to suppose that it included an element of recovery. It would also be reasonable to expect the recovery element to be much smaller in the United States in view of its superior performance in the past. These possibilities are analyzed at length in the next two chapters, but it is worth noting here that the growth rates in the late fifties and early sixties were still very high in Europe. The average growth rate from 1956 to 1961 was 3·9 per cent. Several countries showed some falling off, but Denmark, Italy, Sweden and Switzerland accelerated their growth further.

A striking characteristic of these more recent developments is that the slow-growing countries have had a substantial deceleration in growth so that two distinct groups have emerged. There is a slow-growth group consisting of Belgium, Canada, the United Kingdom and the United States, which are doing badly by past standards, and a fast-growth group made up of the other countries, which are all doing well by any standards. Most European economies have acquired a new momentum of growth which has gone well beyond the point at which recovery might normally be expected to end. Before analyzing the reasons for this, it is necessary to look a little more closely at the historical record, for output movements do not provide an adequate measure of performance in countries where population is increasing at different rates, where other demographic and social forces have influenced the labor supply, and where working hours and holidays reflect a different preference for leisure.

Movement in Population and Output per Head

The variations in the rate of growth of output have not shown any close relation to demographic changes, but the acceleration of output growth seems to have been accompanied in several cases by higher birth rates and immigration, and stagnation seems to have had the opposite effect. As shown in Table I–2, before the first world war, population was growing at a rate of about 1 per cent a year in Europe, and about twice as fast in North America. There was a general slowing down after the first world war, because of a widespread decline in birth rates. Life expectation rose in all countries,

TABLE I–2

POPULATION GROWTH

| | Compound Annual Percentage Change | | |
	1870–1913	1913–50	1950–60
Belgium	1·0	0·3	0·6
Denmark	1·1	1·0	0·7
France	0·2	0·0	0·9
Germany	1·1	0·8	1·1
Italy	0·7	0·7	0·6
Netherlands	1·3	1·4	1·3
Norway	0·8	0·8	0·9
Sweden	0·7	0·6	0·7
Switzerland	0·9	0·5	1·4
United Kingdom	0·9	0·4	0·4
Canada	1·8	1·5	2·7
United States	2·1	1·2	1·7
Average	1·1	0·8	1·1

Source: See Appendix B. The figures refer to constant territory.

and this would have gone a good way to offset the decline in birth rates if there had not been heavy war deaths. The sharp decline in immigration contributed a good deal to the decrease in U.S. growth, though it remained substantially above that in Europe.

In the 1950s, the previous decline in population growth was reversed, and in Canada, France and Switzerland there was a sharp acceleration. Most countries had a higher birth rate in the 1950s than in the inter-war and war period, a change that was particularly marked in France. The death rate continued to decline, and some countries were substantially affected by migration. Italian emigration to Switzerland was on a large scale, and there was a smaller movement to Belgium. West Germany had a substantial migration from East Germany, and France a considerable influx from North Africa. Canadian population growth was extremely rapid, largely because of immigration.

It is clear from Table I–3 that there has been a marked acceleration of post-war European growth in terms of output per head of population. The slower post-war North American growth is even more striking. The two slow-growing European countries, Belgium and the United Kingdom, come out much better on this *per capita* basis than the United States, as they have had the lowest post-war population growth.

TABLE I–3

RATE OF GROWTH OF OUTPUT PER HEAD OF POPULATION

	1870–1913	1913–50	1950–60
Belgium	1·7	0·7	2·3
Denmark	2·1	1·1	2·6
France	1·4	0·7	3·5
Germany	1·8[a]	0·4	6·5
Italy	0·7	0·6	5·3
Netherlands	0·8[b]	0·7	3·6
Norway	1·4[a]	1·9	2·6
Sweden	2·3	1·6	2·6
Switzerland	1·3[c]	1·5	3·7
United Kingdom	1·3	1·3	2·2
Canada	2·0	1·3	1·2
United States	2·2[a]	1·7	1·6
Average	1·6	1·1	3·1

[a] 1871–1913.
[b] 1900–13.
[c] 1890–1913.

Source: Derived from Appendices A and B.

Labor Supply

The movement in output per head of population provides some idea of the increase in potential living standards,[1] but it does not give a picture of productive achievements. In order to measure these, we must consider the changes in labor productivity and the extent to which countries provided employment for those members of the population able and willing to work.

About 95 per cent of the labor force is in the age group 15 to 64. For this reason, it is useful to see how demographic changes have affected the proportion in this group. From 1870 to 1913, changes in the age structure of the population were significant only in Belgium, the United Kingdom, Canada and the United States, where the proportion of people of working age rose substantially (see Table I–4). From 1913 to 1950 this upward movement became general, because of the fall in birth rates and the rise in life expectation. In the 1950s this upward tendency was reversed, except in Germany and Italy, because of rising birth rates and the fact that increasing life expectation now affects primarily those already past working age.

TABLE I–4

POPULATION AGED 15 TO 64 AND ITS LABOR FORCE PARTICIPATION

	Population Aged 15 to 64 as Per Cent of Total Population				Labor Force as Per Cent of Population Aged 15 to 64		
	1870	1913	1950	1960	1913	1950	1960
Belgium	61·7	64·7	68·1	64·5	70·9	60·3	61·3
Denmark	60·8	60·2	64·7	64·2	73·2	74·5	75·7
France	65·5	65·8	65·8	62·2	82·3	73·5	74·0
Germany	61·2	63·1	67·2	67·7	74·7	68·9	71·5
Italy	61·7	60·3	65·5	66·2	78·5	63·8	67·4
Netherlands	60·9	60·1	63·0	61·0	64·9	61·2	62·1
Norway	58·5	57·9	66·0	63·2	67·7	64·2	62·6
Sweden	60·5	60·6	66·3	65·8	68·9	66·5	66·3
Switzerland	63·0	64·0	66·8	66·2	74·7	68·4	70·0
United Kingdom	58·9	64·1	66·9	65·1	70·0	69·4	72·0
Canada	53·5	62·0	62·6	59·0	62·7	61·4	62·9
United States	57·8	63·5	65·0	59·7	62·8	65·7	67·8

Sources: See Appendices C and D.

Not all of the population aged 15 to 64 are able and willing to work. Some are at school, a great many are housewives, and a few are incapacitated. On the other hand, a small fraction of the labor force consists of people above or below the normal working age. The

[1] The increase in personal consumption *per capita* was generally smaller than the increase in income in the 1950s because an increasing proportion of resources was devoted to home and foreign investment and government consumption. The rate of growth of private consumption per head was 6·1 per cent per annum in Germany, 4·0 per cent in Italy, 3·5 per cent in France, 2·3 per cent in the Netherlands, 2 per cent in the United Kingdom; 1·8 per cent in Scandinavia, 1·7 per cent in Belgium and Canada, and 1·5 per cent in the United States.

idea of making any regular or precise measurement of the number able and willing to work is a fairly modern one, and long-term estimates of the labor force are largely confined to the United States and Canada. However, most population censuses have enquired into the economic activity of the population, and census data are the only guide to long-term developments in the labor force.

These changes in activity rates are substantial in some countries and have a considerable influence on the measurement of productivity. The census treatment of economic activity varies between countries and, in some cases, between censuses. These variations mainly affect juveniles and female workers in agriculture. Since there is so much variation between censuses in the coverage of these two groups before 1913, it is simply assumed for this period that the labor force moved parallel to the population of working age.[1]

It can be seen from Table I–4 that, except in the United States and Denmark, there was a general fall in activity rates from 1913 to 1950. In all countries there was a decline in the rate of juvenile employment due to increased schooling. But there was also a decline in female activity in some countries, particularly Belgium, Norway and Italy (see Table I–5). In the United States and Canada, on the contrary, the proportion of women in the labor force increased considerably. In some cases the fall was due to the shift out of agriculture where female activity was higher than in industry, but it may also reflect purely statistical changes in the treatment of family helpers in successive censuses. In the case of France, the successive censuses show an erratic movement in the proportion of female agricultural workers, and the French figure was therefore adjusted as noted in Appendix D. The steady decline in female activity in Italian agriculture was also partly due to changes in definition. Furthermore, the Italian census was more sensitive to the decline in juvenile activity, because it included children 10 years of age and over in the labor force if they happened to be working, whereas other countries generally ignore the activity of those under 15.

[1] Most observers who have attempted to make corrections of census figures tend to produce estimates which show much greater stability in activity rates than does the census. (See Clarence D. Long, *The Labor Force under Changing Income and Employment*, National Bureau of Economic Research, 1958.) Professor Long found a remarkably stable proportion of working-age population in the U.S. labor force after appropriate adjustments to bring juveniles and women to a full-time basis. He also suggested that stability of activity rates may be a fairly general international phenomenon; cf. his findings for Australia, Canada, Great Britain and New Zealand, as well as the United States. K. Bjerke's adjusted figures for the labor force also show greater stability in activity rates than does the Danish census; cf. 'The National Product of Denmark 1870–1952', *Income and Wealth*, Series V, p. 151. See also Jostock's comments on the German census of 1882, which undercounted family workers, 'The Long-Term Growth of National Income in Germany', *Income and Wealth*, Series V, p. 101.

TABLE I-5
PROPORTION OF THE LABOR FORCE CONSISTING OF WOMEN,
1910, 1950 AND 1960

	1910[a]	1950[b]	1960
Belgium	31·4	27·9	30·1
Denmark	31·3		
France	38·3	36·0	
Germany	33·8	35·1	36·9
Italy	31·3	24·9	27·0
Netherlands	31·4	25·6	
Norway	34·4	27·1	27·0
Sweden	27·8		35·0
Switzerland	33·9		30·1
United Kingdom	29·6	31·7	33·5
Canada	13·4	21·4	25·4
United States	19·3	28·8	32·3

[a] Figures for Denmark, France, Italy, the United Kingdom and Canada relate to 1911, figures for Germany to 1907, for the Netherlands to 1909, and for the United States to the average for 1900 and 1920.

[b] Figures for France are for 1954, for Italy 1951, and for the Netherlands 1947.

Sources: Most of these figures are given in the census sources quoted in Appendix D. Others are from the *International Statistical Yearbook*, League of Nations, 1926.

In the 1950s the decline in the activity rate was reversed in many countries, with the biggest increases in Italy, Germany and the United Kingdom. High levels of demand attracted married women and older people into the labor force in sufficient numbers to offset the effects of increased schooling. There appears to have been some increase in the proportion of women in the labor force in all countries except Norway in the 1950s. In the United Kingdom well over half the increase in employment in the 1950s was due to increased female activity, and in Germany about 45 per cent of the increase.

A good deal of the variation in activity rates is therefore due to changes affecting juveniles and females, who probably contribute less to output than do adult males. Some analysts have attempted to refine their estimates of labor force movements by giving a differential weight to the contribution of juveniles and women based on their relative remuneration at some period. Such adjustments are fairly arbitrary, however, as the wage structure has changed over time and differs between countries, and it reflects differences in social attitudes as well as variations in the relative productivity of different classes of workers.

Some writers have also tried to measure improvements in the quality of the labor force. These efforts have been carried furthest by Denison,[1] who has adjusted the U.S. labor force for its degree of

[1] Edward F. Denison, *The Sources of Economic Growth in the United States and the Alternatives Before Us*, Committee for Economic Development, Washington, D.C., 1962.

C

education as well as for changes in age-sex composition. His adjustment for education is made by stratifying the labor force into different educational levels and weighting each group according to its relative income. As a result, he has produced an index of quality improvements which shows a rise of 46·3 per cent between 1909 and 1958. Kendrick has made a different kind of adjustment for changes in the quality of the labor force. He divides the U.S. labor supply into industry segments and weights the labor employed in each segment by its relative remuneration. The difference in remuneration is presumed to reflect a quality difference. Shifts in structure thus defined were responsible for raising his labor input figure by 28·8 per cent between 1889 and 1953.[1] There is little doubt that the educational level has improved in all countries in the century under review, and the improvement has probably affected different countries differently. This is one of the factors influencing productivity which is worth further quantitative investigation. Unfortunately, data on education usually refer to the flow of graduates from different kinds of schools rather than to the stock of educated people, and measurement of the quality of the labor force is, in any case, rather arbitrary because relative remuneration will reflect differences in ability as well as education.

Output developments are influenced not only by the changing amount of labor available but also by the degree to which those willing and able to work are actually used. There have, of course, been wide fluctuations in unemployment in the past few decades, which must be taken into account in estimating productivity changes. Methods of registering unemployment differ between countries and have changed over time. Nevertheless, certain broad conclusions emerge clearly, in spite of the statistical difficulties outlined at length in Appendix E.

The post-war period has been one of very high employment in France, the Netherlands, Norway, Sweden, Switzerland and the United Kingdom, with unemployment usually running below 2·5 per cent of the labor force (Appendix Table E–1). There has been a steady move in the same direction in Germany, which has been a member of the high-employment group since 1959. In Belgium, Italy and Denmark, unemployment has been higher than average, but all three countries have reduced it in recent years, and Denmark is now in the high-employment group.

[1] John W. Kendrick, *op. cit*. It is interesting to compare Kendrick's results with ours, for he has carried out a more refined and painstaking study on the United States than has been attempted or is possible for any other country. His unadjusted figure on employment is close to ours, rising by 196 per cent from 1889 to 1953 as compared with our estimate of 192 per cent. The adjustment to a full-time equivalent basis raises his figure to 208·5 per cent. His quality improvement factor raises this figure further to 297 per cent.

This is in striking contrast with the inter-war years when unemployment was allowed to reach levels which would now be unthinkable in many countries. In the 1930s the unemployment rate averaged about 10 per cent or more. In Germany it went as high as a sixth of the labor force.

The post-war experience of the United States and Canada has been different. Unemployment has been higher on average than anywhere in Europe except Italy and Belgium, and in both Canada and the United States the average level has tended to increase.

In the period since 1870, the working year has been reduced considerably. The increase in leisure has been greatest in the United States where annual working hours declined by about 40 per cent. In Europe the smallest decline was in the Netherlands where hours fell by rather more than a quarter, and the biggest drop was in Norway where it was not far short of that in the United States.

In general, working hours are recorded accurately only for manufacturing industry, and we have assumed that the movement in this sector is representative for the economy as a whole. This is a reasonable assumption over long periods, when the movement in hours reflects an increased preference for leisure which tends to be diffused throughout the economy by collective agreement and the need to synchronize interconnected activities. However, this diffusion process takes more time in some sectors than it does in manufacturing where collective contracts are negotiated more frequently, and in times of rapid change the movement in manufacturing hours may exaggerate the overall change. Working hours in manufacturing are also more volatile than in other sectors because they reflect to a greater extent the involuntary reductions in work which are akin to unemployment and are caused by inadequate demand. Fortunately, this is not an operative consideration in the years chosen as benchmarks, as none of them was a year of recession.

From 1870 to 1913, working hours fell from about 63 hours a week to about 54 hours. They dropped fairly sharply after the first world war when the 48-hour week seems to have become general. In the 1930s hours were reduced by recession—most drastically in the case of France and the United States. Between 1950 and 1960, manufacturing hours declined rather substantially in Germany and Scandinavia, whereas in the United Kingdom, France and Italy they increased slightly. It could well be that the drop in manufacturing hours in Germany and Scandinavia somewhat exaggerated the reduction of hours in the whole economy in this decade, and to this extent exaggerated somewhat their productivity growth. The working week in Europe is now generally between 42 and 46 hours; it is about 40 in North America. There has been a steady increase in the number of holidays. In Europe, about 3 to 5 weeks a year are now devoted to vacations and statutory holidays, and in North America about 4 weeks.

Some analysts have stressed the differential productivity effect of a shorter work week. Denison suggests[1] that a reduction in hours at a level above 48·6 a week is fully offset by a rise in output per man-hour, and that the fall in output becomes fully proportionate to the decline in hours only at levels below 33·9 a week. In between, the impact is graduated. Such a demarcation is arbitrary and implies that it was irrational ever to have had working hours above 48·6 a week. Nevertheless, it is obvious that the impact of reduced working hours on physical efficiency depends on their initial level. Fortunately, the level of working hours has changed in a fairly similar way in most of these countries, and as our major concern is with inter-country comparability rather than with the absolute character of our measuring-rod, we can afford to ignore this finesse.

Total Labor Input

It is now possible to assess the movement in total labor input. It has always grown more slowly than population, with brief exceptions in Germany, Italy and the United Kingdom in the 1950s. Apart from the Netherlands and Scandinavia, the pace of growth dropped sharply in the period 1913 to 1950, mainly because of slower population growth, and the fall in working hours and activity rates. In Belgium, France and Italy there was even an absolute fall in labor input (see Table I-6). From 1950 to 1960 the increase in labor input

TABLE I-6
ANNUAL AVERAGE RATE OF CHANGE IN TOTAL HOURS WORKED
IN THE ECONOMY

	1870–1913	1913–50	1950–60
Belgium	0·7	−0·4	0·3
Denmark	0·6	0·6	0·4
France	−0·2	−0·8	0·5
Germany	0·8	0·3	1·6
Italy	0·2	−0·5	1·8
Netherlands	1·1[a]	1·0	1·1
Norway	0·4	0·3	−0·5
Sweden	0·3	0·3	−0·2
Switzerland	0·8[b]	0·0	0·9
United Kingdom	0·7	0·0	0·6
Canada	1·7	0·7	1·3
United States	1·9	0·5	0·9
Average	0·8	0·2	0·7

[a] 1900–13.
[b] 1890–1913.

Source: These figures are derived by multiplying employment (Appendix F) by annual working hours per man (Appendix G).

[1] E. F. Denison, *op. cit.*, p. 40.

was substantially accelerated except in the Netherlands and Scandinavia—thanks to decreased unemployment and rising activity
rates.

Productivity Growth

Productivity can be measured by dividing output by total labor
input. Table I–7 shows the resulting estimates of output per man-
hour on which much of the following analysis is based. Because of
the statistical problems in measuring working hours and activity
rates, alternative productivity measures are presented in Appendix
H; output per man-hour on the assumption of constant activity
rates, and output per man with no adjustment for changes in working
hours. The following conclusions are developed in terms which are
consistent with the movement of all three measures.

TABLE I–7
ANNUAL AVERAGE GROWTH OF OUTPUT PER MAN-HOUR

	1870–1913	1913–50	1950–60	1913–38	1938–60	1950–55	1955–60
Belgium	2·0	1·4	2·5	1·5	1·9	2·4	2·6
Denmark	2·6	1·5	2·9	1·3	2·4	1·0	4·8
France	1·8	1·6	3·9	2·3	1·8	4·2	3·6
Germany	2·1[a]	0·9	6·0	1·3	2·8	6·0	5·9
Italy	1·2	1·9	4·1	2·6	2·0	4·0	4·1
Netherlands	1·1[b]	1·1	3·7	1·5	1·9	4·1	3·4
Norway	1·8[a]	2·4	3·9	2·7	2·7	3·6	4·3
Sweden	2·7	2·0	3·5	1·7	3·0	3·3	3·7
Switzerland	1·6[c]	1·9	4·2	2·4	2·3	4·4	3·9
United Kingdom	1·5	1·7	2·0	2·1	1·5	1·6	2·3
Canada	2·1	2·1	2·5	0·8	3·9	3·6	1·5
United States	2·4[a]	2·4	2·4	3·0	1·7	2·8	2·0
Average	1·9	1·7	3·5	1·9	2·3	3·4	3·5

a 1871–1913.
b 1900–1913.
c 1890–1913.

Source: Appendix H.

From 1870 to 1913 productivity rose at an average rate of 1·9 per
cent per annum in our countries. The United States was well above
average at 2·4 per cent. Denmark and Sweden also made rapid
progress, and Italy and the Netherlands were the laggards.

From 1913 to 1950 the average rate of growth was slower at 1·7
per cent. The deceleration is even more marked if activity rates are
assumed constant over this period. The biggest retardation was in
Germany, but there was also appreciably slower growth in Belgium,
Denmark and Sweden. American growth did not slacken, so that the
U.S. advantage over Europe was even greater than from 1870 to
1913.

The average growth rate in the 1950s was 3·5 per cent—about

double the rate of 1913–50. U.S. growth continued at its steady 2·4 per cent, but now lagged behind all the others except the United Kingdom. Every country except the United States had much faster growth in the 1950s than in the two earlier periods. This acceleration of the 1950s is demonstrated by all three productivity indices, and it is indeed enhanced by the assumption of constant activity rates.

The foregoing analysis of different periods has been rather crude, as is inevitable in dealing with several series for nine decades for twelve countries. We have tried to choose years for comparison which had comparable cyclical characteristics and where the purely statistical difficulties are minimized. It would be useful to supplement the previous comparisons by contrasting the developments of the 1950s with those of the 1920s, which were also a period of recovery after war. Unfortunately, output data are not available for some important countries for part of this period, and the data on unemployment and hours for the early 1920s are rather too weak to measure short-period changes. However, it is possible to compare the development of 1913–38 with that of 1938–60. These two periods are of roughly similar length, and each was interrupted by a major war. From 1913 to 1938 productivity rose on average by 1·9 per cent and from 1938 to 1960 by 2·4 per cent. The alternative productivity series both show a larger increase from 1938 to 1960 and a smaller one for 1913 to 1938, and in view of the statistical problems they may provide a better guide to developments in this period. The average growth rates of 1938–60 were not remarkably high in most cases, though they were higher than from 1870 to 1913 in all countries except the United States.

The choice of the period 1950–60 may be expected to exaggerate growth because it includes an element of recovery, but it can equally well be argued that to use a period including a major war will also give a misleading though opposite picture of trends. It is therefore worth considering the developments in each half of the 1950s to see whether there was any slackening over the period, while recognizing that such short-period comparisons are affected by cyclical influences to a considerable degree. The average for 1955–60 was fractionally higher than for 1950–55, and half the countries accelerated growth. This is also true if productivity is measured without adjustment for activity rates, but in terms of output per man there was some slight slackening in the later 1950s.

It seems clear that there has been an acceleration in European productivity growth in the post-war period, even after making allowance for considerable elements of recovery. It is difficult to say how much higher this new trend is, when there is such a wide dispersion between countries. It is also dangerous to extrapolate trends from post-war experience. All the long-run averages show that the growth rates of the 1950s are without precedent for any long period. One would need good evidence of basic changes in the economy before projecting such high rates very far into the future. An explanation is also needed of why North American growth did not accelerate in the 1950s and why there was such a wide gap in performance between Belgium and the United Kingdom and the other European countries.

Growth problems cannot be analyzed simply by manipulating time series. An important part of the explanation of the different performance of countries is in terms of the inter-country variation in productivity levels. For this reason, it is legitimate to speak of recovery elements operating in economies which have broken right through their long-term trends. We cannot assess what growth rate should be considered 'normal' in Europe without knowing why European productivity levels lag so far behind that of the United States. For this reason, we need to look at the level of productivity before proceeding further.

Comparative Levels of Productivity

The following comparisons of relative productivity levels should not be confused with measures of real income per head, as the degree to which the population is employed varies considerably, e.g. in 1960 it was 48 per cent in Germany and only 35 per cent in Canada. The gap between real income levels in Europe and America is narrower than the productivity gap because a higher proportion of Europeans work and they work longer hours.

Output levels in different countries cannot be compared by converting national totals at current exchange rates. As a result of differences in price levels the exchange rate does not reflect accurately the relative purchasing power of national currencies. For eight European countries and for the United States there is a detailed O.E.E.C. study of comparative real income levels and of the purchasing power of currencies.[1] This was done by comparing in detail the quantities of different goods and services purchased by consumers, investors and governments, and weighting the quantities purchased in each country by another country's prices for those items. This produces an estimate of the relative level of G.N.P. in real terms. The estimate will vary according to which country's prices are used as weights. Two sets of figures are given in Table I–8, at U.S. relative prices and average European relative prices. If we are considering the problem of closing the productivity gap between Europe and the United States, the figures at U.S. relative prices are preferable. In the process of catching up with U.S. productivity levels, the structure of European prices is getting closer to that in

[1] Milton Gilbert and Associates, *Comparative National Products and Price Levels*, O.E.E.C., Paris, 1958.

TABLE I–8
COMPARATIVE LEVELS OF OUTPUT, LABOR INPUT AND PRODUCTIVITY
IN 1960

	G.N.P.				Output per Man-Hour	
	At 1955 U.S. Relative Prices	At 1955 Average European Relative Prices	Employ-ment	Average Annual Hours	U.S. Relative Prices U.S.=100	European Relative Prices U.S.=100
	($ billion)		(000s)			
Belgium	13·4	11·3	3,457	2,225	54	46
Denmark	7·1	5·9	2,202	2,096	48	40
France	68·5	53·0	19,740	2,166	50	38
Germany[a]	90·7	69·6	25,340	2,197	50	39
Italy	51·5	35·0	19,780	2,001	40	27
Netherlands	16·1	12·6	4,324	2,357	49	38
Norway	5·5	4·5	1,478	1,982	58	47
Sweden	11·9	9·2	3,229	2,040	56	43
Switzerland	8·5	6·4	2,424	2,250	48	36
United Kingdom	84·3	67·2	24,635	2,250	47	38
Canada	31·2	31·2	6,072	1,939	82	82
United States[b]	426·0	426·0	69,177	1,906	100	100

[a] Including the Saar.
[b] Including Hawaii and Alaska.

Source: G.N.P. extrapolated from Milton Gilbert and Associates, *op. cit.*, with the volume movements shown in Appendix A. The Norwegian figure is reduced by 3·5 per cent to eliminate repair and maintenance (see Appendix I on the reasons for this). G.N.P. for Sweden and Switzerland was derived from J. Frederic Dewhurst and Associates, *Europe's Needs and Resources*, Twentieth Century Fund, 1961, p. 948, which gives estimates of real consumption levels for these countries. For Canada it was assumed that the exchange rate reflected purchasing power parity. Manpower estimates are taken from the sources cited in Appendices F and G.

the United States, e.g. cars are becoming cheaper relative to servants. The structure of factor costs and the pattern of demand are geared closely to the level of income and these are the main factors affecting the development of price structures. They are, of course, influenced by differences in resource endowment and trade specialization as well.

The relative size of two economies can also be measured by looking at the pattern of output instead of expenditures. In fact, this is only another way of looking at the same total, for output and expenditure will be identical in each country's own currency when allowance is made for transactions with foreigners. The O.E.E.C. made a study of relative output levels in the United States and the United Kingdom[1] which, in general, confirms the findings of the

[1] Deborah Paige and Gottfried Bombach, *A Comparison of National Output and Productivity of the United Kingdom and the United States*, O.E.E.C., Paris, 1959. Nearly all the other existing comparisons of absolute productivity levels

comparison based on expenditure, though giving a somewhat smaller difference between the output of the two countries (the output of the United Kingdom is 15 per cent higher at U.K. weights and 6 per cent higher at U.S. weights on this basis than in the expenditure comparisons). The authors of the O.E.E.C. study, Paige and Bombach, suggest that this is likely to be a systematic characteristic of such studies, so that we might expect all European countries to be a little higher relative to the United States in terms of an output comparison.

The main problem that arises in comparing employment levels is that the estimate of women workers in the family enterprise sector varies between countries. About 37 per cent of the workers in Germany are women as compared with 27 per cent in Italy. Part of the variation is, of course, due to real differences in social habits or type of agricultural economy. Nevertheless, there are differences in statistical convention which might account for about a third of this apparent inter-country variation in female activity. Other snags arise in comparing unemployment levels and working hours, but these are of smaller importance for a year of high activity like 1960. Some of the errors are offsetting, but it seems likely that Table I–8 understates German productivity somewhat and overstates that of Italy, Norway, Sweden and Canada.

It is apparent that comparisons of absolute productivity levels must be treated with caution. However, it seems clear that productivity levels are fairly similar in the industrial countries of Europe. When output is valued at U.S. relative prices, all the European countries shown in Table I–8 except Italy have an output-per manhour within a range of 47–58 per cent of the United States. The range is narrower in terms of output per man. In terms of European relative prices, the range is similar, i.e. 36–47 per cent, excluding Italy. In view of the statistical difficulties, the differences in productivity levels between European countries shown in the table cannot be regarded as significant, although Italy is clearly below the rest.

It is also apparent that the U.S. productivity level is substantially higher than in Europe—about double the European level at U.S. relative prices. In Canada, too, the level seems very much higher than in Europe.

If these comparisons of 1960 are linked with the estimates of past growth, it appears that a good deal of the present gap between U.S.

for any substantial part of the economy are also confined to the United Kingdom, the United States and Canada. The lack of comparisons between European countries is a curious gap in empirical productivity analysis, although there are, of course, a number of studies of particular industries. The reason why such comparisons are not easy is that most continental countries do not have production censuses comparable with those in the United Kingdom and the United States, but comparisons are not impossible.

and European productivity emerged within the period 1870–1950, and has narrowed again in the 1950s. In 1870 Belgian and British productivity were not too far below the U.S. level. All the other European countries except Denmark and Sweden were within a range of about a third behind the United States. At that time, the spread between European countries was wider, and the Scandinavians were laggards instead of leaders.

The following chapter will attempt to explain why and how the European economy accelerated its growth in the 1950s, why the United States has not shared this acceleration, and why the performance of some European countries has been better than others.

CHAPTER II

THE REASONS
FOR ACCELERATED GROWTH

It is important to try to assess the reasons for the accelerated growth of the European economy to see whether this is likely to be a passing phase, whether it was due to internal or external factors, to policy or to luck, and what factors explain the difference in performance of the various countries. It is convenient to analyze separately the factors on the demand and the supply side.

THE IMPACT OF DEMAND

A striking characteristic of the post-war European economy has been the high level and continuous expansion of demand. Initially, this was a spontaneous aftermath of the war, but its continuance for almost two decades is mainly due to the success of an active governmental policy, both national and international. It is noteworthy that three of the slower-growing countries, the United States, Canada and Belgium, have had a less buoyant level of demand and that they, together with the fourth slow-growing country, the United Kingdom, have also had a much greater cyclical volatility of demand than the fast-growing countries. We shall analyze later the extent to which the relatively poor performance of these countries can be attributed to failures of policy.

The level of demand can be measured in various ways. The most general indicator is the state of the labor market, for which we have tried to present comparable figures.[1] The post-war period has been one of high employment. In France, the Netherlands, Norway, Sweden, Switzerland and the United Kingdom, unemployment averaged less than 2·5 per cent of the labor force in the 1950s (Table II-1). In the early 1950s, Germany had a fair amount of

[1] The conventional statistics tend to understate the unemployment level in Europe as compared with the United States, for European figures are usually based on unemployment registrations and U.S. figures on a sample survey. We have attempted to achieve greater comparability by adjusting the European figures upward with the help of census data. (See Appendix E for a detailed analysis of the comparability problem.)

unemployment because of the difficulties of absorbing the inflow of refugees quickly, but unemployment was steadily reduced and there was very full employment in the latter part of the decade. In Belgium, Denmark and Italy, unemployment was higher than in the other European countries. In Belgium and Denmark, this was due to structural weakness in export demand for traditional products like

TABLE II–1
UNEMPLOYMENT AS A PROPORTION OF THE LABOR FORCE

	Average 1950–60	Average 1958–60
Belgium	5·4	5·0
Denmark	4·3	3·3
France	1·3	1·2
Germany	4·1	1·8
Italy	7·9	5·3
Netherlands	1·9	1·7
Norway	2·0	2·4
Sweden	1·7	1·8
Switzerland	0·2	0·1
United Kingdom	2·5	2·9
Canada	4·4	6·6
United States	4·5	5·8

Source: Derived from Appendix E.

coal and steel, and bacon and eggs. In Italy unemployment did not reflect lack of demand, but the longer-term structural difficulties of putting unskilled Southern workers into industry. All three countries had a lower rate of unemployment in 1958–60 than in the decade as a whole. In fact, most European countries except the United Kingdom, Sweden and Norway, tended to reduce their unemployment levels in the course of the 1950s.

In the United States and Canada, unemployment in the 1950s averaged about 4·5 per cent of the labor force. Furthermore, the rate of unemployment tended to rise at the end of the 1950s, and in 1958–60 was higher than anywhere in Europe.

In theory, it is also possible to measure the pressure of demand by looking at the margin of unused physical capacity, but this is even more difficult to measure than unemployed labor. In the first place, one can assume that all members of the labor force are useable. This is not true, however, of all physical capital. Some of it, e.g. in textiles or railways, is not being used because it has become obsolete through changes in technology or taste. Apart from obsolescence, the problem of measuring the degree of use of aggregate capacity is very complicated. It is difficult to measure the aggregate capital stock because of its heterogeneous character, but there are also very wide differences in the degree of 'normal use' of equipment. Very few industries normally engage in continuous-shift working. Efforts to measure capacity use have been made from time to time; for example, the 1962 report of the Council of Economic Advisers suggests that output in the United States in 1961 could have been 7·7 per cent higher without straining capacity. No comparable figures are available for Europe; it is highly unlikely, however, that any European government would consider that it had this margin of spare capacity.

Slack capacity use is a cyclical manifestation of weak demand. If demand is weaker in one country than in another for a prolonged period, there may well be little difference in the degree of capacity use, but it is likely that weaker demand will be reflected in a smaller pressure for new capacity and a lower rate of investment. This is borne out by a comparison of the European and the U.S. situation. Investment in the United States in the 1950s was lower than in any European country except the United Kingdom and Belgium. Moreover, investment rates exceeded historical records in every European country, whereas U.S. rates were well below previous peaks.

Another manifestation of high demand pressures in Europe has been the balance-of-payments situation. In contrast with pre-war years almost all payments problems have been a reflection of inflationary rather than deflationary pressures. Countries in deficit have generally had sharply rising imports rather than falling exports, and countries in embarrassing surplus have had rapidly rising exports rather than falling imports. There have been other reasons for pay-

TABLE II–2

PRICE MOVEMENTS IN THE 1950s

	Consumer Price Index		G.N.P. Price Index	
	Increase 1950–60	Maximum Annual Fall or Minimum Rise	Increase 1950–60	Maximum Annual Fall or Minimum Rise
Belgium	21·0	−0·3	26·4	−1·9
Denmark	34·2	−1·0	38·0	+0·9
France	73·3	−1·1	86·1	+1·0
Germany	20·6	−1·7	37·3	−0·2
Italy	40·9	0·0	27·7	−0·7
Netherlands	21·0[a]	0·0	38·3	−1·8
Norway	57·2	+1·0	49·4	−3·0
Sweden	57·0	+0·9	59·6	−1·3
Switzerland	15·4	−0·7	12·6	−1·0
United Kingdom	49·0	+0·6	47·9	+0·9
Canada	24·4	−0·9	36·1	+0·4
United States	23·1	−0·2	27·9	+0·9

[a] 1951–60.

Source: Consumer price index from O.E.C.D. Bulletin, General Statistics, September 1962, p. 59; for Italy, cost-of-living index, p. 102. G.N.P. price index derived from issues of September 1961, September and November 1962.

ments difficulties, particularly in the United Kingdom, but the only country to suffer substantially from falling exports has been the United States.

In the 1950s all of our countries experienced considerable price rises, measured in terms of either the consumer price index or the price index for total G.N.P. (Table II–2). The pace of price increase has not been steady and in some years prices stood still. In only one or two years did prices fall by more than a fraction of a per cent, and all price declines were later reversed. This is in contrast to experience before 1913 or in the inter-war period when prices fluctuated in both directions. Such a large, widespread and persistent price increase is new in peacetime experience and can therefore be taken as *prima facie* evidence of higher demand pressure. However, the difference in the degree of price rise in various countries is not at all a precise measure of relative demand pressure. The response of prices to demand depends on the institutional and psychological resistance of the economy. Some price increases are the echoes of earlier inflation which was suppressed by price control. Economies are also affected to a varying degree by foreign inflationary pressures. The steady upward rise in prices cannot, therefore, be taken simply as an indicator of demand pressure; it must rather be considered in its own right as a phenomenon characteristic of the post-war economy.[1] As it is the virtual absence of price declines which distinguishes this recent behavior of prices, it should perhaps be considered in its negative aspect as a 'downward stickiness of prices'. It should be noted that this new characteristic of prices does not apply to the primary producing countries outside our group of countries.

Even more striking than the high level of European demand has been the virtual absence of recession. In terms of total output, unemployment and industrial production, the post-war European record has been markedly better than historical experience, and much more impressive than that of the United States and Canada. There were mild checks to European expansion in 1952 and 1958, due largely to the incidence of government anti-inflationary policies, but, in view of the forces which created these temporary checks, they can hardly be described as recessions. In most of Europe, as Table II–3 shows, G.N.P. did not decline at all in the 1950s, and only in Belgium was there a decline of more than 1 per cent. In the inter-war period, by contrast, G.N.P. was below previous peaks in most countries for about a third or more of the time, and there were falls ranging up to a fifth of G.N.P. The inter-war years were particularly bad, but from 1890 to 1913 output was also below previous peaks for ten years out

---

[1] The causes of this post-war phenomenon, its consequences for internal and external equilibrium, and the policy measures appropriate to deal with it are analyzed in detail in *The Problem of Rising Prices*, O.E.E.C., May 1961.

TABLE II–3
EXPERIENCE OF RECESSION, 1890–1960

	Maximum Cyclical Percentage Fall in G.N.P. from Peak to Trough			Per Cent of Years below Peak		
	1890–1913	1921–38	1948–60	1890–1913	1921–38	1948–60
Belgium		5·9	1·8			17
Denmark		2·6	0·9		18	25
France		19·3	0·0		59	0
Germany	4·0	(16·1)	0·0	17	(46)	0
Italy	5·2	5·4	0·0	44	41	0
Netherlands	(2·1)	12·1	0·0	8	41	0
Norway	(1·8)	8·0	0·2	22	24	8
Sweden	3·3	13·3	0·4	17	24	8
Switzerland	(2·4)	(8·0)	2·2		(50)	8
United Kingdom	4·1	(0·5)	0·5	44	(14)	8
Canada	13·2	29·3	3·6	26	59	8
United States	8·3	28·9	1·6	22	47	25

Note: Figures in brackets refer to part of period.

Source: Derived from Appendix A, supplemented for 1890–1913 from A. Maddison, 'Growth and Fluctuation in the World Economy, 1870–1960', *Banca Nazionale del Lavoro Quarterly Review*, June 1962.

of twenty-three in the United Kingdom and Italy and four in Sweden, and the falls ranged from 1·8 to 5·2 per cent of G.N.P. The U.S. post-war record compares unfavorably with that of Europe. There have been four U.S. recessions, with a slight fall in G.N.P. in 1949, a fall of about 2 per cent in 1954 and in 1958, and a recession in 1960–61 which did not produce a fall on an annual basis. In terms of quarterly movements from peak to trough, the post-war U.S. recessions involved falls in G.N.P. of 2, 4, 4·5 and 2·2 per cent respectively. For most European countries, comparison is not possible on a peak-to-trough basis because of the absence of quarterly or seasonally adjusted data, but in the United Kingdom the fall from the 1957 peak to the 1958 trough was 1·3 per cent—lower than that in any of the U.S. recessions.

A more refined analysis of cyclical movements can be derived by looking at industrial production, for which it is possible to compare quarterly movements in different countries on a seasonally adjusted basis. These figures make possible a crude estimate of business cycle peaks and troughs. There was a mild and short dip in output in a few European countries in the course of the first post-war U.S. recession in 1948–49, but the downward movements were not sufficiently large or widespread to be considered a general European recession. The biggest post-war dip in Europe occurred in 1951–52, somewhat earlier than the second post-war U.S. recession, and it affected all European countries. In Belgium and in the United Kingdom, its intensity was similar to that in the United States in

1953–54, and in many cases it was more prolonged than in the United States. The 1958 setback affected all European countries, but it was generally much milder than that of 1952, both in amplitude and duration. In Table II–4 we have attempted to compare the

TABLE II–4
AVERAGE AMPLITUDE AND DURATION OF POST-WAR CYCLES IN
INDUSTRIAL PRODUCTION
Amplitude measured by percentage change in seasonally adjusted quarterly
index of production. Duration measured in quarters.

	Average of Post-War Recessions		Average of Post-War Expansions	
	Amplitude	Duration	Amplitude	Duration
Austria	−3·5	4·5	62·7	16·0
Belgium	−8·6	3·0	16·4	12·5
Denmark	−5·1	4·0	21·4	14·5
France	−3·0	3·0	39·1	15·0
Germany	−1·0	1·0	92·0	18·5
Italy	−2·2	1·3	47·6	17·0
Netherlands	−4·2	2·3	31·5	14·5
Norway	−3·7	2·7	30·2	13·5
Sweden	−4·7	4·5	16·3	15·5
United Kingdom	−4·8	7·5	18·0	12·5
United States	−9·3	4·7	22·4	12·5

Source: A. Maddison, 'The Post-war Business Cycle in Western Europe and the Role of Government Policy', Banca Nazionale del Lavoro Quarterly Review, June 1960. The data refer to 1948–59.

post-war cyclical experience of the different countries. In no country, except Belgium, was recession nearly as severe as in the United States, and only in the United Kingdom was it more prolonged. Germany and Italy have been virtually free of recession, and their expansions have been both substantial and prolonged. All other countries except Belgium have had recessions with an amplitude only half as wide as the average for the United States, and, except in Belgium and the United Kingdom, the average duration of expansions has also been more favorable than in the United States.

What was the impact of this high level and steady expansion of demand on output? It ensured the full use of available labor and capital resources. High demand also had an effect on productivity. The direct impact of a high level of activity may well be to lower productivity by bringing the least efficient resources into operation, though this is probably offset by the better use of resources made possible by the greater steadiness of demand. But high and steady demand also affects productivity favorably by stimulating investment, research and product development. Market and profit prospects offered to entrepreneurs are good in such a climate. They find existing capacity inadequate, have difficulty finding workers, and foresee a constant increase in money and real wages which points to the need for investment to raise productivity as well as capacity. It is for this reason that post-war levels of investment have been higher in Europe than ever before. The maintenance of high and steady levels of demand has therefore been a major condition for the vastly improved performance of the European economies as compared with the past, and is part of the reason why they have done better than the United States. The fact that in the United Kingdom demand has continually had to be interrupted by deflationary measures to right the balance of payments is one of the major reasons why that country has grown more slowly than the rest of Europe.

Demand, Profits and Profit Expectations

The suggestion that high levels of demand can have such a large impact on growth has rather far-reaching consequences for our interpretation of the past. It implies that the allocation of resources to investment has been consistently too low and that growth has always been below potential. It also implies that different long-term forces have been operative in Europe and America which have led to the seizure of investment opportunities to different degrees.

In fact, it is likely that a private enterprise economy will always tend to underinvest.[1] Entrepreneurs are cautious men who may venture boldly but have a canny awareness of the risks they are taking. Because of the uncertainty of the return on business investment, the average rate of profit is usually twice as high as the rate on long-term bonds. The uncertainty involved in investment decisions is of two main kinds, micro-economic and macro-economic. The first kind of uncertainty is related to the nature of the business—the product, its market and technology. The structure of demand is continually changing towards new goods, new styles and qualities, technology is constantly rendering old equipment obsolete by offering new opportunities for cost reduction, and competitors are always trying to exploit these new opportunities faster. In this type of uncertainty, the entrepreneur is a specialist.

The second type of uncertainty concerns the general conjuncture

[1] This thesis is expounded by Branko Horvat in 'The Optimum Rate of Investment', *Economic Journal*, December 1958. He also draws the conclusion that investment may tend to be pushed too far in a collectivized economy. His optimum rate is one in which the output increment from investment is pushed down to zero, which, he suggests, will happen when output is growing at a rate of 10 per cent a year. This is, of course, an extreme view of the optimum, and its quantitative underpinning makes no distinction between output and productivity, or between economies at different levels of productivity. He is also measuring total output in the Russian sense, i.e., excluding most services. Our own view of the extent of under-exploitation of potential is much more modest, at least for our group of countries.

D

in which his business operates and on which he has no specialized judgment. The movement in the general level of demand will obviously affect the rate of expansion of his market. Volatility in total demand and income will affect his rate of profit considerably, as it will bring variations in his use of capacity. Profits are the category of income most sensitive to recession as most other incomes are fixed contractually. If the prospect of recession within the next three years (the normal pay-off period) is reduced from virtual certainty to virtually zero, then the investment incentive will be greatly enhanced. Profits will also be affected by movements in the general level of labor costs. Wages in any industry must keep pace in the long run with those elsewhere in the economy. If the pace of wage increases is accelerated relative to the change in the price of capital goods, this should increase the incentive to invest. The investment and profit outlook will be better in a situation where price fluctuations are almost invariably upwards than when they move both ways. The dangers of borrowing will be reduced, the risks of keeping liquid funds rather than assets will be increased. As the entrepreneur is not an expert on these macro-economic uncertainties, he will judge them on the basis of experience. After a few years of high and steady[1] expansion of demand, he will change his assessment of these macro-economic risks and respond by raising his rate of investment. He will, in fact, become concerned with the risks of not investing, i.e., lack of capacity to meet expanding demand with consequent loss of market share to competitors, and rising labor costs due to inadequate investment to raise productivity and offset rising wages. What we have said about the impact of demand on risk-taking is particularly true of export markets, where both micro- and macro-economic uncertainties are usually greater than in home markets. The risks of investment to meet export demand are rated very high when import controls, retaliatory tariff and exchange rate changes are common practice. They will obviously be rated differently when trade barriers are being steadily removed and export markets are found to rise faster than home markets.

Our catalogue of uncertainty and profit expectations would not be complete without a consideration of the impact of government policy, or taxation, on investment decisions. The possible impact of government is large, ranging from mild changes in tax rates or monetary policy to expropriation of assets. If government intervenes in the economy erratically, then it is likely to lower investment incentives by increasing risks. In some cases, this factor may be more important now than it was in pre-war years, and it is certainly more important than before 1913. However, government activity is

[1] By steady we mean the absence of declines rather than a steady rate of increase.

usually designed to avoid erratic interference with profit expectations. It has, of course, been argued that investment will be adversely affected if the level of taxation on profits is raised. This is not the place for an examination of changes and inter-country variations in tax structure (Chapter IV). It is enough to point out here that the rate of tax on profits is much higher in post-war Europe than in earlier periods when investment was much lower. There is therefore little evidence that an increase in tax levels necessarily reduces investment incentives. As long as the extra tax burden is not distributed in a way which penalizes investment as compared with other uses of resources, it would seem that the entrepreneur gets adjusted to new levels of taxation and adjusts his concept of normal profit accordingly.

In view of these uncertainties, it is not possible even in the most well-ordered or foresighted society to make a very accurate estimate of future returns, and we cannot therefore hope to illustrate our argument about profits with any quantitative precision. Empirical studies of investment behavior show a low frequency of exact profitability calculations[1] and all decisions will, to some extent, be governed by rule of thumb. It has even been suggested by Lundberg that entrepreneurs consistently expect higher rates of return than they actually realize. If this were so, it would, of course, greatly strengthen our argument about the importance of the factors governing their expectations. As the situation is never in equilibrium, the concept of a normal average rate of return will in any case be vague and conventional. It may vary over time and there is no reason to suppose that it will be the same in every country, although the possibilities of international capital movement are adequate enough to eliminate wide disparities. Because of the fact that uncertainty increases rapidly as the time horizon is extended, many firms will expect investment to pass the test of a minimum recoupment period as well as earning at least the average normal rate of profit over its life. During this recoupment period, gross profits must be adequate to 'recover' the cost of the new assets. Application of this criterion may well eliminate investments which are otherwise satisfactory in that they are expected to earn a normal rate of profit over their whole life. Kaldor and Mirrlees[2] suggest that the length of the pay-off period is normally three years in U.S. manufacturing. If the rate of tax is a third of gross profits, and the pay-off period is three years, a firm would have to expect an *initial* gross profit rate of 50 per cent

---

[1] Cf. Erik Lundberg, 'The Profitability of Investment', *Economic Journal*, December 1959, and Bruce R. Williams, *International Report on Factors in Investment Behaviour*, O.E.C.D., Paris, 1962.

[2] N. Kaldor and J. A. Mirrlees, 'A New Model of Economic Growth', *Review of Economic Studies*, June 1962.

per annum before it undertook an investment. This compares with an *average* gross profit rate of about 18 per cent in the United States in the 1950s.

Thus far, we have been arguing in terms of entrepreneurial expectations and not about the rate of profit actually obtained. It does not follow, from what we have said, that the rate of profit realized on average need necessarily be higher now than it was pre-war, or higher in countries with a more favorable demand situation. The reduction of risk may well lead to an increase in the rate of investment to the point where the average rate of profit, expected or realized, is the same as before. The reduction of risks has two aspects. First, the rate of profit realized on any given investment will be higher in a situation of high and reasonably steady use of capacity than in one of slack and volatile demand. Secondly, the change in the character of uncertainty with greater emphasis on the risks of not investing may even reduce the normal rate of profit which the entrepreneur actually requires, and it will almost certainly lead him to apply a less cautious rule of thumb on the period during which he hopes to 'recover' his investment. How much higher the rate of investment can be pushed will also depend upon technical and organizational factors affecting the schedule of returns. We argue below that for various reasons it was possible to raise the rate of investment a good deal in Europe without any sharp diminution in the rate of return.

Before considering the empirical evidence, we should be clear as to what is meant by profit rates. The average rate of profit on capital is the cumulated return derived over its whole life divided by its life. The profit rate will not be the same throughout the life of an asset but will steadily decline. Apart from the process of physical deterioration and obsolescence arising through changes in taste, the return on an asset will decline because of technical progress. If each successive year's crop of machines is associated with a higher labor productivity, the relative efficiency of old machinery associated with a given level of labor productivity will fall. Eventually, it will be forced out of operation by the general rise in wages, which will raise prime operating costs above gross earnings. Because of this spread of profit rates on equipment of different ages, an acceleration in the rate of investment will raise the average aggregate rate of profit even if the rate of return on individual assets is unchanged. It will do this because it lowers the average age of the capital stock and gives a bigger weight to capital at the stage when it is yielding higher returns.

Empirical evidence on the comparative profit rate in different countries is rather shaky. Less progress has been made in achieving standardization of data on income flows than on other aspects of national accounting. Even if the figures were better, there are institutional and structural differences which make interpretation difficult. The degree to which the corporate form of organization is used varies considerably, being much more widespread in the United Kingdom and the United States than in continental Europe. If we take non-labor income as a whole, it is influenced by the fact that some countries have a much bigger agricultural sector where small-scale enterprise and income from self-employment is predominant. The figure for rent can sometimes not be separated from other property incomes, but its share of the total will be influenced quite arbitrarily by controlled prices. One cannot, therefore, attach too much significance to the fact that the share of non-labor income is much higher in Germany than in the United Kingdom and the United States. It should, however, be possible to get a better idea of profit rates by looking at the non-labor income arising in a sector like manufacturing where the organization of production is fairly similar. As shown in Table II–5, the share of gross profits in gross

TABLE II–5

COMPARATIVE MOVEMENT OF GROSS PROFITS BEFORE TAX
IN GERMAN, AMERICAN AND BRITISH MANUFACTURING

	Ratio of Gross Profits to Gross Value Added in Manufacturing			Ratio of Gross Profits to Net Value of Fixed Capital Stock and Inventories		
	Germany	U.K.	U.S.	Germany	U.K.	U.S.
1950	37·1	35·1	32·4	25·2	22·7	26·2
1951	40·4	36·7	28·9	28·5	22·6	23·1
1952	42·2	31·8	23·2	28·9	18·0	18·4
1953	41·1	32·2	22·9	28·5	18·9	18·9
1954	41·0	33·5	20·6	28·9	20·4	16·1
1955	41·3	33·1	24·8	29·3	20·1	20·9
1956	38·9	31·4	22·8	26·7	18·3	17·8
1957	39·1	31·3	20·9	26·2	18·0	15·6
1958	39·0	30·1	17·6	26·1	16·8	12·3
1959	40·3	31·0	20·4	27·0	17·9	15·7
1960	40·4	30·1		27·4	17·4	14·0
1961		26·8				
Average 1950–60	40·1	31·9[a]	23·5[b]	27·5	19·2	18·1

[a] 1950–61.   [b] 1950–59.

Sources: Germany, profits derived as a residual after deducting labor income, social security payments, income from self-employment and income of independent artisans from gross value added in manufacturing; various issues of the *Statistisches Jahrbuch*. Fixed capital stock figures supplied by courtesy of Dr. Rolf Krengel of the Deutsches Institut für Wirtschaftsforschung, Berlin. Inventories from 'Die Lagerbestände der westdeutschen Industrie', by A. Rischert, *Wirtschafts-Konjunktur*, April 1962, München, p. 38. For 1950–54 it was assumed that the inventory-output ratio was the same as for 1955–60. U.K. profits, gross value and inventories from 1961 and 1962 editions of *National Income and Expenditure*, H.M.S.O., London. Fixed capital stock figures supplied by courtesy of W. Beckerman, National Institute of Economic and Social Research, London. United States, from *Survey of Current Business*, November 1956 and July 1962, and from *National Income, 1954*, and *U.S. Income and Output, 1958*, U.S. Department of Commerce. Profit figures in all cases include depreciation and stock appreciation.

value added in manufacturing averaged about 40 per cent in Germany in the 1950s, as compared with something less than a quarter in the United States, and about 32 per cent in the United Kingdom. If one compares the ratio of profits to the stock of fixed capital and inventories valued at current prices, the return in Germany averaged about 28 per cent, in the United States about 18 per cent, and in the United Kingdom about 19 per cent. These rates of return are based on estimates of the capital stock net of depreciation. There are, of course, different ways of calculating the capital stock which would change the calculation of the rate of profit, but they are likely to affect the three countries in the same way.

It should also be noted that the profit rate in the United States fell steadily in the 1950s. There was not even an upward trend in the absolute level of profits in spite of a cumulative manufacturing investment of about \$125 billion over the decade. In Germany the absolute level of profits rose by 1960 to about three and a half times the 1950 level.

It is also interesting to see how these underlying trends in profits were reflected in the experience of the equity investor in different countries. Table II–6 shows the returns received by investors in several countries in the period 1955–61. It shows the dividend yield and the annual rate of capital gain. These are then added together and divided by the rise in the cost of living index to give a rough indication of the total return in real terms. The result is not necessarily a guide to the underlying profit situation as stock market values are affected by expectations, by the distribution policy of companies, and by the structure of corporate borrowing. Nevertheless, the table provides some guidance as to the investment climate in different countries in the late 1950s. The rate of return on equities was in fact closely correlated with investment rates and productivity growth.

Our explanation of the factors influencing investment is compatible with experience in the post-war period when the slow-growing countries have been the only ones to experience recession, but what accounts for the fact that from 1870 to 1950 U.S. investment rates were higher than in Europe, though recession was at least as frequent? While a healthy conjuncture is a key factor in generating euphoric expectations and a momentum of high investment, this momentum may also be achieved without great stability if there are other factors making for high profit or expectation of profit. The special factors fostering investment in the United States were:

TABLE II–6
THE RETURN ON EQUITIES IN SELECTED COUNTRIES

	Belgium	France	United States	United Kingdom	Netherlands	Italy	Germany	Japan
1. Average Yield on Shares (October 1961)	3·3	1·7	3·0	5·7	3·4	2·5	2·5	4·1
2. Average Annual Increase in Share Prices, 1955–61	2·7	13·3	8·6	8·9	15·8	19·4	23·0	30·5
3. Average Annual Increase in Cost of Living, 1955–61	1·6	5·2	1·8	2·7	2·5	1·9	1·9	2·5
4. Real Annual Return on Capital	4·4	9·6	9·8	12·1	16·8	20·1	23·7	32·6

Source: O.E.C.D., *General Statistics,* and the financial press.

a. Superior natural resources—minerals such as iron ore, coal, oil and natural gas, water power, and, above all, land—gave the United States great advantages over Europe for many decades, and were a stimulus to investment in the nineteenth, and even in the twentieth, century. Some of these resources are now depleted, the frontier has disappeared, and thanks to modern transport Europe's access to cheap energy sources has been improved. Thus the significance of these natural advantages in promoting investment has lessened considerably.

b. The United States has had much faster population growth than Europe. Over the whole of the period since 1870, its population has grown about twice as fast as the European average. This rapid growth was reassuring to entrepreneurs because it meant that few industries were likely to be faced with an absolute fall or stagnation in demand, and there was less likelihood of wasted capacity because of wrong decisions. In addition, the prospects of a steadily growing market probably fostered competition, which is more painful when expansion of a firm can only be achieved at the expense of competitors.

c. In the 1913–50 period, European development was severely disrupted by major wars and their aftermath which created both physical and psychological inhibitions to investment. In the United States the fear of war destruction was not a factor affecting investment decisions.

d. As the U.S. economy is much less dependent on foreign trade than the economies of Europe, it did not suffer as much from the special uncertainties of export markets. The disturbances in foreign trade were particularly acute in the inter-war period, but they were also important before 1913, particularly for the United Kingdom. For similar reasons the United States did not benefit to the same extent as Europe from the great post-war expansion of trade.

e. The absolute size of the U.S. economy in terms of real product has been larger than that of any European country since the mid-1870s, twice as large since 1905, three times as large since the 1920s, and four times as large now. With this bigger size of market there was much less chance of investment being held back by technical indivisibilities which sometimes require a minimum scale of investment which is too large for a small economy to digest easily.

We are not arguing that there has been any exhaustion of investment opportunities in the United States, but simply pointing out that the existence of these special stimuli helps explain why the United States was able to achieve higher investment levels and productivity growth than Europe with a given degree of demand instability.

FACTORS ON THE SUPPLY SIDE

This extensive analysis of the impact of demand is only part of the explanation of the inter-country variation in post-war rates of growth. We must now attempt to identify the main factors which made it possible to evoke the response on the supply side to the high-demand stimuli of the 1950s. It is particularly necessary to segregate the temporary factors from the more permanent changes in order to see what rate of productivity growth can be considered 'normal' in future if policy is successful. The analysis is concentrated on productivity rather than on total output, as our examination of demand has already provided sufficient explanation of high levels of employment, and the factors determining population growth can be treated as exogenous.

Our first concern is to identify elements of recovery which may have operated in the 1950s. These are of three main types—recovery from war and its aftermath, elimination of disguised unemployment accumulated during decades of stagnation, and reduction of the gap between U.S. and European productivity levels which arose from neglect of past investment opportunities. The first element was negligible, except in Germany, while the second was of substantial importance in continental Europe. The third element is not a source of rapid productivity growth in itself but an opportunity to be exploited with the help of investment. Not all European countries have seized these investment opportunities to the same extent, but they are likely to remain important in the next few decades if they are properly exploited with the help of high and stable levels of demand.

Certain structural changes in demand and output have been specially favorable to productivity. Demand increases in Europe have been heavily concentrated on commodity production, whereas in the United States and Canada demand for services has been much heavier. As productivity grows faster in the commodity-producing sectors, this pattern of output has favored Europe at the expense of North America. The pattern of output may have been somewhat more favorable to productivity growth in Europe in the 1950s than in earlier periods, and was probably more favorable in the 1950s than it will be in the future. However, the very wide differences in productivity growth between European countries are not explicable in terms of structural differences, and these structural changes do not play any major role in explaining the acceleration of growth or the inter-country differences in performance.

The reduction of trade barriers has increased European productivity by better resource allocation, and explains some of the intra-European growth differentials. These are largely once-for-all gains, and freer trade is not a magic formula for long-term acceleration of productivity. The least publicized aspects of international cooperation—the establishment of mutual confidence and a payments system which operates without deflationary shocks—have contributed a great deal to productivity growth by promoting confidence and raising investment. If this cooperation is continued, its productivity impact should be permanent.

Most of these sources of accelerated productivity have been exploited only because of extremely high investment levels. Investment has reached unprecedented heights in Europe because it has been nurtured by extremely favorable demand conditions which have been highly conducive to profits and expectations of profit. Some of the special productivity-favoring factors have helped this profitability, and their disappearance may reduce it, and hence the level of investment. However, the growth potential of Europe is likely to remain considerably above any previous long-term trend, and probably above that in the United States. The realization of this potential will depend heavily on the efficiency of government policy.

Recovery Elements

By choosing a period beginning in 1950 it is possible to exclude the immediate post-war elements of recovery, for by this year all countries had regained their pre-war productivity level. In the years just after the war, increases in inventories greatly stimulated the flow of production, and repairs to damaged plant and equipment had a large impact on effective capacity and labor productivity. Productivity benefited from the adoption of technical advances which had been made at home and in other countries during the war—when capital formation fell to very low levels. Work became more efficient as people recovered from the distortions in economic attitudes and incentives induced by the war-time experience of production for an occupying power, service in the army, or black marketeering. These were the main factors influencing productivity in the period in which the pre-war levels were being regained and perhaps even for some time afterwards.

This immediate post-war element of recovery had exhausted its impact in most countries by 1950, but probably continued a little longer in Italy and the Netherlands, where the capital stock suffered badly from war damage, and almost certainly in Germany where recovery was delayed by the arbitrary division of the economy and the stagnation preceding the currency reform. The German capital stock was not fully used in the early 1950s, and was very patchy, so that minor repairs or small investment could readily bring damaged capital back into use. The labor force situation was particularly conducive to growth. As many were unemployed, had lost their assets, and were living well below previous standards, they were willing to work harder than in other countries. Furthermore, there was probably a higher proportion of the population with entrepreneurial and managerial experience than in other countries, as these people, in particular, were squeezed out of the Soviet zone.

Although most countries had recovered from the war before 1950, it is important to note the indirect consequences on productivity of their early post-war achievement of full employment. During the initial recovery period before 1950, there was a shortage of capital equipment as a result of low capital formation during and immediately after the war, and the quality of capital stock was lowered because so much replacement had been delayed.[1] At the same time much fuller use was being made of the labor supply than in pre-war years. Capital per head was therefore abnormally depressed, and higher capital productivity was achieved at the expense of labor productivity. In the 1950s the quality of capital equipment probably increased more rapidly than one would expect in future because an abnormal backlog of old equipment was scrapped.

Disguised Unemployment

Another element of recovery affecting all European countries to some degree in the 1950s was the elimination of uneconomic habits acquired in the inter-war period as a result of prolonged unemployment. One of the effects of a prolonged period of high demand and employment is to attract people from safe but unremunerative jobs.

This second recovery element particularly affects those sectors of the economy where the production unit is the family enterprise, and where employment is difficult to measure. Here, overt unemployment hardly ever exists, but a good deal of manpower can often be removed without loss of output and with little change in existing capital and techniques of production. In many European countries long decades of stagnation or instability had kept people in sectors of the economy where they maintained a modicum of independence and security, even though their living standards were low. The typical case is agriculture, but other sectors have also provided a refuge, particularly retail trade, some services, and even manufacturing in countries where there is a substantial artisan sector as in Germany, where 'handwork' accounted for a quarter of industrial employment in the early 1950s. Some evidence of this phenomenon of disguised unemployment is provided by the fact that in all countries where there is peasant or family farming, agricultural

---

[1] We are speaking here of the capital stock in the sense of the plant and equipment in physical use. If we think instead in terms of the accounting concept of a capital stock after allowance for depreciation, then we would not count the obsolete equipment at all, but simply say that capital per head had been further reduced.

productivity is much lower than in other sectors. It also seems to have been widespread in France where overt unemployment was always small, even in the deep depression of the 1930s, where uneconomic small enterprise has been encouraged by tax privilege and tax evasion, and where small shops and bistros abound.

It is difficult to measure the degree of disguised unemployment, but it is remarkable that in practically every country agricultural productivity rose much faster than total productivity in the 1950s, and agriculture released manpower on a massive scale. Some of the increase in agricultural productivity was, of course, due to increased capital and new techniques, as is clear from the fact that agricultural investment has been high in most countries and agricultural productivity has risen rapidly in Belgium and the United Kingdom where there was little scope for disguised unemployment. It is also true that some of those leaving agriculture were hired workers rather than family members.[1] In spite of this and of some uncertainty about the figures, there is little doubt that many of the 1·4 million who left agriculture in France and Germany and of the million who left it in Italy had been in disguised unemployment.

If, as a compensation for lack of measures for other sectors susceptible to disguised unemployment, we make the crude assumption that all the labor leaving agriculture in the 1950s was previously in disguised unemployment, we would get the productivity figures shown in Table II-7. This reduces productivity growth in all countries, and decreases the spread between the fast- and slow-growing countries. The reduction in France, Germany, Italy and Norway is much larger than in Belgium, the United Kingdom or the United States. However, it has little effect on the Netherlands where productivity growth was fairly fast, and the most effect on Canada where productivity growth was already fairly slow. The once-for-all stimulus from reducing disguised unemployment is only part of the explanation of high growth rates, but it has certainly played an important role and in some cases accounts for about a third of the differential between the fast- and the slow-growing countries. It is probably petering out as a factor affecting Germany, but may have something further to contribute in France and Italy where agricultural employment in 1960 was still 22 and 31 per cent of the labor force, respectively.

The American-European Productivity Gap

The existence of a large productivity differential between Europe and the United States represents another element of recovery which has been exploited by Europe as a source of rapid productivity

[1] O.E.C.D., *Manpower Statistics*, and the special O.E.C.D. report on agricultural manpower, *The Position of the Agricultural Hired Worker*, 1962.

TABLE II–7

THE IMPACT OF DISGUISED AGRICULTURAL UNEMPLOYMENT
ON EMPLOYMENT AND PRODUCTIVITY, 1950–60

	Percentage Increase in Employment from 1950 to 1960	Percentage Addition to Employment from 1950 to 1960 Allowing for Reduction of Disguised Unemployment	Annual Average Percentage Increase in Output per Man-Hour	Annual Average Percentage Increase in Output per Man-Hour Adjusted for Disguised Unemployment
Belgium	4·1	7·6	2·5	2·2
Denmark	10·5	16·1	2·9	2·4
France	3·8	12·4	3·9	3·1
Germany	24·4	33·6	6·0	5·2
Italy	18·9	25·5	4·1	3·5
Netherlands	12·8	15·8	3·7	3·6
Norway	2·3	9·9	3·9	3·2
United Kingdom	6·3	7·2	2·0	1·9
Canada	20·8	29·8	2·5	1·8
United States	12·2	15·7	2·4	2·0

Source: O.E.C.D., *Manpower Statistics*, supplemented by estimates based on the French and Italian censuses. Danish agricultural employment from *Landbrugetsarbejdskraft*, Copenhagen, 1961. U.S., from *National Income Supplement* to *Survey of Current Business*.

growth. This gap existed and widened for decades, so that it could hardly be considered to provide any special reason for a post-war rate of growth faster than that in the inter-war period, even though there has been more awareness of it in Europe in the post-war period, particularly since Rostas made his pioneering studies. There is no doubt that an inferior starting position can be exploited so as to speed the process of growth, particularly if such a position is due to ignorance of the best technical practices, poor management, a poorly educated labor force, and badly organized and uncompetitive markets. If this gap were due to superior American natural resources, or to a larger market, then, of course, it would be much harder to close. However, these elements account for only a small part of the difference between European and U.S. productivity. A major reason for higher U.S. productivity is the larger capital stock per worker. The U.S. productivity growth rate of 2·4 per cent a year from 1870 to 1950, compared with an arithmetic average for the four large European countries of 1·5 per cent, was accompanied by a much higher rate of productive investment. Over this eighty-year period U.S. productive investment averaged about 17 per cent in peacetime as compared with 7 per cent in the United Kingdom. Investment in the United States was favored by a number of special stimuli

TABLE II–8
PROPORTIONATE CONTRIBUTION OF DIFFERENT DEMAND CATEGORIES TO THE 1950–60 G.N.P. INCREASE
Per Cent of G.N.P. Increase at Current Prices over the Decade

	G.N.P.	Consumer Durables	Other Private Consumption	Public Consumption Civilian	Public Consumption Defense	Gross Domestic Investment	Net Foreign Balance	Exports of Goods and Services
Austria	100·0	11·5	44·7	13·0	1·5	29·0	0·2	32·6
Belgium	100·0	8·3	48·8	10·6	4·5	20·6	7·4	51·0
Denmark	100·0	14·8	41·6	11·7	3·6	26·0	2·3	39·3
France	100·0	5·4	58·6	9·6	5·4	19·5	1·5	16·2
Germany	100·0	52·5		10·4	2·8	29·0	5·3	32·8
Italy	100·0	2·6	51·3	17·2		27·7	1·1	21·8
Netherlands	100·0	7·7	39·6	10·7	3·5	28·2	10·2	62·1
Norway	100·0	6·7	48·8	13·1	4·0	27·2	0·3	49·4
Sweden	100·0	6·7	45·1	15·5	5·3	29·5	–2·0	28·7
United Kingdom	100·0	7·9	51·3	11·4	6·4	26·5	–3·5	19·6
Canada	100·0	6·0	57·2	12·3	6·0	23·1	–4·0	15·8
United States	100·0	4·7	54·6	10·9	14·8	14·1	1·0	5·9

Source: September 1962 O.E.C.D. Bulletin, *General Statistics,* except for Belgium and the Netherlands, which are from the September 1961 Bulletin, and Denmark and Norway from the November 1962 issue. The U.S. figures on civilian public consumption were adjusted from 11·1 to 10·9 to exclude purchases of equipment, and the investment figure raised from 13·9 to 14·1 correspondingly. The Norwegian construction and G.N.P. figures were reduced to eliminate repairs and maintenance (see Appendix I on the reasons for these adjustments). The six columns following the G.N.P. column represent the total of G.N.P. The change in the net foreign balance is the differential between the increase in exports (shown in the last column) and imports.

discussed previously, while in Europe it was adversely affected by wars. However, the neglect of past opportunities has in itself provided Europe with a powerful investment stimulus where policy has succeeded in achieving a high and continuously expanding level of demand. To this extent, European growth opportunities are now better than those in the United States, and the relative European advantage has been strengthened by the American failure to achieve a satisfactory level of demand. We shall examine the consequences of this situation in more detail in Chapter III on investment.

Structural Changes in Expenditure and Output
It is worth examining whether variations in the pattern of demand and output increase in the past decade help to explain differences in productivity growth. Table II–8 shows the way in which the total demand increase was distributed in the decade 1950–60. There is a marked difference between the U.S. and the European pattern. In the United States 15 per cent of the increase was devoted to defense spending, twice the figure for any European country and five times the German figure. Investment absorbed more than a quarter of the demand increase in all European countries except Belgium and France, and even in these countries the proportion was well above the 14 per cent figure for the United States. In continental Europe exports provided a powerful stimulus, and the improvement in the

TABLE II–9
PROPORTIONATE CONTRIBUTION OF DIFFERENT PRODUCTION SECTORS
TO THE 1950–60 G.N.P. INCREASE

Per Cent of G.N.P. Increase at Constant Prices over the Decade

	Agriculture	Industry	Other	Total
Austria	8·1	57·5	34·4	100·0
Belgium	2·1	56·9	40·9	100·0
Denmark	13·8	42·6	43·6	100·0
France	6·8	52·7	40·5	100·0
Germany	3·2	62·9	33·9	100·0
Italy	9·5	64·1	26·4	100·0
Netherlands	8·6	49·3	42·1	100·0
Norway	2·9	39·9	57·2	100·0
United Kingdom	4·5	55·8	39·7	100·0
Canada	2·5	35·0	62·6	100·0
United States	2·1	38·2	59·8	100·0

Source: Austria, France, Germany, Italy and the United Kingdom from O.E.C.D., *General Statistics*, September 1962, Norway and the Netherlands from the November 1962 issue. Canada (July 1961 issue) and the United States (September 1961 issue) are not given at constant prices and are estimates; United States figures also include an estimate for depreciation by sector. Belgium and Denmark from 1961 *General Statistics*, September and July issues respectively. The sectors are defined in the same way as in Table II–10.

net foreign balance absorbed a high proportion of resources in
Germany, Belgium and the Netherlands. Here, there is a sharp
contrast with the position of the United Kingdom, Canada and the
United States.

The heavy European demand for investment and exports has, of
course, been concentrated on the manufacturing sector, whereas
American demand has pressed more heavily on the service sector.
This is clear from Table II–9, which shows the distribution of output
increases by sector. In North America 60 per cent of the output
increase has gone to the 'tertiary' sector, and only 40 per cent to
commodity production. In Europe the reverse is true in all countries
except Norway, and the emphasis on commodity production has
been greatest in Germany and Italy.

The effect of these demand changes on productivity can be judged
from Table II–10, which shows how productivity has moved in

TABLE II–10
SECTORAL RATES OF GROWTH OF OUTPUT PER MAN, 1950–60

	Agriculture[a]	Industry[b]	Other	Total
Belgium	5·3	3·5	1·1	2·5
Denmark	5·2			2·3
France	5·5	4·0	2·0	3·9
Germany	5·9	5·7	2·7	5·3
Italy	4·1	5·0	1·5	4·1
Netherlands	5·8	4·4	2·5	3·7
Norway	3·4	2·9	2·6	3·2
United Kingdom	4·1	2·1	1·6	1·9
Canada	4·8	1·7	0·4	2·0
United States	4·4	2·2	1·2	2·1

[a] Agriculture, forestry and fishing.
[b] Mining, manufacturing, gas, water, electricity and construction.

Source: Same as for Tables II–7 and II–9.

different sectors of the economy. The estimates of productivity are
fairly crude, particularly for France and Italy, and are in terms of
output per man rather than output per man-hour. The pattern of
productivity growth is surprisingly similar in spite of the wide
variation in the rate of total productivity growth. With a minor
exception in Italy, all countries show more rapid growth in agriculture than in industry, and more rapid growth in industry than in
services. The spread between agriculture and services is more than
2·5 points in all cases except Norway.

The very rapid productivity growth in agriculture, even in slow-
growing countries, is probably due in large part to the reduction of
disguised unemployment which we have already mentioned, though
it is also due to increased capitalization and technical improvement.
In services, the slow growth is partly due to the convention of

measuring output movements in the government sector by changes in employment, but it is also no doubt a reflection of the fact that productivity gains are harder to achieve in this sector.

One reason why total productivity growth has been slower in the United States and Canada than in Europe is that a greater proportion of the increase in employment has gone into the service sectors where productivity growth has been slower.[1] In the United States and Canada only a fifth of the increase in non-agricultural employment went to industry, as compared with 55 per cent in Germany, 61 per cent in Italy and 63 per cent in the United Kingdom. In other European countries the contrast with the United States was not so marked; nevertheless, the European countries clearly had a structural development more favorable to productivity growth than North America.

We can attempt to measure the impact of structural shifts on productivity by seeing what would have happened to aggregate U.S. productivity if its employment structure had changed in the same way as in Europe and with its sectoral productivity levels moving as they did. We can also apply the change in U.S. employment patterns to European countries. As the implications of the move out of agriculture have already been considered, we can restrict these estimates to non-agricultural movements in order to avoid double counting of structural changes. The results do not suggest that structural shifts have been very important. With U.S. employment movements, German and Italian productivity would have been reduced by only 0·2 per cent per annum, and U.K. productivity would not have been affected at all. Applying the Italian structural shift—which is the most extreme—to the United States, U.S. productivity growth would be raised by 0·3 per cent per annum. Hence, the spread between the best European performers and the United States would be narrowed to a rather modest extent by the elimination of structural shifts, and the gap between them and the United Kingdom would be unchanged.

These hypothetical exercises involve unrealistic assumptions about the transitivity of economic structures. Even when the analysis of structural shifts is confined to one country, the economic significance

---

[1] The productivity effects of structural change do not derive simply from movements of employment between sectors with different growth rates, but also depend on the absolute level of productivity in different sectors. This is not too important in the case of movements between the industrial and tertiary sectors where productivity levels are similar, but in most countries the absolute productivity level in agriculture is about half that in the other two sectors. Hence, the outflow of labor from agriculture—a sector of rapid productivity growth—is not an unfavorable factor for total productivity except in Belgium, Denmark, the Netherlands and the United Kingdom, where agricultural productivity is not too different from that in other sectors.

E

of such statistical manipulation is questionable, because the in-sector productivity movements are not independent of the inter-sectoral shifts (as we have already noted in the case of agriculture), and the division of the economy into three sectors is arbitrary. The impact of structural shift can be changed by choosing a different breakdown, and our 'tertiary' sector is broad enough to conceal a good many divergent movements. Nevertheless, it seems clear that the inter-country variations in overall productivity growth are not attributable to any important degree to structural change, and that they mainly reflect divergences in productivity growth in individual sectors of the economy. The divergence in overall productivity growth is repeated in the industrial sector where the range of performance between countries is at least as wide.[1]

The Effect of European Integration

A major change which affected the European countries in the 1950s was the removal of trade and payments barriers and the rapid expansion of trade. Its greatest impact was in Germany where commodity exports rose from 8·6 per cent of G.N.P. in 1950 to 16·6 per cent in 1960, but the export ratio also rose in many other continental countries (see Table II–11). In the slow-growing coun-tries, by contrast, the share of exports in G.N.P. did not rise in the 1950s, and even declined in the United Kingdom and Canada. The degree to which exports have expanded relative to G.N.P. is fairly closely related to relative rates of growth of G.N.P., but the relation does not hold in all cases. For instance, the export ratio hardly increased in France which has grown fast.

It is difficult to quantify the effect of freer trade on productivity because it stimulates growth in several ways. It permits countries greater freedom to specialize on those commodities which they can produce most efficiently, but it also permits greater economies of scale, and stimulates investment and competition, so that its effects have been felt quite powerfully in France, for example, despite the stable ratio of trade to G.N.P. It is also difficult to separate some of the effects of freer trade from those of high demand. The supply factors we have already noted will tend to raise profits, and the experience of increasing foreign sales in competitive conditions will give entrepreneurs greater faith in the soundness of high investment policies. In several countries such as Belgium, Germany and the Netherlands, export demand was by far the most dynamic element in the economy. Foreign trade was the medium by which the high-

[1] This also happens to be the sector for which we have the best crosscheck on the validity of our figures. Cf. estimates of manufacturing productivity derived from independent sources in Graham Bannock, 'Productivity in Manufacturing', *Productivity Measurement Review*, Paris, November 1962.

TABLE II–11
RATIO OF MERCHANDISE TRADE TO G.N.P. AT CURRENT MARKET PRICES

Imports c.i.f.

	1870	1913	1929	1938	1950	1960
Austria				24·2[a]	20·6	25·0
Belgium-Luxembourg				28·0	25·9	31·2
Denmark	28·7[1]	35·5	29·9	21·5[2]	27·6	30·3
France				10·5	10·4[b]	10·8
Germany	18·5[3]	18·1	14·9	5·9	11·6[c]	14·8[d]
Italy	11·0[4]	16·5	14·5	13·1	10·6	14·7
Netherlands				23·7	41·2	40·4
Norway		32·4	26·8	20·7	32·3	33·0
Sweden	16·3	22·9	20·0	16·2	21·2	23·6
Switzerland				17·3	22·8	26·7
United Kingdom	24·4	24·9	22·7	18·7	18·9	17·5
United States	6·6[5]	5·1	4·5	2·5	3·4	3·1
Canada				10·2	19·6	16·8

Exports f.o.b.

	1870	1913	1929	1938	1950	1960
Austria				24·3[a]	14·1	19·8
Belgium-Luxembourg				26·5	22·1	29·8
Denmark	21·2[1]	29·1	28·1	20·1[2]	21·5	24·9
France				6·9	10·4[b]	11·8
Germany	13·1[3]	17·0	15·0	5·4	8·6[c]	16·6[d]
Italy	10·8[4]	11·3	10·1	6·3	8·6	11·4
Netherlands				17·4	28·3	35·9
Norway		23·0	18·7	14·5	18·6	19·9
Sweden	17·7	22·1	20·3	16·4	19·8	21·0
Switzerland				14·2	19·7	22·4
United Kingdom	18·8	19·8	14·9	8·2	16·3	14·1
United States	6·3[5]	6·1	4·9	3·6	3·5	4·0
Canada				15·7	17·5	14·7

[a] Includes trade with Germany.
[b] Including the Saar.
[c] Federal Republic (excluding the Saar) and West Berlin.
[d] Federal Republic (including the Saar) and West Berlin.
[1] 1874.   [2] 1937.   [3] 1875.   [4] 1872.   [5] 1889.

Source: A. Maddison, 'Growth and Fluctuation in the World Economy, 1870–1960', Banca Nazionale del Lavoro Quarterly Review, June 1962.

demand policies of individual countries spread their effect throughout Europe.

The post-war process of integrating the European economies has had several elements, all of which have affected productivity. There has been co-operation in removing the obstacles to trade and payments erected in the 1930s and during the war. Continuous progress has been made since 1948, when restrictions were practically universal except in Belgium and Switzerland, and the removal of quantitative restrictions on manufactured goods is now virtually complete. All our countries have a high degree of currency convertibility, and have adopted measures to foster mutual credit and international liquidity. Co-operation has steadily grown on general economic policy questions of common interest, and the beggar-your-neighbour policy instruments have been abandoned. There is now constant consultation on matters which would have been regarded as of purely national concern before the war. Governments share information and statistics, and sometimes reveal their policy thinking more freely to each other in private conclave then they tend to do at home. This enables decisions to be taken with full consciousness of the probable external repercussions and reactions, even if it does not guarantee that the policies are the right ones. In the course of the 1950s, there was some progress towards tariff reduction on a worldwide basis in the G.A.T.T., and there were unilateral German tariff reductions in 1956 and 1957. But extensive tariff reduction got under way only at the beginning of 1959 with the creation of E.E.C. and E.F.T.A. Within the E.E.C. steps have also been taken to free movements of labor, capital and enterprise, and to harmonize social policy.

The impact of these developments has been a matter of controversy amongst economists and others, particularly as they have political as well as economic implications. As a result, their consequences are often depicted in rather extreme terms, with little regard for the other factors influencing growth. Thus the effects of E.E.C. tend to be over-emphasized at the expense of other elements in the process of integration. It is difficult to prove much empirically, as there is very little analogous experience of integration on this scale, and economic theory is still in an unsettled state on the dynamic effects of such a process, which are obviously relevant in economies that are growing so fast.

The obvious advantages of integration are those of free trade—a better allocation of existing resources and new investment between high- and low-cost producers. Distortions are involved when this process is regionalized and involves discrimination against the outside world, but in fact the reduction of barriers to European trade and payments in the 1950s was always followed by a reduction in barriers against the outside world. Discriminatory liberalization was later applied to the rest of the world, so that the net effect so far has certainly been to improve resource allocation. These opportunities for concentrating resources on sectors of comparative productivity advantage have been analogous in their effects to the removal of disguised unemployment, except that all factors and all sectors have been affected to some degree. It probably had particularly favorable effects in Germany and Italy where pre-war autarky was most stringently practiced. Freer trade has, of course, increased consumer satisfaction in a non-measurable but important way, by increasing the range of choice and improving design, e.g. in cars and shoes.

The further removal of tariff barriers within the Common Market can be expected to yield additional specialization gains, although, as this will be a discriminatory process, it will have some trade-diverting results which will adversely affect productivity both inside and outside its area. As the external tariff will be lower than the previous average, the diversion effect is likely to be smaller than the positive effect.

These possibilities for increased specialization are not the only effect of integration. It has also brought economies of scale and a stimulus to competition and investment. Before considering these other effects, we should note that there is a curious scepticism amongst economists about the benefits described above. Professor Viner's classic work[1] on customs unions lays heavy stress on the dangers of trade diversion, and Professor Scitovsky, who has written a most illuminating study of the other advantages of integration, is doubtful as to whether the trade-creating and specialization effects are substantial.[2] Professor Viner was, of course, dealing with a more restrictive theoretical situation, and not with the actual situation in which European integration was itself a major stimulus to greater freedom in world trade.

Professor Scitovsky, on the other hand, applies his judgment to what had already happened in the field of liberalization from quantitative restrictions and what was likely to happen as a result of tariff reduction in the Common Market. He suggests that the abolition of quantitative restrictions had little effect in increasing intra-European trade, noting that the share of intra-European trade in the world total was 47 per cent in 1956 compared with 42 per cent in 1938. Apart from the fact that 1938 is not the most relevant benchmark for measuring the impact of post-war policy, it also ignores the impact of European liberalization on the level of world trade. From 1950 to 1961 intra-European trade rose from 41 per cent to 53 per cent of a world total which in the same period had increased in value about two and a half times. As to the impact of tariff reduction, Scitovsky suggests that the 'gain from increased intra-European specialization is likely to be insignificant'. He suggests that the difference in natural resource endowment between European countries is not large, and that transport and other cost variations within countries are greater than those between countries. The main impact of integration, in his view, is as a means of promoting competition. For this reason, integration will have a greater impact in reallocating resources

[1] Cf. Jacob Viner, *The Customs Union Issue*, Carnegie Foundation for International Peace, Stevens & Sons, London, 1950.
[2] Cf. T. Scitovsky, *Economic Theory and Western European Integration*, George Allen and Unwin, London, 1958, pp. 32 and 67.

between high- and low-cost producers within a given country than between countries. We can agree with Scitovsky that the competition effect is important in some cases, particularly in France, but the trade-creating effect of both trade liberalization and tariff reduction can hardly be doubted in view of the rise in the ratio of trade to G.N.P. and particularly of intra-European trade to G.N.P. The impact of greater specialization as a productivity-stimulating factor in this period has been all the greater for the fact that the process of specialization had been severely reversed in the inter-war period of trade restriction.

Before discussing the impact of competition, we should consider the question of economies of scale. Many manufacturing processes have a fairly large minimum level of operation in order to achieve lowest costs. The markets of many European countries are often too small to achieve these economies, though the existing possibilities for trade have clearly offset these difficulties to some extent, for there is no noticeable difference in productivity levels between the small and the large countries of Europe. It does seem that in several important industries the U.S. productivity advantage has in the past derived from a larger scale of production in an economy which is four times the size of Germany and seventy-five times that of Norway. It can hardly be an accident that the U.S. advantage in labor productivity in pre-war years was greatest in mass-produced standardized commodities—radios, automobiles, rubber tires, electric lamps, tins and glass containers.[1] We cannot, of course, assume that relative labor productivity itself is a guide to costs, for these industries are more heavily capitalized in the United States than in Europe. However, since they are also the goods for which U.S. prices have been relatively cheapest, one may reasonably assume that economies of scale have played some role.

In the past decade or so, the growth of intra-European trade has certainly provided scope for exploiting some economies of scale, on both the firm and industry level. The gains in European productivity have been particularly large in mass production industries such as cars and household durables, and trade in these items has greatly increased. However, the rapid growth in income and the high elasticity of demand for durables at European income levels have been a major factor in the expansion of the market, and although these items have increased their share in total trade, the proportion of production of these goods which is traded has not changed a great

---

[1] Cf. Laszlo Rostas, *Comparative Productivity in British and American Industry*, National Institute for Economic and Social Research, Cambridge University Press, London, 1948, pp. 33, 36 and 38. In these industries, U.S. productivity in pre-war years was about four times as high as British, as compared with an overall advantage of about half this.

deal. The rise in productivity due to exploitation of economies of scale is therefore probably a normal consequence of rising income rather than a specific result of increased trade. The new possibilities of exploiting economies of scale and choosing the best location for production afforded by the Common Market policy of freedom for movement of capital and enterprise as well as goods will probably only be utilized gradually. It requires a good deal of investment to achieve such economies, and as part of it will be made abroad, entrepreneurs will probably not take full advantage of the possibilities until the final stage of the Common Market is completed and the extra political and currency risks from investment outside one's own country are considered to have disappeared.

It has been strongly argued, particularly by U.S. economists, that European productivity has suffered from lack of competition, whether in the form of cartels and large monopolies, or the artificial protection of small-scale producers. This is held to have hampered productivity growth by allocating resources inefficiently between low- and high-cost producers, by distorting the pattern of investment, by preventing the achievement of economies of scale or standardization, and even by diverting the pattern of demand away from mass-produced commodities. Sometimes it is suggested or implied that lack of competition has reduced the level of investment, but this aspect is usually given less weight than the argument of misuse of resources. In this situation, the impact of integration is to throw open markets to new competitors who will not observe the existing 'code' of restrictive practices. Domestic producers will then be forced to take a more dynamic attitude to their markets, and high-cost producers will be pushed out by domestic low-cost producers. Productivity and specialization will be increased without any necessary increase in the ratio of output traded.

Some of the descriptions of the European as compared with the American entrepreneur smack of caricature. The dynamic, innovating, ruthless American is contrasted with the European who prefers an easy life, stability of markets, a clubby tolerance of inefficient competitors because of a mutual desire to maintain the social privileges of self-employment, governments willing to subsidize inefficient small enterprises by permitting tax evasion and giving tax privileges, the production of traditional quality articles rather than mass-produced goods, and a hierarchical social structure which prevents standardized consumption patterns. There is some truth in this, but there is a good deal of mythology. Many European firms are very large, and many are actively seeking to increase their share of the market. In spite of barriers intra-European trade has always been very large, and the lag in mass production and consumer credit is, or was, due more to the lag in income levels behind the United States than to lack of initiative.

Empirical evidence on competition is hard to muster. We would like to know how wide are the spreads in cost between different firms in each country, whether production is concentrated on the most efficient firms, and whether the spread has narrowed as a result of integration. Here, there is little comparative evidence, but Scitovsky cites French reports that excess capacity is present in similar degree for both high- and low-cost producers, though this may well be true in the United States as well. He suggests, on the basis of analysis of miscellaneous productivity reports, that the cost spread, at least as indicated by labor productivity, is wider in Europe than in the United States. Spreads in labor productivity are not, of course, an adequate reflection of the spread in unit costs. To a large extent, the inter-firm spreads are a reflection of the age distribution of the capital stock they are using. There will, of course, be a spread even within a firm owing to its use of capital of different ages, and the distribution of these in-firm spreads will affect the range of inter-firm spread. We have no measure showing what has happened to these cost spreads in the process of integration, although it is obvious, in some cases, e.g. in the motor industry, that competition has eliminated many smaller firms and promoted economies of scale in the past few years.

Although the evidence on European competition is not as well documented as one would like, there is undoubtedly a good deal of truth in some of the American descriptions of European behavior. We must, however, ask why the European entrepreneur reacts this way. If it were simply due to a difference in social attitudes and structure, there is little reason to suppose that integration would help, for entrepreneurs would merely be competing with more people having the same background. Scitovsky seems to argue that a major reason for lack of competition in Europe is to be found in the substantial indivisibilities in investment opportunities in markets of the European size. The adoption of the best technique would therefore necessarily involve the capture of a substantially larger share of the market for a particular producer. The prospect of a costly struggle to deprive rivals of their share of the market induces entrepreneurs to settle for a second best. In other cases, it may encourage the formation of a monopoly whose share of the market is guaranteed by protection and whose further incentives to develop productivity are thereby limited. The enlargement of the market would lead to the exploitation of economies of scale which are technically possible within the framework of national markets, but inhibited by lack of competition.

There is, however, another explanation of the behavior of European entrepreneurs and of the existence of wider cost spreads in

Europe than in America. We have argued that the maintenance of very high and steadily expanding levels of demand is sufficient reason for the acceleration in investment in post-war Europe. It is natural that the contrast in the historical demand situation faced by entrepreneurs in Europe and America, and the post-war acceleration of growth in Europe, should be manifested by an apparent difference in the motivations of entrepreneurs. Their attitudes have, in fact, been a reflection of the general momentum of the economy rather than of any fundamental difference of approach to the economic process. The divergence in productivity levels between different firms is also a consequence of differing growth rates and not necessarily a reflection of different competitive situations. The inter-firm productivity differences arise largely because firms work with capital of different vintages. In an economy which is growing more rapidly, as was the case in the United States until the 1950s, there will be a younger capital stock on average, a greater concentration on firms with the higher productivity levels, and a smaller spread between best-practice and worst-practice firms than in Europe because of faster amortization.

The acceleration of European demand would itself tend to lower the cost spread between firms and increase the number of firms using best-practice techniques, because it stimulates investment. It will change the attitude of entrepreneurs to investment and to their markets and enhance competition.

Hence, we reject the idea that the size of markets has been the major force restraining European competition, or that removal of trade barriers is the main cause of any increase in competition. We also reject the idea that the European entrepreneur is a basically different animal from the American (except, perhaps, in France, which in this, as in other respects, is *sui generis*), although in some important senses the greater stratification of European society has no doubt been a hindrance to productivity, both in standardizing products and in making the best use of human resources.

The maintenance of high levels of demand and the prospect of fairly continuous expansion have made the major contribution to changing European attitudes. Without this high demand, integration itself would never have taken place. However, international trade has played an important part in influencing entrepreneurial expectations in Europe. All European countries are heavily dependent on external trade, and the experience of the years 1914–48 was extremely unsettling. Trade and, hence, a substantial part of demand, was interrupted by wars and by the vagaries of commercial policy. In this situation, European entrepreneurs became wary of risky investment decisions. It was the bad climate of demand, to which external trade dependence contributed a good deal, rather than the limited size of domestic markets, which induced this caution. By contrast, the postwar expansion in trade gave a fillip to European expectations and investment which was not felt in America.

Foreign trade has helped to improve the climate in which entrepreneurs operate, not primarily by creating a wider area of competition, but by the elimination of external deflationary shocks,[1] and by the security induced by the feeling that export markets would steadily increase. This new optimism about exports has affected productivity mainly by raising the level of investment and not primarily by improving its allocation. It has been experienced unevenly by different countries, and has had its greatest relative impact in Germany, Italy and the Netherlands. It is curious that most commentators on integration have attached little weight to this, and its impact on investment levels has been discussed largely in connection with the possibility of encouraging a larger inflow of U.S. capital.

In assessing the impact of integration on productivity, importance should, therefore, be attached to the old-fashioned advantages of better resource allocation through freer trade. The gain from economies of scale or greater competition has probably been of minor importance, but integration has strengthened the forces making for buoyant entrepreneurial expectations and has helped raise the level of investment. Insofar as integration means the reduction of trade barriers, its economic effects are likely to continue for a few more years, but must obviously cease at some stage and be once-for-all in their impact. Integration in the wider sense, i.e., the reduction in entrepreneurial risks brought about by a new mode of international behavior and the avoidance of external deflationary shocks, should continue to promote high levels of investment and bring a permanent improvement in productivity growth. The effect of a wider freedom of movement for capital, labor and enterprise, and of integration of tax systems remains to be seen. The level of productivity in European countries is not sufficiently different for factor movements to play a major income-equalizing role, and investment is not limited by the capacity to save in any country. These benefits of integration will probably accrue mainly to small countries which are centrally located, such as the Netherlands and Belgium, where projects may have been neglected in the past because of the limited size of the home market.

The Role of Investment

The factors thus far examined—recovery elements, structural changes and increased integration—have in themselves only partially explained the acceleration of European growth and the difference

[1] Balance-of-payments difficulties have not been avoided, but they were almost all due to internal inflationary pressures.

between the post-war performance of countries. Our basic problem is to explain why Germany could get productivity to grow at 6 per cent and France, Italy, the Netherlands, Norway and Switzerland at around 4 per cent. The factors examined so far probably do not account for more than about 1 per cent of these growth rates, except in Germany. Some of these elements are not independent, and some of them are opportunities that could be exploited only with the help of investment. High investment has, in fact, been the major factor explaining the acceleration of post-war output in response to high demand. In all European countries considered here, the rate of investment in the 1950s was half as high again as it had ever been before on any sustained basis. In Germany and the Netherlands, investment averaged a quarter of G.N.P. in the 1950s, in Norway it was even higher, and in several other countries it was a fifth of G.N.P. The investment ratio was lowest in the United Kingdom and the United States. In the United States it was, in fact, lower than the historical average. Because of its importance, the role of investment is analyzed at length in the next chapter.

CHAPTER III

INVESTMENT AND GROWTH

The role of investment is so important in growth and so much a matter of controversy in both economic theory and empirical analysis that it deserves lengthier treatment than the other growth factors so far considered.

From the evidence available in Table III–1 and Appendix I, it is

TABLE III–1
TOTAL GROSS DOMESTIC INVESTMENT AS A PROPORTION OF G.N.P.
AT CURRENT PRICES

| | Average of Years Cited | | |
	1900–13	1914–49	1950–60
Belgium			16·5
Denmark	15·0	12·6[a]	18·1
France			19·1
Germany		14·3[b]	24·0
Italy	15·4	13·5	20·8
Netherlands			24·2
Norway	12·7	15·4[c]	26·4
Sweden	12·3	15·5	21·3
United Kingdom	7·7	7·6	15·4
Canada	25·5	16·0[d]	24·8
United States	20·6	14·7	19·1

[a] 1921–49.　[b] 1925–37.　[c] 1914–38.　[d] 1926–49.

Source: See Appendix I.

clear that all European countries devoted a higher proportion of G.N.P. to investment in the 1950s than in any earlier recorded period. Only at the height of previous booms has investment reached the levels which are now normal. Furthermore, the rate of investment rose throughout the decade in almost every country. Investment was highest in Germany, the Netherlands and Norway, which are among the fastest-growing countries, and lowest in slow-growing Belgium and the United Kingdom. The U.S. investment rate in the 1950s was below that of the fast-growing European countries and no better than the rates it had achieved steadily over several decades before the first world war. Canadian investment was as high as in Europe, but no higher than had been achieved historically in Canada. In both Canada and the United States investment rates fell during the 1950s and are now well below their peak for this period. Thus there seems to have been a distinct association between the acceleration of growth and the increased level of investment in the 1950s.

The relationship between the share of resources devoted to investment and the output growth achieved is not uniform. This is clear from Table III–2, which shows the investment-output ratio.[1] These

TABLE III–2
INVESTMENT–OUTPUT RATIO[a]

	1900–13	1913–50	1950–60
Belgium			5·7
Denmark	4·1	5·0[b]	5·5
France			4·3
Germany		4·1[c]	3·2
Italy	5·7	10·4	3·5
Netherlands			5·0
Norway	4·9	5·3[d]	7·5
Sweden	3·3	7·0	6·5
United Kingdom	6·4	4·6	5·9
Canada	4·6	4·6[e]	6·4
United States	5·2	5·1	5·8

[a] Average ratio of total gross domestic investment to G.N.P. at current prices divided by rate of growth of output in real terms.
[b] 1921–50.   [c] 1925–37.   [d] 1913–38.   [e] 1926–50.

Source: Appendices A and I.

ratios have varied a good deal between countries and over time, but there was a tendency in the 1950s for the faster-growing countries to have lower investment requirements per unit of extra output. The range of these ratios is so wide that some analysts discount the role of capital in growth and instead attribute major importance to the independent effect of technological innovation. In such explanations, changes in growth rates are due to waves of innovation which are unevenly dispersed over time and in their impact on individual countries. Others attribute differences in growth to variations in the skill and technical ability of entrepreneurs, or simply to differences in national character—though the latter explanation can hardly be applied to countries whose growth rate has greatly accelerated. As we consider investment to be of major importance in explaining the acceleration of growth and believe that the impact of technical progress will depend largely on the rate of investment, we are under some compulsion to explain in detail why the relation of investment to output has varied between countries, and to see how it may move in future.

[1] This ratio is sometimes called the gross incremental capital-output ratio (I.C.O.R.). We use the term 'capital-output ratio' in this chapter to refer to the total depreciated capital stock divided by output.

The Pattern of Investment
The investment-output relationship may vary because of differences
in the structure of investment. Residential construction contributes
little to increasing the output potential of the economy, but its
importance in capital formation is large. It is therefore useful to
exclude this from the investment ratio and concentrate the analysis
on 'productive' investment. This reduces the investment-output
ratio, but it does not change the general picture. The acceleration of
investment in the 1950s is just as strong, and there is an even wider
range of investment-output ratios between countries (Table III–3).

TABLE III–3
ALTERNATIVE INVESTMENT–OUTPUT RATIO[a]

	1950–60
Belgium	4·0
Denmark	4·2
France	3·1
Germany	2·1
Italy	2·6
Netherlands	3·6
Norway	6·2
Sweden	4·6
United Kingdom	4·3
Canada	4·8
United States	4·1

[a] Average ratio of fixed non-residential investment to G.N.P. in current prices
divided by the rate of growth of output in real terms.

Source: Appendices A and I.

Some investment is destined to increase amenities rather than output,
e.g. hospitals. There are no comparable data on such investment, but
it is rather small and there is no reason to suppose that its exclusion
from 'productive' investment would change the picture.

Investment requirements may vary because of different patterns
of industrial development. Capital requirements in energy and
transportation are usually about four times as high as in manufacturing and services, so that a heavy bias towards the first two sectors,
which might well arise temporarily from large indivisible projects,
should raise the ratio. This seems to have been the case in the 1950s
in two of the smaller countries with a high ratio: in Norway[1] and
Sweden about half of non-residential investment went to energy and
transport, compared with a third or less in France, Germany, Italy
and the United Kingdom (see Table III–4). For North America, data

[1] The influence of structural factors as a cause of the high Norwegian capital-
output ratio is denied by O. Aukrust, 'Investment and Economic Growth',
Productivity Measurement Review, February 1959, p. 42. But he is comparing
with the past and not with other countries. Investment in shipping has also risen
since his reference period.

TABLE III–4
INDUSTRIAL BREAKDOWN OF FIXED NON-RESIDENTIAL
INVESTMENT, 1953–59[a]

	Agriculture, Forestry and Fishing	Mining, Manufacturing and Construction	Transport	Electricity, Gas and Water	Other
France[b]	10·2	34·9	19·0	12·8	23·2
Germany	10·7	38·9	20·0	8·2	22·2
Italy	16·8	33·3	21·7	7·9	20·3
Norway	9·7	22·4	37·8	8·7	21·3
Sweden	6·3	28·1	32·0	15·8	18·0
United Kingdom	4·9	36·4	15·1[c]	14·5	29·2[c]

[a] Cumulated gross capital formation in each sector as a percentage of total fixed non-residential investment at constant (1954) prices.

[b] Figures for France refer to 1956–60 and are in current prices.

[c] Road construction and road goods vehicles are included in 'Other'.

Source: O.E.E.C. Bulletin, General Statistics, March 1961, except for French figures, which are derived from O.E.C.D., National Accounts Division.

on the industrial distribution of investment are not available in the same form as for Europe. It seems, however, that U.S. investment was distributed in much the same way as in the big European countries, whereas Canadian investment was biased towards capital-intensive industries. There was thus no substantial difference between the structure of investment of the four big countries of Europe and the United States, though their aggregate investment-output ratios differed a good deal. For the smaller countries, however, structural factors seem to have played a role in producing high investment-output ratios.

The distribution of investment by type of asset might be expected to affect the investment-output ratio. Buildings have a much longer life than machinery and equipment and contribute less directly to increased output. There was no marked association of investment distribution by type of asset and the investment-output ratio in the 1950s, but Sweden and Canada devoted more than half of investment to construction compared with only a third in the United Kingdom and Germany (see Table III–5). It is, in fact, likely that construction investment was relatively higher in Canada and Sweden for climatic reasons, both because more solid buildings are required and because bad weather raises construction costs.

The Measurement of Investment

The figures on investment rates might, of course, differ for purely statistical reasons. Investment includes producers' durable goods, transport equipment, buildings and inventories. It excludes consumers' durables, government expenditure on military equipment

TABLE III–5
BREAKDOWN OF TOTAL GROSS DOMESTIC INVESTMENT BY
TYPE OF ASSET, 1950–60[a]

	Machinery and Equipment	Non-residential Construction	Change in Inventories	Residential Construction
Belgium	7·3	4·3	0·5	4·3
Denmark	9·0	4·7	1·6	2·9
France	8·1	5·4	1·8	3·9
Germany	11·1	5·2	2·7	5·0
Italy	9·0	6·2	0·9	4·7
Netherlands	11·0	6·8	2·2	4·3
Norway	15·5	6·3	1·2	3·4
Sweden	7·5	7·7	1·1	5·0
United Kingdom[b]	7·4	3·7	1·0	3·0
Canada	8·3	10·4	1·4	4·7
United States	7·2	6·2	1·2	4·5

[a] Average ratio of each type of investment to G.N.P. at current prices.
[b] Excludes property transfer costs (stamp duty), which amounted to 0·3 per cent of G.N.P. and are not allocable by type of investment.

Source: O.E.C.D. Bulletin, General Statistics.

and military buildings, and expenditures on repairs and maintenance unless they involve major additions to structures. It is difficult to achieve comparable definitions in such a complex field, but the O.E.E.C. did a great deal to standardize the estimates for different countries, so that the figures can be treated with reasonable confidence. There remain minor possibilities of variation mainly because of different accounting practices in the treatment of major repair work and the allocation of car purchases between consumption and investment. These possibilities are examined in detail in Appendix I, which describes a number of adjustments that have been made to enhance the comparability of the figures.

The relative price of investment goods varies between countries. The extent to which this was so in 1950 can be gauged from Table III–6,[1] which shows investment ratios in eight European countries in terms of U.S. relative prices as well as their own prices. The main point that emerges from this table is that investment goods were relatively more expensive in all European countries except Belgium than in the United States (i.e. column 1 is higher than column 2). This U.S. advantage was probably reduced somewhat in the course of the 1950s. Nevertheless, it is clear that the other tables at national prices understate the investment effort of the United States relative to that in Europe. A comparison of national investment efforts in real terms

[1] Derived from Milton Gilbert and Associates, op. cit., p. 87. This source also gives figures for 1955, but they are not as reliable as the figures for 1950 as they are fairly crude extrapolations for a period in which the relative price of certain capital goods was changing rapidly. The figures are also too crude to permit significant comparisons between prices in different European countries.

TABLE III-6
RATIO OF NON-RESIDENTIAL FIXED INVESTMENT TO G.N.P.
AT NATIONAL PRICES AND U.S. RELATIVE PRICES IN 1950

	Investment Ratio in National Prices	Investment Ratio in U.S. Relative Prices
Belgium	11·5	13·2
Denmark	12·3	10·4
France	13·6	11·3
Germany	14·3	9·7
Italy	14·8	9·5
Netherlands	16·3	11·5
Norway	22·9	17·2
United Kingdom[a]	9·9	7·9
United States	13·9	13·9

[a] Excludes stamp duty.

Source: Column 1 from O.E.C.D., General Statistics, September 1962, and 1961. Column 2 from Milton Gilbert and Associates, op. cit., p. 87.

would serve to reinforce our later argument about the higher level of U.S. investment over many decades in the past and the better opportunities which Europe now has of achieving productivity gains.

General Influences Affecting the Productivity of Investment
The major differences between investment-output ratios are not due to structural differences or to faulty statistics, but to the following macro-economic reasons:

a. The use of capacity is one important factor. Variations in capacity use were significant in the 1950s, and help to explain why Germany had a lower investment-output ratio than the United Kingdom or the United States.

b. The proportion of gross investment going to replacement is lower in fast-growing countries, and helps explain why their gross investment-output ratios were lower in the 1950s.

c. Countries have differed widely in the contribution of increased employment to output. These variations have a considerable impact on capital requirements. A given output increase requires less capital if more labor is used.

d. Because of technical progress, the effect of different types of investment cannot be separated quite as neatly as has just been suggested. In particular, the distinction between replacement and new investment is blurred. Technical progress cannot be given any substantial independent role in explaining differences in economic growth in Europe in the 1950s. The technical possibilities open to the European economies are substantially similar. There is, however, an important difference in the role of technical progress in Europe and in the United States. European countries should get a better productivity return for a given rate of investment than the United

F

ates because they have a lower absolute level of capital per worker, ïd are therefore exploiting existing technical knowledge to a lesser extent.

e. Inter-country variations in the productivity of investment can arise from differences in the quality of management, but there is little reason to suppose that in this particular group of countries the basic attributes of management are very different. If anything, there are reasons for supposing that the quality of management is better in the slow-growing United States than it is in France or Italy. In fact, the capacity of management to absorb investment in an advanced industrial country will depend to a large extent on the economic climate. This is conditioned primarily by government economic policy whose impact is examined in the next chapter.

Capacity Use

Most countries started the 1950s with a strain on capacity which was reduced over the decade. In Germany, however, there was a good deal of spare capacity in 1950, and a fair amount of shadow capacity, i.e. capital, particularly buildings, which could be reactivated by minor repairs.[1] Krengel has estimated that in 1950 only 78 per cent of German industrial capacity was being used as compared with 90 per cent in 1960.[2] Most attempts to measure capacity use, such as this one of Krengel's, refer to 'normal' capacity and not to physical potential. Use of capacity is lower in modern industry than in the early days of the industrial revolution when shift working was standard practice. If the capital stock were used every day for twenty-four hours, it would be used 8,760 hours a year, whereas the average working year for capital cannot be very different from the average working year for labor, as shown in Table I–8, because shift working is limited to only a few industries like iron and steel, and electricity, where capital costs are particularly high. It is therefore likely that the capital stock must be used on average less than 2,500 hours in Europe and even less in the United States. If we allow 15 per cent of the year for repairs and maintenance, normal capacity use would be about a third of potential capacity. It is clear, therefore, that entrepreneurs always have some scope for growth without investment, particularly in the short term.

The concept of a normal degree of capacity use is therefore bound to be somewhat arbitrary and it will change over time. There are

[1] From 1950–55 German capital costs per unit of steel capacity were half of those in the United Kingdom because Germany was developing existing sites, whereas new British developments were largely on green field sites. Cf. *Europe in 1960*, O.E.E.C., 1956, p. 51.

[2] 'Produktionskapazitäten, Kapitalintensität und Kapitalausnutzung der Westdeutschen Industrie', *Vierteljahrshefte für Wirtschaftsforschung*, Berlin, 1962, p. 58.

several reasons for expecting the 'normal' capital-output ratio to have changed in the post-war period, apart from any changes in technical requirements,[1] structure of output, or cyclical pressures of demand. Capital equipment was intensively used in wartime and in the early post-war years when demand and employment were very high and investment low. The productivity of capital was increased at the expense of labor productivity. As conditions became more normal and labor input grew more slowly, the use of capacity became less intense. Part of the investment of the 1950s has gone to provide amenities which were generally curtailed in wartime as their main effect is to increase the comfort of workers and management rather than their productive efficiency, e.g. better office space and furniture, more and newer cars for the managerial and sales staff, improved canteen facilities, etc. A greater margin of spare capacity is needed in more normal market conditions where capacity to meet demand quickly is an important factor in maintaining sales and where seasonal variations in demand, e.g. in motor cars, have re-emerged. There has also been some reduction in normal working hours which will lead to a minor increase in capacity requirements.[2]

In view of these difficulties of defining 'normality' it is for practical purposes impossible to compare the degree to which actual use of capacity in different countries has deviated from a 'normal' situation. We have to content ourselves, therefore, with seeing how the average capital-output ratio changed during the 1950s. Estimates of these

[1] There may, of course, be technical reasons which would change the capital-output ratio. These would probably be operative only in the rather long run as it takes some time to change the characteristics of a stock with a fairly long life. The long-term movement of the capital-output ratio will not reflect purely technical influences. If inventions are predominantly capital-saving, this may tend to make investment more profitable and there may be an offsetting incentive to invest more. The average capital-output ratio in the United States was considerably lower in the 1950s than in pre-war years. In 1929 it was $2 \cdot 2$ (excluding housing and inventories) as compared with $1 \cdot 5$ in 1950. In Germany the comparable ratio (i.e., excluding depreciation) was $2 \cdot 2$ in 1929 and $1 \cdot 4$ in 1955. The fall in the German ratio net of replacement was from 4 to $2 \cdot 5$ in this period. No fall is observable in the U.K. ratio. The fall in the United States seems to have been due mainly to structures, the ratio for equipment being about the same as pre-war; cf. G. Terborgh, various numbers of the *Capital Goods Review*, Machinery and Allied Products Institute, Washington, D.C., particularly No. 22, for the private sector of the economy. D. G. Wooden and R. C. Wasson show the same finding for U.S. manufacturing in 'Manufacturing Investment since 1929', *Survey of Current Business*, November 1956. The estimates of the National Bureau of Economic Research are summarized by E. D. Domar in *The Theory of Capital*, edited by F. A. Lutz and D. C. Hague, International Economic Association, Macmillan, London, 1961. It is clear from this that the most dramatic reduction in the United States has been in public utilities and transport industries.

[2] A 10 per cent reduction in working hours would not mean a 10 per cent reduction in capacity use but perhaps a 3 per cent reduction, as most equipment is idle for two-thirds of the day in any case.

average ratios for the whole economy are available for Germany, the Netherlands, Norway, the United Kingdom and the United States.[1]

The figures do serve to confirm our general expectations. In Norway and the United Kingdom, the average capital-output ratio seems to have risen substantially in the 1950s. In Norway it rose by about 14 per cent from 1950 to 1959,[2] and in the United Kingdom by about 12 per cent from 1950 to 1960.[3] In Sweden it has also been suggested that the capital-output ratio rose during the 1950s.[4] In the United States the ratio was fractionally higher in 1957 than in 1950, and has probably risen somewhat since then.[5] In the Netherlands the ratio appears to have been the same in 1958 as in 1950.[6] In Germany it fell by 11 per cent between 1950 and 1955, but the evidence suggests that it has risen somewhat since then.[7] As evidence for other countries is lacking, we can only guess what might have happened elsewhere. The German experience is likely to have been exceptional, although in Italy the investment-output ratio was very high from 1913–50 (see Table III–2), and this may reflect the creation of excess capacity which was fully used only in the 1950s. Most other European countries probably had some increase in the average capital-output ratio in the 1950s, and this was almost certainly the case in Canada.

The effect of these changes in the average capital-output ratio on the investment-output ratio can be illustrated as follows: If a country

[1] These estimates generally refer to the stock of capital calculated by the perpetual inventory method after allowance for straight-line depreciation, though the length of life assumed for different assets varies between countries to some extent. As long as the assumptions about length of life of assets are constant over time for each country, the figures will serve our purpose well enough as we are not interested in the absolute level of the ratios but only in their movement. For the United Kingdom the ratio of net fixed capital stock (excluding housing) to G.N.P. was 1·4 in 1951 and 1·6 in 1960, in Germany it was 1·5 in 1950 and 1·4 in 1955. In the United States it was 1·5 in 1950 and 1·6 in 1957, and in the Netherlands it was 1·6 in 1958. Figures net of replacement would be higher than this. For Germany, Grünig has calculated a figure net of replacement as well as net of depreciation. His capital-output ratio net of replacement was 3·1 in 1950 and 2·5 in 1955.

[2] *Statistical Yearbook of Norway 1962*, Central Bureau of Statistics, Oslo, 1962.

[3] P. Redfern, 'Net Investment in Fixed Assets in the United Kingdom 1938–53', *Journal of the Royal Statistical Society*, 1955, extended to 1960 from *National Income and Expenditure 1962*, H.M.S.O., London, 1962.

[4] E. Lundberg, *Economic Journal*, December 1959, p. 666.

[5] J. W. Kendrick, *op. cit.*, pp. 301 and 322. The Council of Economic Advisers, in its *Economic Report to the President*, January 1962, p. 55, suggested that there was 7·7 per cent spare capacity in the economy in 1961.

[6] *Statistische en econometrische onderzoekingen*, third quarter 1960, p. 114, Central Bureau of Statistics.

[7] F. Grünig, *Versuch einer Volksvermögensrechnung der Deutschen Bundesrepublik*, Deutsches Institut für Wirtschaftsforschung, Berlin, 1958. Some evidence for 1955–60 movements can be gathered from Krengel's figures for industry.

started in 1950 with 10 per cent spare capacity and its normal capital-output ratio were 2·5, it could economize its investment effort over the 1950s by an amount equal to 25 per cent of the initial G.N.P. If the spare capacity were absorbed gradually over the decade, the country would be able to economize on its investment effort each year by 2·5 per cent of the initial year G.N.P. Another country with the same 'normal' capital-output ratio of 2·5 which reduced its use of capacity by 10 per cent over the decade, either because it started with overstrained capacity and/or ended the decade with some slack, would have to add correspondingly to its investment effort. In the case of Germany, for instance, the absence of spare capacity would have meant having a non-residential fixed investment rate of about 18 per cent instead of 16·3 per cent of the average G.N.P. of the decade to sustain its rate of growth. This would have raised its investment-output ratio from 2·1 to 2·4. Similarly, if the United States had avoided the creation of excess capacity in the 1950s, its ratio would probably have been nearer to 3·3 than to 4·1. It is clear, therefore, that changes in capacity use can explain substantial differences in the investment-output ratio between some of the fast- and slow-growing countries, even if their 'normal' capital-output ratio is the same.

Replacement

Another reason why the gross incremental capital-output ratio can vary is because of differing proportions of replacement investment. If the life of capital is fixed and is the same in all countries, the rate of replacement will vary according to the age structure of the capital stock, which will depend on past rates of growth. A country which has had a steady growth rate of 2 per cent a year and an average life of capital of thirty years will need to replace 1·8 per cent of its capital stock each year. A country which has had a steady growth of 5 per cent a year will need to replace only 0·8 of its capital stock annually as it will have a newer stock. If the capital-output ratio is 2·5, then the first country would spend 4·6 per cent of G.N.P. each year on replacement and the second 1·9 per cent.

Not only does a slow-growing country have to devote a larger fraction of G.N.P. to replacement than a fast-growing country, but the share of replacement in total investment will be higher because the slow-growing country has a lower rate of new investment. A country with a growth rate of 2 per cent and a capital-output ratio of 2·5 will need to devote 4·6 per cent of G.N.P. to replacement, and it will need to invest another 5 per cent of G.N.P. in new investment. Its total investment rate will be 9·6 and its investment-output ratio 4·8. A country growing at 5 per cent will be spending 1·9 per cent of G.N.P. on replacement and 12·5 per cent of G.N.P. on new investment. Its investment rate will be 14·4 per cent of G.N.P. and its investment-output ratio 2·9.

This hypothetical illustration is based on the case of countries which are set on a given path of growth for a very long period—long enough for their capital stock to have acquired a 'normal' age structure for that rate of growth. This is unrealistic as applied to countries which have all experienced phases of acceleration and deceleration in the past thirty years and have had widely differing rates of capital formation at different periods. Acceleration of growth and capital formation will reduce the replacement burden, and deceleration will increase it.

There are no data on actual rates of scrapping, but some idea of its probable size can be gained from information on past investment rates. If all non-residential fixed capital had a life of exactly thirty years, the capital invested in 1925–30 would have been scrapped during the years 1955–60. If this assumption is applied to Germany, the United Kingdom and the United States, we find the following rates of replacement as a fraction of G.N.P. in 1955–60: Germany 3·9 per cent, the United Kingdom 3·8 per cent, the United States 5·5 per cent. This goes some way to explaining the spread in the gross investment-output ratios between these three countries. If we assume that these replacement rates are valid for the 1950s as a whole, then the investment-output ratio net of replacement would be 1·6 for Germany, 2·8 for the United Kingdom and 2·4 for the United States, compared with a gross ratio of 2·1, 4·3 and 4·1 respectively. However, this calculation ignores the effect of war damage. The German capital stock was probably reduced by about a quarter by war damage and post-war dismantling. This reduced the need for replacement correspondingly so that the spread between the German and U.S. investment-output ratio net of replacement is further narrowed, being about 1·8 in Germany and 2·4 in the United States.

Capital Widening and Deepening
Incremental capital-output ratios also vary between countries because of differences in the relative importance of the employment increase. The extreme cases are Germany with an increase in employment of 24·4 per cent in 1950–60 and Norway with an increase of 2·3 per cent (see Table II–7 of Chapter II). The rate of increase in employment was higher in Europe in the 1950s than in earlier periods and it was particularly high in the fast-growing countries. Since less investment is required to achieve a given increase in output with more labor than without it, it is useful to distinguish between the costs of capital widening and capital deepening. Capital widening

means equipping additional workers with the same amount of capital per head as the average for the existing labor force, and capital deepening refers to investment destined to raise the average capital stock per head above existing levels.

If the capital-output ratio for capital widening is 2 and the ratio for deepening is 3, then a country with a 2·5 per cent increase in employment and a 3 per cent productivity growth will have a new investment requirement of 14 per cent of G.N.P., whereas a country with no increase in labor supply would need a 16·5 per cent investment rate to get the same rate of output growth. This is a rather crude example, for the investment requirements involved in capital deepening will depend on how much is done. This is not the case for capital widening as it involves no change in factor proportions or production techniques. The reason for the difference between the investment ratios for widening and deepening will be clearer after the analysis of technical progress, the influence of which we have so far ignored. This process of technical improvement must be kept in mind in any realistic explanation of economic growth.

The Nature of Technical Progress

In practice, it is difficult to separate technical progress and capital accumulation, but they are analytically different. Most technical progress is embodied in improvements in the design or arrangement of capital equipment and can only be obtained by installing new plant or equipment. The rate of technical progress may well be uneven in any particular sector of the economy, but as it is mostly a matter of adopting a large number of improvements, which are small in relation to the combined economy of our group of countries—now approaching a trillion dollars a year at U.S. prices—we can assume that it is not erratic in its aggregate impact, and for simplicity, that it is a constant rate of improvement. Even dramatic innovations are adopted gradually. Improvements are brought about by a widely diffused international process and there is little that any one country can do to accelerate this.

In a closed economy the rate of technical progress is not a simple function of time but depends mainly on the rate of investment. However, our economies are not closed, and this dependence of technical progress on the rate of investment is only true of the investment rate in the technically advanced world as a whole but not of any one country, except, perhaps, a giant like the United States. For any single country in our open system, therefore, technical progress may well appear to be largely a function of time. It may, of course, be true that the generally high rate of investment in the post-war world has quickened the pace of technology somewhat, but there is no way of testing this. The high level of research and development expenditures is often cited as evidence, but much of this is for military purposes and is concerned with the remote frontiers of knowledge whose impact on production techniques is small as yet. The fact that the rate of technical advance is largely independent of an individual country's efforts does not mean that all countries derive the same benefit from it. It is an opportunity which is seized by countries in different degrees according to their rate of gross investment. There is, of course, some progress in knowledge which can raise productivity without being embodied in new capital. This is not likely to be of great importance in developed countries. If it were a major source of progress, we would not expect such large inter-firm or inter-country productivity differentials to exist unless there were differences in the quality, education and know-how of labor and management.

At any given time the capital stock presents a fossilized history of technology with capital of differing vintages associated with differing levels of labor productivity.[1] All new investment, including replacement and capital widening, will bring productivity gains because new capital is more efficient than old. Because of technical progress, the life of capital will not be determined primarily by wear and tear but by obsolescence. Old equipment will be retired when it can no longer earn enough to meet the labor and other prime costs of production. It will be replaced by new machinery whose productivity is high enough to ensure that the entrepreneur can not only cover labor costs but earn a profit. Labor costs will rise steadily over time as the average productivity of the economy rises and permits increases in the wage rate. The productivity rises will, in turn, be determined by the pace of technical progress and capital accumulation. As productivity rises, all labor costs rise throughout the economy, and the price of capital goods falls relative to labor, thus opening new possibilities of profitable investment and rendering old capital obsolete. The faster investment proceeds, the faster will be the growth of labor cost and the shorter the economic life of equipment.

This basic situation of technical change affected all our countries in a similar way, as can be seen from the sector pattern of productivity increase already noted in Chapter II, as well as from a more detailed comparison of individual industry growth rates in the United Kingdom and the United States. In modern conditions there cannot be widely varying degrees of technical advance due to differences in technical knowledge. The existence of a wide variation in productivity levels between the United States and Europe, and of

---

[1] Cf. W. E. G. Salter, *Productivity and Technical Change*, Cambridge University Press, London, 1960, for a highly illuminating discussion of the impact of technical progress on investment.

equally large variations within individual countries,[1] is not due to lack of intellectual contact or differences in the quality or efficiency of management but mainly to differing amounts of capital per employee and a differing age structure of capital.

As technical progress is a diffused process offering more or less equal opportunities to different countries, it is necessary to explain why these opportunities were not seized in equal degree, and why the productivity gap between Europe and America was permitted to become so wide. The reasons for this were discussed in Chapter II. Various factors have in the past led European entrepreneurs to take a different view of market and investment risks. During the period 1870–1913 the United States advantage was largely in terms of superior natural resources and more rapid population growth. For about two decades of the 1913–50 period the major European countries had a depressed investment level because of the claims of war and its aftermath. The United States suffered more than European countries from low demand levels in the depression of the 1930s, but most European entrepreneurs had a more prolonged experience of depression in their export markets. In the United Kingdom, this dates back to the 1880s. Apart from these factors which affected entrepreneurial capacity to invest and take risks, we must recognize that an initially high impetus to invest will carry its own momentum, when the original causes have disappeared and whatever they were, if it is carefully nurtured by government policy. In a high-investment economy, entrepreneurs are more conscious of the risks of not investing. They know from experience that real wages have been rising rapidly and they expect the process to continue. This pressure of changing factor costs is the reason why the process of high investment is generalized throughout the economy in the first place. The high rate of investment and the rate of growth of real wages will also reduce the age at which old capital is scrapped.

Apart from having a lower rate of investment, a slow-growing country will also tend to have a wider range from poorest- to best-practice firms in any industry because the assets will have a longer life in a country where relative labor costs are rising slowly. This appears to be true of the United Kingdom as compared with the United States, and it is noteworthy that Krengel's estimates of the German capital stock assume some acceleration of replacement in the 1950s accompanying more rapid growth. There will not only be a

---

[1] Salter quotes figures for the U.S. blast furnace industry showing a labor productivity in best-practice firms roughly twice as high as the average for the industry (*op. cit.*, p. 48). For the United Kingdom he quotes a range of up to 4 to 1 in the variation between best-practice and worst-practice firms. The range is biggest in the most capital-intensive industries (p. 96). By contrast, the difference between average productivity levels in the two countries is about 2 to 1.

wider range but a smaller concentration of output on best-practice firms due to lower investment rates. These wider inter-firm spreads do not reflect differences in managerial efficiency nor do they necessarily reflect lack of competition, for the pursuit of best-practice techniques in terms of productivity does not mean a lowering of total costs if real wages are rising slowly. These spreads are not determined by the competitive urges of individual entrepreneurs but by a constellation of circumstances affecting entrepreneurial attitudes to risk and determining the momentum of the economy. In modern conditions it is government policy which is primarily responsible for this momentum.

Replacement and Technical Progress. We must now consider how technical progress affects the different types of investment, starting with replacement. We assume that the quality of capital goods is improving every year in such a way that a given amount of new capital per worker in money terms[1] will carry with it a higher average level of labor productivity than the previous year's capital. If technical progress has thus raised the labor productivity potential of capital by 1 per cent a year and the life of capital is thirty years, then the labor productivity associated with a given amount of the current year's vintage of capital will be 34·8 per cent higher than that of the thirty-year-old capital now due for replacement. The average level of labor productivity will also have risen. If replacement has taken place steadily, and if we assume for the moment that no widening or deepening has taken place, i.e., that the capital stock has been constant, then the average productivity level will be 18 per cent higher than the initial productivity level of thirty years ago. The impact of 1 per cent replacement will therefore be to raise the average productivity level by 0·3 per cent. In this case, 3·3 per cent of capital is replaced every year and the productivity bonus is 1 per cent. If there has been an abnormal delay in replacement, as was the case in the 1950s, then the productivity bonus will be increased, because the difference between the end-year and initial-year productivity of capital will be greater, the average productivity of the capital stock will be lower, and more replacement will be necessary.

If the capital stock is growing, the productivity bonus from replacement will be smaller than in the case just described for two reasons: (1) the proportion of the capital stock to be replaced will be smaller; and (2) the average level of productivity will be higher with a lower average age of capital. For example, if the capital stock had

---

[1] We could, of course, define capital in terms of efficiency units rather than financial ones, but we have tried to stick as closely as possible to the type of convention likely to be used in practice.

been widened steadily by 2 per cent a year, then replacement requirements would be 1·8 per cent of the capital stock, and average productivity would be 25 per cent higher than that of thirty years ago. The bonus on 1 per cent replacement would be 0·28 per cent and the total bonus would be 0·51 per cent.

The impact of this productivity bonus on the gross investment-output ratio is clear. Without technical progress, replacement contributes nothing to output, but in our second case if the average capital output ratio were 2·5, then replacement investment would be 4·6 per cent of G.N.P. and it would raise output by 0·5 per cent.

Capital Widening and Technical Progress. If the initial ratio of capital per employed person is 2·5, an increase of 1 per cent in the employed labor force will require investment of 2·5 per cent of current G.N.P. to maintain the average capital/worker relationship in value terms. However, the increase in output will be bigger than 1 per cent because the new capital is more efficient than the average of the existing stock. If the new workers were to have the same productivity as the existing workers, they would, in fact, need less equipment per head than the existing average.

The rate of productivity bonus on capital widening is smaller than on replacement. The widening bonus is the difference between the productivity of the current year's vintage of capital goods and the average level of productivity of the capital stock. If technical progress improves the labor productivity potential of capital by 1 per cent a year, the life of assets is thirty years, and the capital stock and employment are growing by 2 per cent a year, then the labor productivity associated with the current year's vintage of capital will be 34·8 per cent higher than that of thirty years ago and the average productivity level will be 24·8 per cent higher than that of thirty years ago. The average annual productivity gain from 2 per cent widening will be 0·21 per cent.

If widening had been going on at a faster pace, the total productivity bonus would be bigger, but not proportionately bigger. The rate of productivity bonus would have been lower because the existing average productivity level would have been higher. However, this is true only of the comparison of two equilibrium rates of growth. In the process of accelerating from one rate of growth to another, the rate of productivity bonus is temporarily increased because the impact of acceleration will be bigger on the margin than on the average. The productivity bonus for a steady 1 per cent widening is 0·13 per cent as compared with 0·21 per cent for a steady 2 per cent widening, but if widening is accelerated from 1 per cent to 2 per cent, the impact in the first year is to raise the bonus to 0·27 per cent. In the longer run the bonus will fall back to 0·21 per cent when the economy has worked itself into an equilibrium for this new rate of growth.

Capital Deepening and Technical Progress. Thus we see that productivity can be raised to some extent by replacement and widening. The bigger these two types of investment are, the less will be the burden of capital deepening. The return on investment designed purely to increase labor productivity (i.e., capital deepening) will depend on the age and amount of the existing capital stock per head (which will determine the existing level of productivity) and on the rate of progress of technical knowledge in the world in general. The return will also depend on the scale of the productivity gain which is aimed at. The higher the productivity gain, the more costly is it likely to be in terms of investment.

Technical progress is constantly improving the opportunities for investment. Over time, therefore, capital deepening can be increased without any necessary increase in the investment-output ratio. At any given time, however, diminishing returns are bound to set in if capital deepening is pushed beyond a certain limit. The schedule of returns will depend on the size and age of the existing capital stock, which will reflect the degree to which existing technology is being exploited. A country operating near the fringe of known technology will have a more steeply progressive investment cost schedule than one which has lagged behind. There would appear to be an initial phase of increasing returns to capital deepening if all productivity gains were attributed to it and the productivity bonus from capital widening and replacement were ignored.

The productivity returns from deepening investment should not normally be too different for the industrial countries of Western Europe which have similar income levels, similar demand and industrial structures, and no wide differences in resource endowment. In some of the smaller countries, the limited size of markets may have raised investment costs, particularly when trade opportunities were more restricted and indivisible units of investment were large. From time to time, there will be special factors which will change the schedule of returns. In the past decade or so, the increased specialization and improved resource allocation in the European economies via trade may well have produced a phase in which the returns were particularly high. This process has affected some countries more than others. The recovery elements which we mentioned in Chapter II may also have lowered capital requirements temporarily in some countries, particularly in Germany. In Italy the development of newly discovered natural resources of oil and natural gas had some impact in lowering capital costs in the 1950s, and the same is true to a smaller degree in France. It is also true that the countries to which these special factors apply—France, Germany, Italy and the Netherlands—had a markedly lower starting level of productivity in 1950 than the other European countries, and for this reason may have been operating on a more favorable schedule than their European neighbours.

In the United States the existence of a better natural resource endowment would probably have produced a bigger productivity return from investment in the past (or even now) if the age and amount of existing capital per head had been similar to that in Europe. However, the amount of capital per head in the United States is much higher than in Europe as a result of higher investment rates over a number of decades. Because of this neglect of past investment opportunities, it is likely that European countries can now get better returns from a given rate of capital deepening than the United States.

Although the average age of the U.S. capital stock may now be higher than in some European countries, the fact that it has a lot more capital per worker means that it is operating nearer to the fringe of known technology, for technology is not just a matter of age of machinery but of operating it in different combinations with labor. In the United States, therefore, technical progress is largely a matter of adopting the newest discoveries of science and technology, or of using existing types of machine, in new factor combinations. In Europe there is a vast range of the economy working well below known best-practice technology. In some activities like steel making, motor car assembly or aircraft production European technology is nearer American. The divergence is wide, however, even in manufacturing, as Rostas showed years ago. We are not suggesting that the whole U.S. economy is operating at a technical frontier. Even if technical progress dried up altogether, the United States would continue to show productivity gains for a long time as the worst sectors and firms caught up, but in Europe productivity would grow for several decades longer as the best firms would also have a great deal of leeway. In underdeveloped countries the process of growth would hardly be perceptibly affected for decades.

Apart from the fact that the United States is nearer to the technological fringe, it is also operating on the margin of consumption experience. Entrepreneurs have to take more risks in guessing what demand patterns will be, and the risk of wasting resources due to taste obsolescence, or sheer mistakes, is much greater.

The Quality of Management and the Capacity to Absorb Investment

The fact that Europe has a much lower productivity level than the United States does not mean that it can carry out any degree of capital deepening annually at a lower cost than the United States until it reaches the U.S. ratio of capital per worker. An important factor limiting the extent to which European countries can exploit their low starting position in order to grow faster is the absorptive capacity of management and labor. It is not easy to adapt to a faster rhythm of change, which often means changing jobs faster, or being thrown out of a job more often. The fact that a technology is already known does not eliminate the need for new types of training and skill on the part of those employing it for the first time. This is primarily a question for management, and depends on the type of people and on their level of education. It also depends upon whether workers' organizations maintain a restrictive attitude to changes in technique.

If the managerial group is drawn from a narrow circle or does not attract its fair share of the most gifted members of society, then the cost of capital deepening will be higher than in a country with wider openings or better education.[1] There is little doubt that U.S. management has had, and probably continues to have, advantages over Europe in this respect both because access to business leadership depends less on social origins and because business has a higher social status than the professions or the civil service. In post-war Germany, the division of the country, the flight of people who lost their property and social position in the Eastern portion, and property losses in the currency reform, all tended to make a business career more attractive to the most able people and strengthened the urge to succeed quickly. The experience of German management in the early 1950s, when production soared after enforced stagnation, was a useful conditioning to the process of rapid growth. In this respect, experience of growth probably generates its own momentum, for growth has also been rapid in France and Italy where the social barriers inhibiting entrepreneurship and good management have been just as great or greater than in a slow-growing country like the United Kingdom. There is, therefore, no reason to suppose that the basic quality of management has been a hindrance to growth in the slow-growing countries. The management of British nationalized industries in the 1950s was, however, a distinct weakness of the United Kingdom economy, as noted in Chapter IV below.

Conclusions

The high rates of investment in the 1950s were a major factor responsible for the acceleration in European output and productivity. High investment took place in circumstances which enhanced its productivity in the fast-growing countries. This happened because

---

[1] These social factors inhibiting European entrepreneurship are given considerable weight by Professor H. J. Habakkuk, *American and British Technology in the Nineteenth Century*, Cambridge University Press, London, 1962.

the burden of replacement was reduced and because the increase in employment was very large. In Germany the possibility of calling on spare capacity also helped reduce the investment cost of growth. There were in addition some temporary factors which increased the returns on investment destined to raise productivity. The most noteworthy of these was the improved allocation of resources brought about by the increase in the relative size of international trade.

It is not possible to quantify with any certainty the importance of the different kinds of capital formation we have distinguished or to quantify the schedule of returns on capital deepening. We have, however, established the probable direction of the influences operating in the 1950s, and our examples are probably adequate to cover the observed range of variation. It is clear that the investment-output relationship is too complex to be interpreted satisfactorily in terms of simple aggregative ratios or production functions. We have tried to show that some of the apparent lag in technical progress in the slow-growing countries is largely a reflection of low investment rates in the past. It reflects a difference in investment dynamism and not in technical dynamism or entrepreneurial efficiency. It is also clear that the aggregate investment-output ratio is the net result of several influences which do not all operate in the same direction. In particular, we should not be led to suppose that the key to faster growth is always an increase in investment, or that the productivity of investment will always be increased by doing more of it. Some things are already fairly clear. Countries with a higher increase in labor supply are likely to have lower I.C.O.R.s. (This is true of productive investment, but it will be offset somewhat by increased housing needs if faster growth of labor supply is due to more rapid population growth.) Capital widening will contribute something to productivity, and so will replacement. Countries which start with excess (deficient) capacity will have lower (higher) I.C.O.R.s (*ceteris paribus*) than those which do not. The cost of capital deepening can be expected to be higher in a country which is operating near the fringe of known technology (the United States), as reflected in its higher labor productivity, than in a country which is catching up to U.S. levels.

We might now ask how investment costs are likely to develop in future, and whether the incentive to invest is likely to be modified. These questions are closely linked, and the answer will depend on the state of demand that is assumed, and, to some extent, on the way taxes affect investment incentives. We will assume for the moment that high and stable levels of demand can be maintained and that there will be no specially favorable or unfavorable developments affecting the structure of demand or investment. There is, in fact, nothing to suggest any significant shift in future demand patterns towards more or less capital-intensive sectors. There may, of course, be large indivisibilities which will raise capital requirements temporarily, particularly in small countries, and there may be cases, e.g., in Norway, where past indivisibilities or heavy concentration of recent investment on long-lived assets will reduce future capital requirements.

As far as the investment costs of growth are concerned, we may examine each of our types of investment in turn. In nearly all European countries, and particularly those which grew fastest in the 1950s, the scope for capital widening is likely to be reduced. Although the natural increase in the labor supply should continue at a similar pace, there is not the same possibility of drawing on unemployed manpower, whether overt or disguised, or for immigration, as there was in the 1950s. This is particularly true of Germany, France and Italy. As capital deepening is more expensive than capital widening, this should increase the investment-output ratio in these countries. Furthermore, the rate of productivity bonus from widening should drop slightly.

Replacement investment makes the least contribution to output, and if its share of total investment should fall, this will lower the investment cost of growth. It is difficult to say what will happen to the share of replacement. In the 1950s replacement was higher than normal because of retirement of assets whose lives were prolonged during the war and early post-war years of full employment and capital scarcity. On the other hand, this abnormal replacement also brought a higher than normal productivity bonus. As the rate of capital formation has been accelerated, the stock of old assets due for replacement in the next few years should be smaller than in the 1950s and smaller than it will eventually be when the age structure of assets has become attuned to the new high rate of growth. We might therefore expect the share of replacement to fall temporarily. In all European countries it is likely to be lower than pre-war because of the much higher level of investment. On the other hand, we might expect the average life of assets to be shorter in present conditions of rapid productivity growth than it was in pre-war years—but this shortening of life had probably already taken place in the 1950s. It could, therefore, be that replacement will absorb less of G.N.P. than it did in the 1950s. The share of replacement in total investment will, of course, also depend on what happens to other types of investment.

Some of the special growth-stimulating factors of the 1950s reduced the costs of capital deepening in a temporary way. This is true in the case of the benefits of increased specialization through trade. It would also be true of the apparent productivity gains from disguised unemployment, had we not treated this as an employment increase accompanied by capital widening. These benefits of trade specialization are not yet exhausted, and higher returns on deepening investment in Europe than in the United States are likely to continue for some decades more. The schedule of returns on capital deepening may therefore be somewhat less favorable than it was in the 1950s, but not too different from what it was in the late 1950s. There is no reason to expect it to be significantly different between European countries. For example, there is no technical or psychological reason why the United Kingdom should not push its capital deepening as far as Germany. Whether it does so will depend on the economic climate in which entrepreneurs operate. The same schedule of potential returns on deepening does not mean the same aggregate investment-output ratio. This depends on how much deepening is actually done and on the relative size of other investment. There are, of course, limits to the process of capital deepening which will depend upon how hard the frontier of technical knowledge is being pushed and on the absorptive capacity of management. It is clear that the United States is closer to this frontier than Europe. It is difficult to say how much harder the United States should push this frontier, but in Europe no country except Norway seems to have pushed it to excess, in spite of the high rate of investment.

The use of capacity is no longer strained as it was in 1950, and in fact there is some slack in the slower-growing countries, i.e., the United Kingdom, the United States and Canada, which may reduce the capital costs of their expansion in the next few years, particularly by contrast with the 1950s, when the creation of excess capacity increased growth costs. In Germany the reverse applies and investment costs of growth should be higher than in the 1950s because of this.

The net result of these different influences is therefore a rise in growth costs in the fast-growing countries and a potential reduction of costs in the slow-growing countries if they accelerate growth. An influence which works against such convergence is that this decade of rapid growth has given workers and management in the fast-growing countries a greater capacity to absorb capital-deepening investment. This is an important factor in enabling high investment to continue, and this self-induced momentum of growth is the equivalent on the supply side to the momentum effects on risk-taking which fast growth generates in respect to entrepreneurial demand for investment.

We should now ask how a change in the cost of growth in this aggregative sense will affect the incentive to invest and the amount of investment. A change in the aggregative capital-output ratio may indicate the way profit potentialities are moving, but this is not necessarily true. For instance, a rise in the cost of growth in Germany

G

due to a reduction in capital-widening possibilities does not mean a lower rate of profit on deepening investment, although it may have indirect repercussions on profit if the bargaining position of labor is strengthened by greater pressure in the labor market. The shortage of labor and the pressure on profit from higher labor costs may even enhance the incentive to capital deepening. Nevertheless, we cannot assume that all of the investment funds devoted to widening will be switched to deepening, and there may be a fall in the investment rate.

It is likely that the exhaustion of the factors which temporarily cheapened the cost of capital deepening will lead to a fall in profit rates and some lowering of investment incentives. The reduction in the productivity bonus on widening and replacement should also tend to lower profit rates. However, the basically better opportunities of the low productivity countries of Europe vis-à-vis the United States have not changed.

A major reason for a potential reduction in the cost of growth in the slow-growing countries is the existence of excess capacity. Although this is a production opportunity, its existence is hardly an incentive to invest. Here we have a clear example of the inter-relation of demand, investment incentives and growth.

CHAPTER IV

THE ROLE OF GOVERNMENT
IN PROMOTING GROWTH

THE AIMS OF POLICY

A major reason for the post-war acceleration of economic growth in Europe was the action of governments in sustaining high and steady levels of demand and investment. Government policy helped to offset the recessionary or inflationary tendencies of the private sector, instead of exaggerating them as was often the case in pre-war years. Government has assumed so important a role in the economy that its own operations largely determine the general economic momentum, and what appears as the business cycle is nowadays mainly a reflection of phases in government policy.

The acceptance of responsibility for aggregate economic management was a conscious act in most countries. For most of the 1950s this responsibility was not conceived in terms of raising the production potential but simply of securing a level of demand adequate to attain a full use of resources, particularly labor. This is a fundamental requisite of any growth policy, and it was highly successful in most cases. By keeping resources fully employed and adding to the stability of the economy, governments succeeded in reducing the uncertainties of economic life to a degree which promoted high investment and raised the growth trend itself. This was a result of full employment policies that was not fully foreseen. Some countries—the United States, Canada and Belgium—failed to maintain adequate demand. This failure has been a major reason for their relatively slow growth, and it must be attributed largely to the weakness of policy.

Full employment was not the only goal of policy. In all countries considerable weight was given to the need to attain price stability. This was an important aim in its own right, and also an integral part of a policy for growth. All these economies are heavily engaged in international trade, and their price competitiveness directly affects their export performance. If this is poor, growth will be held back by payments difficulties. Policy was not too successful in maintaining price stability, and price rises were everywhere substantial. The failure to check price rises was partly due to the difficulty of reconciling this objective with the policy of maintaining high levels of demand. In some years governments allowed demand to rise to levels higher than the economy could supply and prices were forced up. When this happened, demand needed to be curbed. But price rises also occurred in years when demand was not excessive, and here demand management was not a remedy. In a few countries governments tried to tackle this second problem by direct intervention in the process of price and wage fixing, but attempts were also made to check the process by depressing demand and output below full potential. This policy of trying to check the second type of pressure by repressing demand was not successful in avoiding inflation and was a major hindrance to growth in both the United Kingdom and the United States.

The major emphasis in government policy in the 1950s was on maintaining equilibrium in the short term, i.e., pushing or restraining demand to what seemed to be a position of full capacity use, consistent with reasonable stability of prices and the balance of payments. In most countries there was no attempt to formulate any goal or perspective as to the longer-term growth potential of the economy or the likely pattern of future demand. At the end of the 1950s it became generally realized that this lack of perspective could lead to mistaken emphasis in short-term policies. It was a handicap in investment decisions in both the public and the private sector. It also prevented governments, employers and workers from formulating any clear view as to the size of wage increase which was likely to be compatible with price stability. 'Planning' in the sense of an articulate set of policy goals for future growth played an important role in the growth achievements of the 1950s only in France, the Netherlands and Norway. Nevertheless, there were a number of very important ways in which governments tried to increase the supply potential of the economy. In the first place, some governments strove to increase the share of investment in total spending. This was particularly true in Germany and Norway. In Germany and France there was a considerable effort to affect the pattern of investment to promote growth. In all countries an important contribution to economic efficiency was made by reducing barriers to trade. There was also a general attempt by governments to promote productivity growth by fostering the spread of best-practice technology.

In an advanced industrial economy a fully rounded growth policy consists of three main elements: (1) managing the level of demand, (2) keeping the economy competitive, (3) fostering the growth of production potential. In all of these aspects of policy the short-term and long-term problems cannot easily be segregated, and the quality and scope of a country's growth policy can only be measured broadly by a general survey of its response to a series of challenges over the years and by an examination of the range of policy weapons it has been willing to use. Such an assessment is necessarily crude and impressionistic, particularly if it deals with a group of countries. Comparative study is, however, of particular value in this field.

In individual cases it will often seem that policy was thwarted by force of circumstance or succeeded more by luck than by judgment. However, if a country appears consistently to run into difficulties which others manage to avoid, one is entitled to assume that bad policy played a role. The two big countries where this was the case are the United States and the United Kingdom. It is not, of course, easy to say how much was lost by bad policy in these countries, but the analysis of supply potential of the first three chapters of this study can provide some guidance here.

In the United States it is clear that policy allowed demand to flag and that resources were wasted through unemployment. The productivity losses from bad policy are more difficult to judge, but there is little doubt that they did occur. The situation in the United Kingdom was more complicated. The losses of the 1950s were due to slow productivity growth rather than to unemployment. They were due not so much to inadequate demand but to constant interruptions in its momentum, and to a low rate of investment. British growth could not, of course, have been expected to be as fast as Germany's either in terms of employment or of productivity, nor would it have been reasonable to aim at the same rate of investment. However, our analysis of supply conditions provides no reason why British productivity growth should not have been something like that achieved in Sweden or Switzerland—3·5 instead of 2 per cent a year. British policy was lacking in two very important respects: in maintaining competitiveness and in fostering production potential. In both these aspects of policy some other countries made greater efforts and overcame difficulties faced by the United Kingdom. On the other hand, the United Kingdom had a special problem not experienced elsewhere: it had to carry the responsibility of a reserve currency with inadequate reserves. The implications of this are considered in the next chapter, which deals with the purely external aspects of policy. It will be clear from that discussion that the fast-growing countries also had some responsibility for the special payments difficulties which hindered growth in the United Kingdom, and which may hinder future U.S. growth. Thus it is true that some countries find it harder to reach their growth potential than others, and that the responsibility for achieving this is not entirely a national one. The greatest problem in a growth policy seems to be to generate the right initial momentum. It is more difficult to get rapid growth started than to keep the economy on a high-growth path. For this reason the policy problems of the slow-growing countries are particularly difficult, and they may now need a much more energetic effort than their neighbours.

If we attribute slow growth largely to the failings of policy, must we attribute fast growth to the successes of policy? Here again the answer must be qualified. In some countries the rapid growth of the 1950s probably could have been somewhat faster. This was the case in France where an inflationary policy distorted resource allocation and impeded productivity growth. In Italy it would probably have been possible to cut down the size of unemployment somewhat by a more active policy to foster the shift from Southern agriculture. Even where the economy can reasonably be assumed to have fully realized its potential, as in Germany, this was not due entirely to the superior efficiency of domestic policy but partly to the policy failures of other countries. One reason for the full employment of resources in Germany was that the high level of foreign demand led to a large export surplus throughout the 1950s. Part of German success was due to luck, but a good deal of the apparent luck was due to the fact that a successful growth policy has strong self-reinforcing elements. There is a tendency to discount the role of policy in Germany and to exaggerate the economic 'miracle'. This is partly because the Minister of Economics, Dr. Erhard, was wont to expound Germany policy in simplified terms, and partly because the techniques of policy were different from those used in the slow-growing countries. However, the German authorities followed a vigorous line of action in each of the three major aspects of growth policy: management of demand, maintenance of competitiveness, and fostering output potential by policies favoring high investment and foreign trade.

This chapter examines in some detail the types of policy instrument which governments can use to influence the pace of economic growth, and assesses their effectiveness in meeting contemporary needs. It deals largely with internal policy problems. The international problems of growth policy are left to the next chapter. However, the two aspects of the problem are so closely linked that the analysis is full of cross references.

MANAGING THE LEVEL OF DEMAND

Public Spending

Before analyzing the policies affecting private demand, it is useful to examine the scope of government spending and see how it has varied. Government spending is, in fact, so large that a consideration of its role immediately suggests that the cyclical or growth momentum of the economy cannot nowadays be set independently by the private sector. However, government spending decisions are not monolithic but are widely diffused between different departments and local authorities which are often unconcerned with the problem of economic stability or growth.

Government spending can be classified under several different headings: government consumption, i.e., spending on current goods and services—both civil and military; transfer payments; capital spending on public works; and spending in those parts of the production or enterprise sector which happen to be publicly owned.

TABLE IV–1
GOVERNMENT CURRENT EXPENDITURE ON GOODS AND SERVICES
AS A PROPORTION OF G.N.P. AT CURRENT PRICES

	1870	1913	1938	1950	1960
Belgium				9·8	12·1
Denmark			9·3	10·3	12·6
France			13·0	12·9	13·3
Germany			23·1	14·4	13·6
Italy	9·7	9·8	16·3	11·1	14·5
Netherlands		11·0ª	11·4	12·6	13·5
Norway	3·8	6·3	9·9	10·6	14·6
Sweden	4·7	5·6	10·4ᵇ	13·9	17·7
Switzerland					12·1ᶜ
United Kingdom	4·9	7·2	13·5	15·6	16·6
Canada	4·6	8·1	10·9	10·6	14·4
United States	3·7ᵈ	4·2	10·1	10·6	17·2

ª 1921. ᵇ 1938–39 average. ᶜ 1959. ᵈ 1869–78 average.

Sources: 1950 and 1960, O.E.C.D., *General Statistics.* 1938 from *Statistics of National Product and Expenditure, No. 2,* O.E.E.C., Paris, 1957. The U.S. figures of O.E.E.C. and O.E.C.D. were adjusted to exclude government investment in machinery (see Appendix I). Earlier years from national sources cited in Appendix A.

Government Consumption. It can be seen from Table IV–1 that the relative size of government consumption in 1960 had increased over pre-war in all countries except Germany and Italy, where it was considerably below the level prevailing under the totalitarian regimes. The rise was biggest in Sweden, Norway and the United States. In nearly all European countries public consumption is smaller than in the United States, largely because U.S. defense expenditure is so much bigger than that elsewhere.

TABLE IV–2
SHARE OF CENTRAL GOVERNMENT IN TOTAL GOVERNMENT
CONSUMPTION, 1958

(Per Cent)

Belgium	65	Norway	68
France	87	Sweden	66
Germany	44	United Kingdom	79
Italy	85	United States	68
Netherlands	70		

Source: Statistics of Sources and Uses of Finance 1948–58, O.E.E.C., 1960.

In the course of the 1950s government expenditure on goods and services increased faster in money terms than private demand in all countries except Germany. The biggest increase in the government share of total demand was in the United States and was mainly due to military spending. Government consumption was not expanded with a view to raising total demand to a level adequate to make full use of resources but was changed in response to what was currently needed in the public sector. In fact, public consumption has quite often moved in a way that was inconvenient from the point of view of economic growth and stability. This was particularly true of military spending, which was subject to large variation because of changes in the degree of international tension or in technology. Greatly increased defense expenditures were the major cause of the boom in 1950-51 in all these countries, and the decline of these expenditures was mainly responsible for the 1953-54 recession in the United States. The cancellation of orders for conventional aircraft just before the missile program got under way in 1957 was a similarly disturbing feature. Military spending has also had destabilizing balance-of-payments effects in several countries. In fact, government expenditure changed in response to current needs and required compensatory tax action as much as did variations in private spending.

Productivity growth in the government sector was slower than elsewhere in the economy so that from this point of view the increased share of government spending was a drag on the average rate of growth. Some government consumption expenditures do of course help to improve the long-run growth potential of the economy. This is particularly true of the 3 per cent or so of G.N.P. which government spends on education. However, education was not the most dynamic element in government spending, and governments showed little concern during the 1950s with the role which education can play in fostering growth.

To some degree governments were directly concerned with fostering the growth of productivity in the economy. In Europe all governments created productivity centres for the exchange of information on best-practice production techniques and this helped to enlighten European entrepreneurs as to the productivity gains they had missed in the past by inadequate investment. In the United States, substantial government funds were spent on research and development expenditures, but much of the impact of this was in the military field.

Transfer Payments. In some European countries—Germany, France, Italy and the Netherlands—government transfer payments are larger than current spending on goods and services. The bulk of transfer payments are intended to raise the consumption level of

TABLE IV–3
GOVERNMENT EXPENDITURE AS A PROPORTION OF G.N.P. IN 1957

G.N.P. = 100

	Current Civil Expenditure on Goods and Services	Defense Expenditure	Subsidies	Other Transfers	Interest on Public Debt	Total Current Expenditure	Total Current Surplus	Gross Asset Formation	Overall Government Surplus
Austria	11·2	1·4	1·7	11·9	0·5	26·7	6·9	3·7	3·2
Belgium	7·4	3·4	1·2	8·8	1·7	22·6	1·3	1·8	−0·5
Denmark[a]	9·6	3·3	0·3	6·6	1·4	21·0	4·5	2·1	2·4
France	7·5	6·8	1·9	13·0	1·4	30·6	1·5	1·8	−0·3
Germany	10·0	3·0	0·8	14·8	0·6	29·2	7·3	2·7	4·6
Netherlands	8·8	5·1	1·7	8·2	2·5	26·2	5·7	3·2	2·4
Norway	8·4	3·5	4·3	5·6	0·9	22·7	7·5	2·8	4·7
Sweden	12·6	5·0	1·1	6·5	1·5	26·7	4·7	3·0	1·7
United Kingdom	9·8	7·0	1·9	5·9	3·6	28·2	2·8	1·1	1·7
Canada	8·2	5·9	0·3	6·7	2·3	23·5	3·4	3·7	−0·3
United States	6·6	10·0	0·3	4·3	1·4	22·6	3·4	2·8	0·6

[a] 1955.

Source: Statistics of Sources and Uses of Finance 1948–58, O.E.E.C., 1958.

people with low incomes. In most European countries there are substantial family allowances, particularly in France. In Germany and Sweden comprehensive government pensions were introduced in the course of the 1950s, and in several continental countries unemployment benefits amount to as much as two-thirds of a worker's normal earnings. Sickness benefits are general, and medical expenses are largely paid by the state. These payments were highest in some of the fast-growing countries. European transfers are notably higher than those in North America, and they are higher on the continent than in the United Kingdom, which is often erroneously considered as the extreme example of the welfare state. There is no evidence here of a weakening of economic incentives through social security. These transfer benefits undoubtedly contributed to the stability of post-war consumption expenditures and to the general pressure of consumer demand in the earlier post-war years. But in the latter half of the 1950s the propensity to save was probably as high as it has ever been. This is partly because social transfers are not financed by progressive taxation but largely by poll taxes. They have narrowed the spread between very low and medium incomes, but have not reduced the spread between medium and high incomes. In a high-employment situation their net effect in raising consumption is small because the taxes financing these transfers are taken from people who would have spent the money if they had not been taxed. When employment falls off, their role in maintaining demand is greater, particularly that of unemployment benefits. The main growth contribution of these social transfers has been to promote confidence amongst the population generally. Fear of unemployment or of sudden destitution has been greatly diminished, and this has encouraged European entrepreneurs to feel that major depressions are no longer in the cards and that recessions will be brief and modest.

The stabilizing role of transfer payments was a built-in feature of the economy of the 1950s and they were seldom used in Europe as a discretionary means of offsetting demand fluctuations. In a few cases, however, such payments were deliberately raised to foster demand: in the United Kingdom in 1959 'post-war credits' (i.e. the compulsory savings levied during the war) were released to foster demand, and in the United States in 1958 and 1960 unemployment benefits were extended for similar reasons. Apart from social payments, governments make other transfers which may or may not contribute to economic growth and stability. In several countries subsidies provided some incentive to people to move out of declining sectors of the economy, and promoted productive investment or housebuilding. Often, however, subsidies have had an anti-growth rather than a pro-growth impact, because they are designed to bolster or protect the income or activity of sectors with weak markets such as agriculture, coal or textiles. The other major transfer payment is interest on government debt, which obviously has little to do with growth. Its size depends on the relative burden of debt and the rate of interest.

Public Works. Government capital spending on public works has not been a major factor in total demand, though it has been varied from time to time to compensate for variations in the total pressure of activity. Some governments have had an elaborate program of anti-cyclical public works, as in Switzerland, but in most countries, public works were often held back for most of the post-war period to allow room for other types of investment, and in many cases public investment has lagged to an extent which has hindered productivity growth. This is particularly true of roads, as most governments did not foresee the massive increase in private car ownership, and there has also been a backlog in the school building required because of the widespread increase in birth rates.

Public Enterprise. A big difference between the scope of government activity in the United States and Europe is that European countries have more publicly and municipally owned enterprise and a substantial nationalized industry. In France and the United Kingdom a good deal of nationalization has been carried out since the war, but in other countries the scope of government enterprise has not changed substantially. In France and the United Kingdom public enterprises absorb about a fifth of total fixed capital formation. In other European countries the proportion is smaller, but in almost all of them there is public ownership of electricity, gas, water, railways, airlines, city transport, radio and television broadcasting, telephones and telegraph. In the United States most of these utilities are privately owned though there are some municipalities which own city transport systems and there are some government-subsidized public utility systems.

French post-war nationalization included electricity, gas, coal, atomic energy, the Renault motor works, and four banks—Crédit Lyonnais, Société Générale, the Banque Nationale pour le Commerce et l'Industrie, and the Comptoir Nationale d'Escompte de Paris. The government also owns the railways, airlines, some shipping lines, radio, television, telegraph, telephone, city transport and the tobacco industry, as well as parts of the insurance, aircraft, armaments and petroleum industries. The state is a shareholder in about 500 industrial and commercial undertakings. In the United Kingdom post-war acquisitions included electricity, coal, gas, atomic energy, railways and airlines. Road transport was nationalized and denationalized, and the same is true of steel, though some companies are still in government hands. The government also owns radio, telephone and telegraph, and part of television.

In Italy the government controls a considerable portion of industry via a system of holding companies established before the war. The biggest of these is the I.R.I., which covers a good deal of engineering, steel, shipping and public utility enterprises. The other large government company is E.N.I., which controls the petroleum, atomic energy and chemical industries. In 1962 the electric power industry was nationalized. The state also owns railways, and the telephone, salt and tobacco industries; some enterprises are under mixed government-private ownership.

In Scandinavia there has been no post-war nationalization, and the nationalized sector is smaller than in the United Kingdom or France. Nevertheless, the public sector is fairly large in Sweden and Norway, even though it affects only a tiny fraction of the manufacturing sector. In Sweden government ownership covers the railways, telephones, tobacco, wines and spirits, airlines, a large iron-ore mining company and a fifth of the forest lands. The gas and electricity industries are owned by municipalities. In Norway the government controls sales of wines and spirits, 51 per cent of hydroelectric investment, and it owns the railways. Gas and electricity are municipally owned.

In the other countries government ownership is much smaller. In Germany the government owns the railways, telephones and a mixed-bag of industrial enterprises of which the most important are in the mining industry. In 1961 the government made a public share issue for part of the equity of the Volkswagen motor works and it sold shares in the Preuszag company in 1959 by the same means. Gas, electricity and city transport are under municipal ownership. In Denmark the government owns the railways, and municipalities own gas and electricity. In the Netherlands public enterprises consist of airlines, railways, coal mines, gas, water and electricity. In Belgium the public sector is confined to railways and some public utilities.

The role of public enterprise in economic growth has varied a good deal. Nearly all public enterprise has been in capital-intensive sectors whose investment is a substantial part of final demand and an important contribution to the growth of production potential. In France, public enterprise played a major role in securing the dynamism of the economy. In the early years of reconstruction, these enterprises were given priority in the allocation of funds, and their expansion ensured a sound infrastructure for the economy as a whole. Furthermore, they generated a spirit of enterprise and faith in France's capacity as an industrial nation which was indispensable to expansion. Public enterprises have been managed by men of high intellectual capacity, technical ability and entrepreneurial spirit. They have been in the forefront of technical innovation, e.g. in the motor industry, the electrification of railways, and the production of the Caravelle. They have been free to fix their own pricing policies to a great extent, and have never had serious difficulty in finding capital. Nationalized industries played a leading role in making the plan work, and in generating momentum in an economy faced with many uncertainties and a perverse fiscal policy.

In the United Kingdom, the process of nationalization dragged out over a much longer period than in France. The coal mines were nationalized in 1945, but steel was not nationalized until 1950. Nationalization was a matter of violent controversy between the major political parties, although the Conservative Party in office denationalized only steel and transport. This controversy had no counterpart in France where all the nationalization was done by decree in 1945, and nationalization ceased to be a live political issue.

The motives for nationalization were rather mixed in the United Kingdom. It was carried out partly because certain industries, such as mines, were inefficient or had treated their workers badly, and partly because monopolies were thought safer when in state hands. In some quarters it was regarded as a first step in a general move towards state ownership of productive assets. There was no move to introduce workers' control in the nationalized industries, nor were they regarded as a leading sector in the economy which by exemplary management or a dynamic investment policy would provide an example for the private sector. The future of the enterprises was uncertain, they had large bonded debts which made them financially insecure, managerial salaries were well below those in private business, and management had nothing like the freedom of M. Dreyfus in Renault or Signor Mattei in E.N.I. In many cases their pricing policies and the location of their investment were determined by considerations of 'public interest' rather than by normal market forces. The cost situation of these industries was also worsened because their wages policy was influenced by their position as public employers. Policy is now changing, and the quality of management has been improved. The controversy over public ownership has become much less of a real issue. There can be little doubt that the lack of any clear policy for public enterprise was a major weakness of the British economy in the 1950s. Its result was not so much a waste of resources in the public sector, but rather that it added to the uncertainty and indecision of the general outlook for the economy, weakened investment incentives generally and contributed to the inspissated gloom of British entrepreneurs.

In Italy the role of public enterprise has been dynamic. As a whole, the public sector has made profits and contributed greatly to the investment effort of the country and the broadening of the industrial base. The role of the state in technical innovation was substantial, largely because of the discovery of new resources of natural gas and oil.

It is clear that the growth impact of public enterprise has varied. It played a dynamic role in providing leadership in the previously stagnant economies of France and Italy. In Germany, too, the public sector as represented by Volkswagen was very dynamic, but in the United Kingdom the lack of a policy for public enterprise contributed to the slow pace of growth.

Housing. In European countries the volume of housebuilding is virtually dictated by government policy, as the majority of houses are built with some kind of government financial support. Residential building has generally constituted a higher proportion of total demand than in pre-war years, and government policy had a great deal to do with this, both by providing finance for new housing and by increasing the pressure of demand by rent controls. The methods of providing finance vary considerably from country to country. In the United Kingdom, the local authorities are heavily engaged in direct construction of publicly owned dwellings, with financial support from the central government. Public ownership is also important in Italy and the Netherlands, but in these and other

TABLE IV–4
GOVERNMENT FINANCE FOR HOUSING

	Year	Per Cent of Housing Expenditure Financed from Public Funds	Per Cent of New Dwellings in Receipt of Public Financial Assistance
Belgium	1956	44	53
Denmark	1955	55	85
France	1957	46	91
Germany	1957	28	52[a]
Italy	1955	13	21
Netherlands	1957	64	95
Norway	1956[b]	47	66
Sweden	1956	49	97
Switzerland	1955	1	7
United Kingdom	1957[c]	56	58

[a] Excludes dwellings built with tax concessions only, which are considerable, and cover 90–95 per cent of total construction.
[b] First column refers to 1957.
[c] First column refers to 1955.
Source: E.C.E., *Financing of Housing in Europe*, Geneva, 1958.

European countries, governments give financial support of some kind to houses built for private ownership by granting loans at low interest rates, and by giving interest subsidies or tax remissions. These incentives were most substantial in Germany where savings devoted to housebuilding were virtually freed from tax liability.

In most European countries, therefore, a government-stimulated housing boom has contributed to the pressure of post-war demand. In general, there has been a reluctance to apply anti-cyclical controls to this sector, even though it was often a leading source of inflationary pressure and was a competing bidder for the scarce resources needed for productive investment. This reluctance was an important failing of anti-cyclical policy in both the United Kingdom and Germany. Apart from the fact that the government-stimulated housing boom contributed to cyclical problems, it may also be questioned whether it represented the best use of resources in other respects. Rent control often led to misallocation of existing housing, and many of the housing subsidies were given indiscriminately without due priority for slum clearance or urban planning. Because of rent control there was also too little spending on repair and maintenance. This policy of stimulating housebuilding was in strong contrast to growth policy in Communist countries where housing is usually cut to a minimum to release investment resources for productive purposes.

In the United States public housing construction is negligible and financial support for housing smaller than in Europe. However, the government provides insurances for F.H.A. mortgages and guarantees V.A. mortgages as well as providing a secondary mortgage market. U.S. interest rates have also been much lower than in Europe. The fact that the U.S. government had a fixed interest ceiling on the mortgages it insured made the mortgage market highly sensitive to interest rate changes, and U.S. housing construction has shown much greater anti-cyclical variation than anywhere in Europe except the Netherlands. It has been suggested in the C.M.C. report on monetary policy that this sensitivity is in fact too great and should be mitigated. By contrast, the anti-cyclical variation of housing construction in Europe might well be strengthened and could usefully include direct government regulation of mortgage terms on minimum deposits and loan maturities.

Conclusions on Public Demand. It is clear that government is directly responsible for a good deal of the final demand of the economy. Government consumption varies from 12 to 18 per cent of G.N.P. and government investment in public works and public enterprise from 3·5 per cent in Belgium to 9 per cent in the Netherlands (see Table IV–5). Government finance for housing may also amount to up to 3 per cent of G.N.P. European governments directly control from 40 to 60 per cent of total investment activity, as compared with about 30 per cent in the United States and Canada. Governments thus have considerable power to determine the investment momentum of the economy, but these powers were seldom fully used in the 1950s. A better use of these powers should emerge as perspective planning techniques improve.

TABLE IV-5
GROSS DOMESTIC INVESTMENT BY TYPE OF USE IN 1957
AS A PROPORTION OF G.N.P.

Fixed Domestic Investment

	General Government	Public Enterprise	Private Enterprise	Total	Of which Residential	Inventories
Belgium	1·8	1·7	13·7	17·2	5·2	1·2
Denmark	2·1	1·9	13·4	17·4	2·9	1·8
France	2·1	(4·3)	(12·2)	18·6	4·6	1·8
Germany	2·6			21·8	4·9	2·5
Italy	2·4			21·9	6·2	0·5
Netherlands	4·2	4·7	16·7	25·6	5·2	2·6
Norway	2·9			28·7[a]	4·5	0·9
Sweden	3·5	4·7	11·9	20·1	5·1	2·3
United Kingdom	1·5	5·3	8·8	15·5	2·8	1·3
Canada	3·9	3·9	19·2	27·0	4·4	0·6
United States	2·4	0·4	14·5	17·3[a]	4·1	0·2

[a] The figures are not consistent with those given in Appendix I.

Source: U.N. Yearbook of National Accounts Statistics 1960. French figures on public and private enterprise derived from Statistiques et Etudes Financières, April 1959, p. 391, Ministère des Finances, Paris. Germany from O.E.C.D. National Accounts Division.

The Management of Private Demand[1]

As government demand is not designed primarily with a view to

[1] A more detailed account of the development of economic policy instruments and the business cycle can be found in the following sources: 'The Postwar Business Cycle in Western Europe and the Role of Government Policy', A. Maddison, Banca Nazionale del Lavoro Quarterly Review, June 1960; Nationale Konjunkturpolitik in Europa 1945–56, C.E.P.E.S., Frankfurt, 1958; O.E.E.C. Ninth Annual Report, Chapters I, II and V, Paris, April 1958, O.E.E.C. Tenth Annual Review, Chapters II and III, Paris, March 1959, and O.E.E.C. Eleventh Annual Review, Chapter II, Paris, April 1960. The following analyses of the policies of individual countries are most helpful: Growth in the British Economy, a P.E.P. report, Allen and Unwin, London, 1960; Bert G. Hickman, Growth and Stability of the Postwar Economy, The Brookings Institution, Washington, D.C., 1960; Money and Credit, The Report of the Commission on Money and Credit, Prentice-Hall, N.Y., 1961, and the Congressional Hearings on the Report before the Joint Economic Committee, August 14–18, 1961; Erik Lundberg, Business Cycles and Economic Growth, Allen and Unwin, London, 1957; Henry C. Wallich, Mainsprings of the German Revival, Yale University Press, New Haven, 1955; Christopher Dow, The Management of the British Economy, 1945–60, National Institute of Economic and Social Research, London, 1964; John and Anne-Marie Hackett, Economic Planning in France, Allen and Unwin, London, 1963.

exercising a growth or stabilizing influence, governments must seek to influence the level and growth of private spending to attain their ends. Private demand represents up to three-quarters of G.N.P. and there are three main ways in which governments influence it. In the first place, they can vary taxation. Most governmental income is not derived directly from production but by taxes levied on the private sector. Taxation is therefore almost as large as government expenditure—about a quarter to a third of G.N.P. Changes in tax rates can have a powerful influence on private income flows and spending. The second weapon of governments is monetary policy. Spending decisions of the private sector are influenced by the availability and cost of credit. Monetary policy may also be used by the central government authorities partly with the idea of influencing the spending decisions of other parts of the government sector, particularly local authority spending. Finally, governments can influence the pattern of private spending by direct controls, and if these controls are extensive they will also affect the general level of private spending.

Fiscal Policy. Taxation takes about a quarter to a third of total G.N.P. in these countries (see Table IV-6). In North America the tax burden is somewhat smaller than in most European countries. There is no evidence that a high tax burden has hindered growth, for the fastest-growing country—Germany—has had the highest tax burden, and a slow-growing country—Belgium—the lowest. High taxation gives the government great leverage in influencing the volume of private activity, and it has been extensively used in Europe in order to achieve the aims of economic policy. Fiscal policy has been mainly directed at short-term stabilization problems, but it has, of course, conditioned growth. In Europe it has proved easier to change taxes than government expenditure, and although most government budgets are still presented in their old pre-war accounting framework, governments are mainly concerned with their general economic effect and the budgets are generally accompanied by a set of supporting financial documents or national accounts showing their impact on economic activity.

The main emphasis in post-war fiscal policy has been on the achievement of a level of total spending—public and private—which ensured reasonably full use of resources but was not so excessive as to cause balance-of-payments difficulties or inflationary price increases. In pre-war years in all countries except Sweden, which was more sophisticated and successful, the main emphasis had been on the need to secure balance in the public accounts. This led to some extremes of folly. In the great depression of 1932 when there was mass unemployment, U.S. income taxes were increased to help balance the budget, thus pushing demand and employment even

H

TABLE IV–6
CATEGORIES OF GOVERNMENT REVENUE AS A PROPORTION OF G.N.P. IN 1957

	Total Current Revenue	Social Security Levies	Indirect Taxes	Income from Property and Entrepreneurship[b]	Direct Taxes		
					Total	Taxes on Corporations	Taxes on Persons
Belgium	23·1	6·0	9·2	0·9	7·0	2·0	5·0
Denmark	25·8a	1·3	11·4	1·6	11·5	1·3	10·2
France	32·7	9·3	17·1	0·6	5·7	2·3	3·4
Germany	36·9	9·4	14·7	3·3	9·5	3·2	6·3
Italy	29·3	8·5	13·8	1·2	5·8		
Netherlands	32·6	7·5	10·0	2·2	12·9	3·8	9·1
Norway	31·3	2·4	13·5	0·8	14·6		
Sweden	31·7	2·8	9·4	2·1	17·4	3·6	13·8
United Kingdom	31·0	3·0	13·5	2·7	11·8	4·4	7·4
Canada	27·1	1·9	12·6	2·7	9·9	4·2	5·7
United States	27·7	3·3	8·8	1·9	13·7	4·7	9·0

a 1956.
b Includes current transfers from the rest of the world.

Source: Statistics of Sources and Uses of Finance 1948–58, O.E.E.C., 1958, except for corporate taxation which is derived from O.E.C.D., General Statistics, November 1962. Taxes on persons derived as a residual. For Belgium the figure on corporate taxation is derived from the U.N. Yearbook of National Accounts Statistics, 1960.

lower.[1] At the same period, British unemployment benefits were cut for similar reasons, and equally perverse policies were followed in many other countries. The commitment to pursue full employment policies was usually undertaken during or immediately after the war. These commitments were embodied in employment acts in the United Kingdom, the United States and Sweden, in the institution of planning offices in France and the Netherlands, and in the Vanoni plan in Italy. Even in countries where the commitment to active economic policies was less overt, and where the main stabilization weapon was monetary policy rather than the budget, as in Belgium and Germany, there was by no means a policy of *laisser faire*.

Fiscal policy has been most actively used for stabilization purposes in Scandinavia, the Netherlands and the United Kingdom. In the United Kingdom, for instance, there were important tax changes in nine of the eleven annual budgets from 1950 to 1960, and there were two special budgets in 1955 and 1960 with other tax changes. The average tax change in post-war budgets has been about £150 million,[2] or 0·75 per cent of G.N.P. Apart from the tax changes, there were six major changes in depreciation allowances in the 1950s. Most of the tax changes were reductions. There were tax increases in 1951 and 1955, but when policy was restrictive, the main emphasis was on cuts in public expenditure or on monetary restraint. As taxes were changed so much, the two standstill budgets of 1954 and 1956 can also be properly regarded as acts of fiscal policy.

In Germany there is a constitutional requirement of budget balance, to which little attention has been paid in practice, but German fiscal policy has been hampered by the fact that a large share of taxes and expenditures is in the hands of local government and the Länder. Nevertheless, German fiscal policy has played a major role in ensuring a high level of investment in both industry and housing. In the course of the 1950s, German tax rates were changed several times. The overall effect of such changes was always to reduce the tax burden, though some of the changes involved restraint on particular types of demand. The steady reduction in tax rates was due to the fact that government spending increased less than private spending in the 1950s, and that the government share of total saving was reduced as personal saving increased. This was also true in several other countries, and, of course, if the general burden of the tax system is progressive and national income is rising fast, governments would, in any case, have to reduce tax rates to avoid taking a larger slice of each year's income.

After a prolonged period of recession in 1952 and 1953, govern-

---

[1] U.S. pre-war fiscal policy is described in the *Annual Report of the Council of Economic Advisers*, Washington, D.C., January 1963, p. 71.

[2] Christopher Dow, *op. cit.*

ment spending in France was a constant inflationary force in the years 1954–58. Taxes were frequently changed, and there was a good deal of juggling with subsidies and price controls in an attempt to suppress inflation, but fiscal policy was usually perverse. From 1958 onwards, French fiscal policy was successful first in ensuring the success of devaluation, and then in promoting a sound expansion of output.

In Belgium and Italy the tax system of the 1950s was rather antiquated and unsuitable for a modern fiscal policy. Nevertheless, the Belgian authorities made some attempt at anti-cyclical policies, and tried to stimulate investment by special tax favors. These measures were not vigorous enough to stimulate an adequate level of total demand or to promote structural adjustments in depressed sectors. The Belgian economy was also inhibited by the rigidities of the monetary system. In Italy the main emphasis in fiscal policy was to stimulate public and private investment for long-term growth, and taxes were not changed for stabilization purposes.

In Switzerland federal powers are too exiguous for an active fiscal policy in the sense followed in other countries, and to some extent this is true of monetary policy too. However, the authorities were able to control the movement of foreign labor by the labor permit system, and to influence foreign capital flows by understandings with the Swiss commercial banks. As foreign labor is a third of the Swiss labor force, as most materials are imported, and as foreign capital movements are enormous in relation to domestic savings, the Swiss authorities had a unique opportunity to vary the supply situation of the economy. This they used unobtrusively but firmly and succeeded in getting fast growth without inflation.

By contrast with Europe, the United States can scarcely be said to have had a fiscal policy for most of the 1950s, although public discussion and governmental consideration of tax changes were extensive. U.S. tax rates were raised in 1950 and 1951 during the Korean war, and were lowered in 1954, but there was no attempt to compensate for the 1958 or 1960 recessions by fiscal policy or, indeed, to offset the longer-term tendency from 1957 onwards for the economy to work below full-capacity level. This happened in spite of the fact that the U.S. tax structure is more progressive than that in most European countries, and has a built-in tendency to damp the growth of private demand.

Why was the U.S. economy untouched by fiscal policy over eight years in spite of two recessions? Why have the U.S. authorities accepted fluctuations in activity involving absolute falls in output and substantial increases in unemployment as a fact of life, and restricted active policy intervention to the monetary field or to minor variations in public spending? This seems to have been due in part to a misjudgment as to the causes of rising prices, in part to a more old-fashioned attitude to fiscal policy than in Europe, in part to the intellectual influence of a fatalistic school of 'business-cycle' analysis, and in part to special constitutional difficulties in wielding a fiscal policy. The existence of inadequate demand during the 1950s was fully admitted by the Council of Economic Advisers in its 1963 report:

'In the past five years, the economy has been consistently out of balance—with too little demand to match our supply capabilities. In the first post-war decade, when demands were considerably stronger, the balance was frequently tipped in the other direction.'[1]

The U.S. emphasis on the virtues of a balanced budget has had no post-war counterpart in Europe, where there are no statutory limits on fiscal policy such as the ceiling on government debt and on the interest rates payable on longer-term government securities as in the United States. The constitutional system of checks and balances in the United States makes it more difficult for an administration to change taxes quickly than is the case in Europe. Reliance has therefore been placed on the automatic capacity of the U.S. tax system to stabilize the economy by cushioning income fluctuations in the private sector. It has even been suggested that the reliance on 'built-in stability' has been an advantage because a more active discretionary fiscal policy would probably have been perverse.[2]

Built-in stability refers to the capacity of the tax system to provide automatic compensations for fluctuations in money incomes in times of recession or boom. If the tax rates are progressive, if tax rates are high on specially volatile incomes, or if social transfers are paid out when income falls, then the tax system is compensatory. It has been estimated[3] that in the 1953–54 U.S. recession the potential decline in G.N.P. was offset by about 30 to 40 per cent because of the automatic compensatory variation in revenues and transfer expenditures. In the 1930s, by contrast, U.S. government fiscal operations aggravated recessionary influences because of the much greater relative

[1] *Op. cit.*, p. 22.
[2] See the views of Senator Proxmire, p. 202 of the Hearings of the Joint Economic Committee on the Report of the Commission on Money and Credit.
[3] See David Lusher, 'The Stabilizing Effectiveness of Budget Flexibility', a chapter in *Policies to Combat Depression*, National Bureau of Economic Research, Princeton, 1956. See also *National Income and Outlay*, National Income Supplement to *Survey of Current Business*, U.S. Dept. of Commerce, 1959. Unfortunately, such sophisticated studies are not available for most European countries. For the United Kingdom see Peter Pearse, 'Automatic Stabilization and the British Taxes on Incomes', *Review of Economic Studies*, No. 79, February 1962. In any case, the frequency of discretionary changes in Europe makes such studies more difficult and less rewarding.

importance at that time of state and local finance which relies on regressive taxation.

Tax revenue in the United States is sensitive to cyclical movements because of the importance of federal income and corporate tax. Corporate profits are the most volatile source of income, are taxed more heavily than in pre-war years and form a bigger proportion of total revenue. As a result, the fall in corporate profits tax in recession can now offset about a fifth of the total fall in incomes.[1] Companies themselves cushion the impact of falling profits on personal incomes by a policy of relatively stable dividends. Personal income tax collections are a much less important stabilizer and have usually offset only a twelfth of the recession drop in income.[2] Both of these stabilizers are bigger in the United States than in Europe where corporate taxes and income taxes are generally lower.

Another reason for the sensitivity of tax collections to income movements is that the bulk of U.S. tax on personal or corporate income is now paid at or near the time that income accrues, under the pay-as-you-go and quarterly corporation withholding (self-assessment) tax systems. Thus taxes go down almost as soon as there is a recession and vice versa in a boom, and there are also provisions for carrying over losses, whereas in pre-war years payment in arrears often accentuated the cycle. In this respect, too, the U.S. system has a more automatic effect than that of most European countries.

On the expenditure side, the main compensatory item is transfer payments, which in the United States have tended to offset about a fifth of income declines in post-war recessions.[3] The major one is, of course, unemployment benefits. These are more important now than pre-war, but not as important in the United States as in Europe. In the United States some further stability is provided by the private sector in which a number of industries, particularly automobiles, pay substantial compensation to workers who are dismissed in times of recession. The U.S. steel industry also provides supplementary unemployment insurance to its unemployed workers. In this respect European industry has lagged, but in several continental countries there are substantial legal guarantees of employment, and in Italy particularly it is very difficult to dismiss workers. It is also true that the higher level of employment at which the European economies have been operating has itself been a source of stability, for employers faced with a continuing labor shortage are reluctant to dismiss workers when demand falls off. This stickiness of the labor market has been particularly noticeable in the United Kingdom.

[1] See David Lusher, *op. cit.*
[2] See Lusher, *op. cit.*
[3] *Ibid.*

The U.S. stabilizers work to check expansion as well as recession. Their impact depends on the level of money income and does not necessarily respond to changes in the degree to which the economy is using its output potential. Hence the stabilizers can work against economic growth even when the economy is operating below capacity, particularly if prices are rising.

Furthermore, the whole philosophy of relying on such automatic stabilizers implies taking the business cycle for granted, and this is not particularly settling to expectations.

Since 1961, the emphasis given to built-in stability in official U.S. policy has diminished. There were changes in corporate taxes to foster investment in 1962—a change in depreciation allowance schedules and an investment tax credit—and the administration introduced proposals for rather substantial reductions in income tax and corporate tax at the beginning of 1963. These were brought forward explicitly with the idea of sustaining the longer-run growth of demand and supply, and were not geared to the current situation. The President also requested standby powers to initiate a temporary reduction in personal income tax rates subject to Congressional approval, and to accelerate and initiate public works in times of serious unemployment. The first of these powers was proposed by the report of the Commission on Money and Credit in 1961, but the second goes beyond its suggestions. It is clear, therefore, that an attempt is being made to move U.S. fiscal policy closer to the European pattern. This effort will have to go much further if it is to succeed, for the U.S. economy no longer has a high momentum of growth and investment and needs a bigger stimulus than European countries.

In Europe, tax changes in the 1950s were mainly restricted to the annual budget, but there was growing support for the use of tax changes for stabilization purposes between budgets. It was generally felt that the restriction of stabilization measures to a fixed budget date is an arbitrary and undesirable restraint on the freedom of action of the authorities, and in many cases sets up adverse effects from the expectation of tax changes. There are, of course, ways in which governments can vary the tax burden between budgets without changing tax rates. Tax collections can be speeded up or slowed down, social security levies can usually be adjusted, depreciation allowances can be changed or exemption limits for income tax may be varied. These adjustments are usually not nearly as useful as the power to vary tax rates. In the Netherlands taxes were changed between budgets, tax collections have been accelerated and temporary taxes were voted in budgets which could be changed afterwards according to the government's judgment of the economic situation. In Sweden the government made considerable use of investment levies and subsidies between budgets to retard or stimulate investment.

In the United Kingdom the 1961 budget gave the Chancellor two new discretionary powers to vary all indirect taxes and tariffs by 10 per cent, and to impose a 10 per cent payroll tax between budgets. These regulators gave him power to vary taxes by an amount equivalent to 1 per cent of G.N.P. The power to vary indirect taxes was used in the summer of 1961. These tax changes were consolidated in the 1962 budget, so that the Chancellor was once again given his power to vary taxes by 10 per cent. In November 1962, the British Chancellor used his power to reclassify rates of purchase tax to reduce the tax on cars from 50 per cent to 25 per cent. This type of action had been theoretically available throughout the 1950s, but had never previously been used outside a budget. At the time the regulators were introduced, there was some discussion of the possibility of giving the Chancellor powers to vary income tax rates as well. It was felt that this was technically too difficult to do because of the complications in the system of weekly tax deductions which cannot be changed easily at short notice, although this power to vary direct taxes is the one recently requested in the United States by the President.

The frequency with which taxes need to be changed depends on the basic structure of the tax system, as well as on economic developments. If the tax system is progressive and incomes are rising fast, the maintenance of existing tax rates will tend to depress demand unless government demand rises faster than G.N.P. It was for this reason that most European countries with progressive tax systems reduced direct taxation rates over the 1950s. Another reason for this was that private savings increased, and a smaller proportion of government saving was required. In the United States the failure to reduce tax rates meant that the progressive tax system acted as a damper on expansion.

Although the total tax burden is not dissimilar in these countries, tax structures differ considerably. In Scandinavia and the United States, about half of total revenue is derived from direct taxation, whereas in France only a sixth of tax receipts is derived from direct taxation (see Table IV–6). In Scandinavia and the United States direct taxes are highly progressive and entail a considerable narrowing of the pre-tax spread of personal incomes. In one or two countries there are capital gains taxes as well as income taxes. In Belgium, France and Italy direct taxes have a much more modest impact in equalizing incomes. Direct taxes have been varied occasionally—usually downwards—to affect the level of consumption, but direct taxes on persons have been varied much less than corporate taxes or indirect taxes for anti-cyclical purposes. Curiously enough, the heavy social security levies of European countries have not been varied for anti-cyclical purposes though they affect nearly all income earners.

Corporate taxes are those which most directly affect investment incentives. They also affect the flow of funds available for investment as profits are the major source of investment funds. Several countries attempted to influence business investment by varying the rate of depreciation allowance, by imposing taxes or giving subsidies on investment, or by discrimination between tax rates on distributed and undistributed profits. Apart from these stimuli to investment, several European governments gave special tax incentives to saving which were varied for anti-cyclical purposes.

The Swedish system seems to have worked best as it actually secured a considerable increase in investment in the 1958 recession. In the United Kingdom, corporate tax rates and depreciation allowances were changed six times in the 1950s. The 'initial' allowances (accelerated depreciation) were removed in 1952, restored at half the rate in 1953, and substituted by 'investment' allowances (investment subsidies) in 1954. These were withdrawn and the initial allowances substituted in 1956. The initial allowances were twice increased in 1958, and in 1959 the investment allowance was restored and the initial allowance curtailed a little. Because of the slowness of tax collection, the change in the flow of funds available for investment was not always changed at the time the new incentives or disincentives were created, and the incentives were not always powerful enough or timed properly to offset the profit expectations of entrepreneurs.

Indirect taxes are of several kinds. In most continental countries, i.e., Germany, Italy, Belgium and the Netherlands, they mainly consist of turnover taxes levied consecutively on the total value of output at each stage of production. France had this type of tax until 1954, but it was then abolished as it hit investment adversely and promoted an artificial tendency to vertical integration. In its place a tax on value added was introduced. In some countries taxes are concentrated on retail sales as with the Swedish sales tax, and in the United Kingdom they are heavily concentrated on particular items in the form of purchase tax (wholesale sales tax) or the older excise duties on tobacco, beer, wine and spirits. Within the Common Market, an attempt is being made to standardize indirect taxes on the French system. Changes in indirect taxes and subsidies have been used a good deal to influence consumption and have usually worked promptly. Changes in purchase taxes have been used for anti-cyclical purposes in the United Kingdom, and these have had a very marked influence because of the high rates of tax and the high elasticity of demand for the products involved. The Swedish government introduced a sales tax in 1960 in order to increase its control over consumption.

Conclusions on Fiscal Policy. Thus far, we have merely described the degree to which fiscal policy has been used. It is not so easy to assess the degree of its success. However, European demand was sustained at a higher level for a longer period in the 1950s than had ever previously been recorded, and the two recessions of 1952 and 1958 were of a very minor nature and more obviously influenced by government policies in restraining inflation than by any spontaneous demand forces of the private sector. There seems little doubt that an active fiscal policy played a major role in nurturing high levels of demand and investment in Europe, and these high levels of demand themselves did something to moderate the volatility of private spending. The lack of an active policy in the United States was a major reason for the slacker demand, greater fluctuation and slower growth there. In some respects the need for an active policy to promote demand was even more necessary in the United States than in Europe because the post-war pent-up demand which sustained European growth to some degree in the early 1950s had disappeared much earlier in the United States.

An active fiscal policy was not in itself enough to secure rapid growth, for the United Kingdom grew slowly in spite of having a very active fiscal policy. In fact, fiscal policy was expected to carry too great a burden in the United Kingdom and at some phases mistakes in policy were the major obstacle to growth, as in 1957 when fiscal and monetary restraint were pursued while the economy was working below capacity. British policy also placed too little emphasis on the need to foster a steady rise in investment over the long run, and its attempts to influence investment spending in a compensatory way were probably harmful to growth and not particularly helpful in promoting stability. The United Kingdom was not, of course, the only country to make mistakes in fiscal policy. French policy was often quite perverse, and the lack of a policy in the United States was also worse than the U.K. record.

Certain major problems of fiscal policy emerged clearly in the 1950s. It became apparent that the annual budget exercise did not give enough leeway to policy makers to intervene at the right time, and that within limits they must have some additional discretionary powers to modify taxes if they are to do their job properly. Too much emphasis was placed on control of demand as an anti-inflationary weapon, and output was sometimes unnecessarily restricted when the sources of inflationary pressure lay elsewhere. This was true even though tax increases were fairly rare, because lack of tax reduction was often deflationary. In some countries there was a lack of public understanding as to the aims of policy and an inadequate effort on the part of the authorities to educate public opinion. As a result, some of the more difficult policy decisions were shirked or delayed, and there was an over-reliance on automatic devices or the more anonymous weapons of monetary policy to meet the responsibilities which fiscal policy should have faced.

Another respect in which policy was deficient in the 1950s was lack of adequate perspective which could have been provided by a long-term 'plan'. Fiscal policy is mainly and necessarily concerned with short-term problems, but a better idea of the longer-term perspective of investment demand, spending on consumer durables, or the level of exports required would have probably helped orient the choice between different policy decisions. In spite of these problems and the relative crudeness of policy weapons, there can be little doubt that governments were highly responsible in trying to maintain the growth momentum of the economy. Their mistakes in most cases involved excess demand, because the basically buoyant state of demand made the economy very sensitive to marginal expansionary stimuli. In dealing with inflationary problems none of the European countries took so much steam out of the economy that this buoyancy disappeared, though this seems to have happened in the United States.

Monetary Policy. Monetary policy played a major role in government attempts to direct the general level of activity in the 1950s. It was the main anti-cyclical weapon used in the United States and Germany and was extensively used in other countries as well.

Monetary policy fell out of favor in the 1930s as it was not very effective against the severe depression of that period. The relative quiescence of monetary policy continued well into the post-war period, in spite of the prevalence of inflation and balance-of-payments difficulties. There were several reasons for this, apart from a general preference for budgetary policy or direct controls. The existence of large public debts would have made dear money expensive, and many of the inflationary problems were so severe in the early post-war years that direct controls were more effective than monetary policy. The return to more normal conditions in the early fifties made it possible for monetary policy to be used more effectively as the liquidity of business was reduced and the dependence on the banking system increased. The emphasis on the desirability of low interest rates disappeared after a prolonged period of rapid growth and inflation. A fairly high rate of return on assets with a fixed money value was felt to be normal in such circumstances, and to be no particular deterrent to investment.

Moreover, it was felt that monetary policy was more flexible than fiscal policy, as it does not require parliamentary sanction, can be administered in smaller doses, and its direction easily shifted. Its impact is more anonymous, and an attempt to enhance this was made in some cases by fostering a deliberate mystique.[1] There is also a tradition in some countries that the Central Bank is independent of the government, and monetary policy was therefore relied upon to do some of the more unpopular jobs of policy, particularly measures to restrain demand. As a result, central bankers have at some points acquired a mysterious or Mephistophelian character, and have taken some of the onus of unpopular policies from ministers. Curiously enough, some central bankers seem to have enjoyed this role, perhaps because they resented the alternative suggestion by the opponents of monetary policy that their actions were unimportant. This mysticism, of course, is not a real advantage in any policy, because the authorities need to be as well informed as possible about its impact in particular sectors of the economy in order to judge when it should be relaxed or augmented, and it is a positive disadvantage to confuse the public as to the aims of policy.

Monetary policy was felt to be a useful expansionary weapon when the economy was suffering from mild recession, as well as an anti-inflationary instrument. The greater convertibility of currencies also revived its international role in influencing short-term money movements. In pre-war years, the main impact of monetary policy was thought to be concentrated on business investment in inventories; more recently, monetary policy has also been aimed at fixed investment, consumers' durable expenditure, housing or even local government spending.

The scope and impact of monetary policy have varied a good deal between countries. In most cases, monetary controls are applied directly only to the commercial banks, and the impact on other financial institutions is usually indirect. These other financial intermediaries are more important now than they were in pre-war years, and the role of the commercial banks has diminished correspondingly. Commercial banks are more important in supplying long-term finance to industry on the continent than in either the United Kingdom or United States, which have well-developed capital markets and where commercial banking is more heavily concentrated on short-term lending. The effective leverage of monetary policy is therefore greater in the continental European countries.

The freedom of action of the authorities has varied to some extent because of the differing importance of the national debt. A tight

---

[1] See the remarks of Sir Robert Hall, Economic Adviser to the U.K. government throughout the 1950s: 'There is still a tendency to speak in magical rather than scientific terms of the use of interest rates and monetary controls generally.' *Economic Journal*, December 1959, p. 648.

monetary policy will raise the interest burden of the national debt, and make the government unpopular with existing bondholders, who will see the value of their assets fall. The reverse is true of an easy monetary policy. In the United Kingdom, the national debt was much bigger than G.N.P. throughout the 1950s, and in Belgium, the Netherlands and the United States, it was usually well over half. In Germany, by contrast, it was only a sixth of G.N.P., and in France about a quarter. The existence of national debts is not always a restraint on the freedom of action of the authorities. In the United Kingdom the price of government bonds varied considerably in the course of the 1950s, and the yield on irredeemable bonds (Consols) ranged from 3·4 to 5·6 per cent. This is about the same range as that experienced by 'rentes perpetuelles' in France—which is a similar type of government security. In the United States the national debt was probably more of a politically felt constraint on policy than in the United Kingdom, though here too there was a considerable variation in long-term bond prices in the 1950s. Although the existence of a large national debt means that the monetary authorities must constantly organize the refunding of large bond issues which may be embarrassingly timed from the point of view of stabilization policy, there is a technical advantage in having a well-organized government securities market that provides a sensitive medium of interconnected markets which rapidly transmits the effects of government actions to all sectors of the economy. The effectiveness of monetary policy is also affected by the liquidity of the banking system and of the economy in general. Early post-war inflation or currency reforms reduced liquidity in several continental countries more quickly than in the United Kingdom and the United States and increased the amenability of the banks to pressure from the monetary authorities.

The techniques of monetary policy have varied a good deal—so much in fact that what passes for monetary policy in Europe would hardly be recognized as such in the United States. Some countries have wielded a much larger range of weapons than others, the frequency of changes has varied, the weapons have been used both gently and massively. The range of policy weapons used is illustrated synoptically in Table IV–7. Open-market operations are a major weapon of monetary control in the United States, the United Kingdom and Germany, but in other European countries this weapon has not been used because the market in government bonds is not large or well organized. In the United States, such operations were confined to short-term securities from 1953 to 1961, with the idea of causing the least possible disturbance to free market forces and of exercising only an indirect influence on medium and longer-term interest rates. In Germany, such inhibitions were not felt and there was no reluctance to cause major disturbances in the bond market when the authorities felt that the economic situation warranted a change.

The traditional bank rate weapon was used in all countries, but most often in Germany, the United Kingdom and the United States. In Italy, Norway and Switzerland, however, it was hardly ever used. The use of the bank rate weapon in the United States was much more delicate than in the United Kingdom and Germany. The range of bank rate changes, and the average size of changes, was half that in the United Kingdom.

In the United States, compulsory reserve ratios were changed several times in the 1950s in a downward direction. The United Kingdom used reserve ratios and compulsory special deposits with the Bank of England both to contract and expand credit. In continental countries, compulsory reserve ratios have been used more frequently and have been more stringently and selectively applied than in the United Kingdom or the United States, particularly in Belgium, France and Germany. The monetary authorities on the continent have also imposed the obligation on commercial banks to hold government securities, they have enforced rediscount ceilings on the commercial banks with penalty rates for excess discounting, and have made gentlemen's agreements with the commercial banks to restrain particular kinds of credit. In Germany and France there has been detailed regulation of bank-lending policies, and prescription of the reserves required for different kinds of lending. In the United Kingdom, frequent use has been made of consumer credit regulation of down-payments and maturities, and this has been done in Sweden, the Netherlands, Belgium and France as well; powers to regulate this type of credit also exist in most other European countries. In the United States, such powers were dropped after the Korean war. In Norway, Sweden and France, the authorities have had a large say in the investment policies of financial institutions other than commercial banks.

There has recently been a reconsideration of the role of monetary policy in both the United Kingdom and the United States in the shape of the Radcliffe Report[1] and the report of the Commission on Money and Credit.[2] Both studies have stimulated a great deal of academic and official discussion on the role of monetary policy. In general, the Radcliffe Report is sceptical of the power of traditional

---

[1] *Committee on the Working of the Monetary System*, Cmd. 827, London, August 1959. This is the report of a Royal Commission established by the Chancellor of the Exchequer, Mr. Peter Thorneycroft, in May 1957.

[2] *Money and Credit, Their Influence on Jobs, Prices and Growth*, Prentice-Hall, 1961. This is an authoritative private report of the Commission established by the Committee for Economic Development. The report was extensively discussed in the Congressional Hearings of the Joint Economic Committee.

TABLE IV-7
INSTRUMENTS OF MONETARY POLICY USED IN 1950–60

	Number of Changes in Bank Rate	Range of Bank Rate Changes	Average Size Bank Rate Changes	Use of Open Market Operations	Use of Reserve Ratios	Compulsory Holding of Government Securities	Rediscount Ceilings	Gentlemen's Agreements	Consumer Credit Controls	Other Selective Credit Controls
Belgium	15	2·75–5·0	0·4		x	x				x
Denmark	9	3–5·5	0·6					x		
France	12	2·5–5	0·5		x	x	x	x	x	x
Germany	19	2·75–6	0·7	x	x	x	x	x	x	x
Italy	2	3·5–4·5	0·5		x			x		x
Netherlands	16	2·5–5	0·5					x		x
Norway	1	2·5–3·5	1·0		x			x	x[a]	x
Sweden	7	2·5–5	0·6		x			x		x
Switzerland	2	1·5–2·5	0·8		x			x		
United Kingdom	18	2–7	0·8	x				x		
United States	22	1·5–4	0·4	x	x				x[b]	

[a] Exercised under gentlemen's agreement.
[b] Consumer credit control was used in the United States during the Korean war.

monetary instruments to influence economic activity and attributes more importance to new instruments such as consumer credit control. In its view, the main general management weapon of government is fiscal policy, and monetary policy must be relegated to a very secondary role. By contrast, the C.M.C. report considers that U.S. monetary policy has exerted a significant influence on the level of activity:

> 'The Commission believes that the restrictive monetary policies in 1955–57, and again in 1959, demonstrate that monetary policy can have a very substantial effect on the level and rate of growth and of demand. In both periods monetary restriction seemed to induce a decline in the annual rate of growth of residential construction of $3 to $4 billion. Business investment was lower than it would have been if credit had been freely available at low rates. If allowance is made for the indirect effects that the restraint on some investment had on consumption and on types of investment not directly affected, monetary restraint seems to have had an important effect on the level and rate of growth of economic activity'.[1]

The C.M.C. report does not provide such a specific example of the effectiveness of monetary policy in compensating downswings, but seems reasonably satisfied that its stabilizing powers are substantial in both directions. The report would have been more convincing in this respect if it had contained more evidence. It should also be noted that the effectiveness of U.S. monetary policy in influencing residential construction, a point particularly stressed by the C.M.C., is due in major part to the special character of government intervention in the mortgage market.

The C.M.C. report makes some suggestions for modifying U.S. monetary policy weapons, but by comparison with the powers used in Europe, the changes suggested are minor. It proposes a widening of open-market operations to cover longer-term bonds, but no selective controls are recommended. In fact, it suggests a modification of mortgage regulations which would reduce the counter-cyclical impact of monetary policy, and it also suggests that changes in reserve requirements are undesirable.

The contrast between the Radcliffe Report and the C.M.C. report is quite striking, particularly when it is remembered that the former deals with a country where monetary weapons have been wielded more drastically. In the first place, the Radcliffe Commission is sceptical about the possibilities of assessing the effectiveness of monetary policy, both because of statistical and analytical difficulties and also because of the British practice of making monetary changes

[1] *Op. cit.*, p. 55.

part of 'package deals' in which a number of policy weapons are used. Radcliffe is sceptical as to whether interest rate changes affected investment decisions and suggests that the effect of quantitative credit restraints was offset by changes in the velocity of circulation. It believes that the only quick or major influence of monetary policy on demand was exercised by consumer credit controls, which were felt to have had an undesirably heavy influence on a particular sector of the economy that was not always the most relevant from the view-point of stabilization policy. As a result, the Radcliffe Commission's findings are rather negative:

'Our review of monetary measures has not led us to any positive and simple recommendations. No method, new or old, provides the remedy for all our troubles. We do not find any solution of the problem of influencing total demand in more violent manipulation of interest rates; we find control of the supply of money to be no more than an important facet of debt management; we cannot recommend any substantial change in the rules under which the banks operate; we do not regard the capital issues control as useful in ordinary times; and we believe there are narrow limits to the usefulness of hire purchase controls ... monetary measures cannot be relied upon to keep in nice balance an economy subject to major strains from both without and within.'

The Radcliffe Report did not suggest that monetary policy could not be used to exert a major or prompt influence on demand, but in order to do so, it felt that it would have to be used 'with a vigour that itself creates an emergency'. Such drastic measures would include effective changes in commercial bank reserve ratios, backed by restrictions on all classes of lenders, and much bigger changes in interest rates. As the Radcliffe Commission did not consider that in normal times monetary policy should play 'other than a subordinate part in guiding the development of the economy', it confined itself to recommending that the authorities should operate on long-term interest rates as well as short, and that they should use consumer credit regulation to a lesser extent. The report gave brief considera-tion to direct controls which were thought to have a useful function in controlling housing investment, but apparently placed its main faith in fiscal policy.

The recommendations of the Radcliffe Report and the C.M.C. Report are similar, but their assessment of the stabilization role of monetary policy is strikingly different. This is partly due to different standards as to what the economy should attain, and partly to the fact that the penalties for policy mistakes were much higher in the United Kingdom in the 1950s than in the United States because of

I

the shaky external position. It is also partly due to the fact that the Radcliffe Report was dealing with a limited aspect of the stabilization problem. If it had given more consideration to the difficulties of fiscal policy, it might well have been as pessimistic about its potential as it was about monetary policy. Both the reports reflect a major concern with the management of demand. As in most of the official policy statements in these two countries in the 1950s, there is little sign of an interest in the possibility of an incomes policy or of policies to enhance the supply potential.

These two reports deal with particular national situations, and were heavily influenced by the academic controversies and traditions in their respective countries on many questions of monetary theory which are not clearly settled. As a result, the Radcliffe Report was subtle and ambiguous, and had difficulty in finding enough facts to judge the efficacy of post-war policy measures. Obviously a similar official enquiry on the efficacy of monetary policy in a continental country could well have reached totally different conclusions, not only because of a different academic tradition, but because of a different monetary system and a wider scope of monetary policy. There are several reasons already mentioned for thinking that monetary policy had more teeth in France, Germany and other continental countries than in the United Kingdom or the United States. In any case, even if the scepticism of the Radcliffe Report about the potency of monetary policy is correct, there is little doubt that governments used it actively in the 1950s with the aim of managing demand in both directions. It is also true that government regulation of the operations of financial institutions ensured that the 1950s were relatively free of the speculative financial collapses which greatly enhanced the difficulty of maintaining stability in the pre-war period. The improvement here was, of course, greatest in the United States. In some cases the soundness of European financial institutions could well be improved by further regulation. This applies particularly to consumer credit.

Direct Controls. In addition to fiscal and monetary weapons, direct controls were used to some extent in the 1950s. In the early 1950s direct controls over resource allocation and imports were fairly widespread, particularly in the United Kingdom. But these were found cumbersome administratively and arbitrary in impact, so that they tended to distort resource allocation if retained for a long period. They were felt to be unsuitable once the period of desperate shortages was over, and were largely abandoned. In the Netherlands, however, building licensing was retained, and was frequently and fairly successfully used as a control weapon. The Radcliffe Report suggested that such controls might be useful to the United Kingdom.

In France extensive controls over the location of industry and access to the capital market were a major instrument of policy. In Switzerland too, controls over migration and the capital market were the main instrument of economic management.

Conclusions on the Management of Demand

In the course of the 1950s the main aim of governments in their efforts to control demand was to ensure that resources were reasonably fully used, and that demand was not so excessive as to lead to payments deficits and rising prices. The degree to which they succeeded in maintaining high demand can be judged by the state of employment and the experience of recession. Both were extremely good by previous standards in most European countries. The only serious case of persistent unemployment was in Italy, and this arose largely because of structural difficulties in absorbing the labor surplus of the underdeveloped South. There was a phase in the first half of the 1950s when German unemployment was also high, but this, too, was mainly due to structural difficulties in absorbing a large and continuing flow of refugees, which swelled the volume of employment by a quarter in the 1950s. Belgium and Denmark had unemployment which was due to inadequate demand and lack of sufficiently active policy, although in both countries there were major structural difficulties in exporting some traditional commodities. By European standards, the United States and Canada were unsuccessful in maintaining adequate demand. Both had several recessions and an increasing unemployment trend.

There were periods in the 1950s when demand was excessive. This was universally true in 1950–51, at the time of the Korean war, and it was true in most countries in 1955–56.[1] The momentum of activity in the economy had gathered such steam that there was less of a problem in stimulating activity than in checking it.

Although the basic elements of private demand—durable and nondurable consumption, fixed productive investment, exports, inventories and house construction—remained volatile, the basic rhythm of activity was set by government. The fluctuations in 1952 and 1958 and the boom of 1955–56 were not business cycles in the spontaneous or self-generating sense, but were policy-determined.[2] Both of the 'recessions' were due to policy restraints, and a good deal of the boom was due to special investment stimuli. The business cycle in

---

[1] The periods of excess demand in individual countries are catalogued in the O.E.E.C. Experts report, *The Problem of Rising Prices*, O.E.E.C., Paris, May 1961, p. 35.
[2] For an interpretation of European developments in this sense, see Milton Gilbert, 'The Postwar Business Cycle in Western Europe', *American Economic Review*, May 1962, p. 93.

the classical sense has virtually disappeared in Europe. In the United States it still remains, and acceptance of its existence was a fundamental characteristic of U.S. policy thinking in the 1950s.

It is true that some elements in the high-demand situation of the 1950s were due to spontaneous forces. Europe had reached an income level where the elasticity of demand for durables was very high, and the industries producing these goods in their turn have heavy investment requirements. In this sense, the buoyant demand experience of the 1950s might be interpreted as an expansion phase of a 'Kuznets cycle' rather than as a reflection of policy. However, government policy was constantly augmenting or checking the demand stream, and some of these dynamic demand factors would clearly have waned if policy had been passive. There is no reason to suppose that the particular constellation of private demand forces of the 1950s had any uniquely dynamic characteristics. And it must also be remembered that stabilization policy was successful in conditions where the most volatile elements in demand—investment, exports and consumer durables—were relatively much more important than they had been in most earlier periods.

In exercising control over private demand, governments used weapons affecting both aggregative demand and specific types of demand. Both were necessary. At times it was the aggregative pressure which was too high or risked becoming so. But some kinds of demand are more volatile than others, and supply of some kinds of resources is less flexible than others. The flexibility of resources and the usefulness of general measures to control demand are enhanced by international trade. This makes it possible to meet demand excesses by imports, though of course this possibility is limited by the size of exchange reserves. In spite of rather substantial efforts, governments were not too successful in controlling fixed investment, but their power to influence consumer durable spending was amply demonstrated. As housing construction uses similar resources to those needed for other kinds of construction, the effectiveness of policy in controlling investment would have been enhanced by a greater readiness to influence housing expenditures in an anti-cyclical way.

European governments made a number of attempts to improve the effectiveness of fiscal and monetary policy in the 1950s. The range of monetary policy instruments was steadily broadened, a wide variety of fiscal devices was used to influence particular types of demand, and fiscal policy was made more flexible by introducing tax changes between budgets. The main emphasis in Europe was on discretionary changes in policy, and very little was heard of built-in stability. In Sweden where there is a heavy reliance on direct progressive taxation and a Social Democratic government, there was an interesting change in the tax structure in the direction of that existing in the other European countries. In January 1960 a general 4 per cent sales tax was introduced to curtail consumption, and this has since been increased. It was felt that changes in such taxes are more effective than modification in direct taxes in securing a quick response in private expenditure. They affect the whole population, and are not subject to leaks through savings. It was also felt that direct taxation was so high that it was destroying incentives.

The biggest problem in controlling demand is in the investment field. It is here that fluctuation is most marked and production least elastic. It is also here that the interaction between growth and stability action is most sensitive. Action to control investment spending that is powerful enough to have a short-term influence will affect entrepreneurial attitudes for some time to come. It may well happen that the short-run impact is negligible and the long-run effect perverse. This was probably true in the United Kingdom, where the frequent changes in depreciation allowances and company taxation were slow in taking effect and had an adverse effect on growth by rendering expectations uncertain. The Swedes have had greater success with their various schemes for subsidizing investment. The impact of investment fluctuations on domestic production was less in smaller countries because many of their capital goods are imported.

In several cases the investment problem has been exacerbated by the reluctance of the authorities to vary residential building for anti-cyclical purposes. This is particularly true in Germany where inflationary pressures have usually originated in the capital goods sector. In the United Kingdom, control over housing has not been easy to exercise for anti-cyclical reasons, in spite of the large amount of government building—which is dispersed amongst local authorities. In the Netherlands, active use has been made of building controls. The U.S. system of interest rate ceilings on F.H.A. mortgages has made building highly responsive to monetary policy.

It seems likely that swings in investment and stocks will remain the most difficult aspect of domestic demand management. Apart from better compensatory management of residential demand, the only other major way of improving the situation is by development of a better long-term perspective for the investment requirements of both government and industry, so that likely excesses of demand can be checked well in advance or steps taken to improve the supply potential.

To some degree, one could hope to improve the effectiveness of government policy measures by improving the flow of statistical information. It is distressingly clear in the Radcliffe Report that the effects of policy changes cannot easily be measured in a quantitative way. In the case of monetary policy, there seems to be difficulty in providing even a qualitative assessment. This vagueness is not due simply to the use of several policy measures at once, but to a weakness of statistical information. For most of the 1950s, European governments made their policy decisions without any quarterly estimates of national income, and without benefit of seasonally adjusted figures for other key indicators. In many cases, forward indicators, such as orders figures, were not collected. There was little effort to set up the budgetary accounts in such a way as to quantify the impact of discretionary policy measures as distinct from the impact exerted by the existing tax structure. There is such a heterogeneity in government accounts that it is not possible to compare the effect of policy in different countries in any quantitative way. The situation in Europe is now improving, but in this respect, at least, the United States is generally much better equipped than Europe.

In view of the difficulty of measuring the effect of policy with any precision, one cannot point to any particular deficiency in the policy-mix used in Europe to manage demand in the 1950s, except the absence of control over housing. There were, of course, respects in which policy could have been further refined. In the United States the situation was different. Fiscal policy was quiescent at times of recession. Whatever the policy-mix, the United States should have aimed at higher targets in terms of resource use and economic stability. There is a danger that the relatively passive acceptance of the business cycle as a natural phenomenon will not only slow down U.S. growth but may well leave the United States susceptible to a major recession in investment. This would undoubtedly spur the authorities into action, but their leverage would be greatly reduced by the lack of natural momentum and the fact that the U.S. government has a smaller influence in the economy than do European governments.

A major defect of policy in the 1950s was that the growth of output was sometimes checked unnecessarily when the major problem was the excessive growth of incomes. This was a fault of U.K. policy in 1957 when taxes were raised, government investment spending cut, nationalized industries restrained and the bank rate kept at 7 per cent when the economy was stagnating, and it was a more long-standing fault of U.S. policy.

MAINTAINING COMPETITIVENESS

In the course of the 1950s, inflation was a continuing problem and there were substantial price rises in all these countries. The varying pace of inflation was reflected in the international payments position, and in several cases payments difficulties were the major obstacle to faster growth. For a good deal of the 1950s there was an active and sometimes bitter discussion about the causes of inflation. Although the debate did not lead to any precise conclusion on the theoretical plane, there was, by the end of the decade, a fairly clear and sharp switch of emphasis in the official appreciation of the nature of the problem. For most of the 1950s inflation was regarded as a manifestation of excess demand and treated with the policy weapons described in the previous section. This diagnosis was correct in some cases, but as prices continued to increase in situations where there was evidence of slack capacity, it became evident that policy should also be aimed more directly at the process of income determination rather than being concerned exclusively with demand management.

It was true, of course, that the climate of high demand of the 1950s was favorable to inflation, and some analysts suggested that there was some level of demand (usually measured in terms of an unemployment percentage) at which inflation would disappear. The precise level at which this would happen was never clear, just as it was never too easy to determine what level of demand was excessive. Professor Paish has suggested a margin of 2 to 2·5 per cent unemployment,[1] but Professor Brown had earlier suggested that this might involve 10 to 15 per cent unemployment,[2] though the latter was interpreting figures which included a recovery from the great depression of the 1930s. Whatever the level of unemployment involved, it is clear that such a policy would cost something in terms of output—not only the output lost through the extra unemployment, but the reduction in output potential caused by any reduction in investment due to the lower level of activity. The proponents of such a policy have several answers to this. Some of them would be indifferent to the loss of output, counting it a reasonable outlay in securing the positive advantage of stable prices. Others would argue that the ending of inflation and payments difficulties would stimulate investment and enhance growth.

However, it was clear that the price response of the different economies to a given degree of demand pressure varied considerably, because of the attitudes and habits of entrepreneurs and workers. The inflationary momentum of an economy will depend on its own psychological and institutional background, its previous price history, the presence or absence of traumatic shocks such as a currency reform, the degree of price collusion which is legally possible or habitually practised, the degree of foreign competition,

[1] F. W. Paish, *Studies in an Inflationary Economy*, Macmillan, London, 1962, p. 327.
[2] A. J. Brown, *The Great Inflation 1939–1951*, The Royal Institute of International Affairs, Oxford University Press, London, 1955, p. 94.

the presence of elements of previous inflation suppressed by price control, the power and bargaining tactics of trade unions, and the expectations of entrepreneurs and workers about future price levels.

As all these factors play a role in the pace of inflation, it is not really possible to define an equilibrium level of non-inflationary demand. It is clear, however, that the inflationary momentum can be moderated if these institutional and market mechanisms can be influenced by government policy. It is not likely that full success can be attained, but it is necessary to push further in this direction than was attempted in the 1950s. Policy must also be supported by better information; for the available figures on different kinds of income flows, particularly profits, are usually poor.

There is now general recognition that the problem of rising prices is a complex one.[1] One of the causes of inflation is excess demand, which was general in the Korean war period and again around 1955–56, and was quite properly tackled with disinflationary policies. But inflation can also arise from excessive income increases at times when demand is not too high. For this kind of problem an incomes policy is relevant. It is inappropriate to tackle this second type of pressure by deflation, which will exacerbate the problem by holding down output and productivity unnecessarily. An incomes policy implies having a sufficiently articulate view of the economy's potential as to require an explicit growth objective. It needs a widespread public sympathy for the general line of government economic policy and some harmony of social interests as to the goals to be achieved.

The conditions required for an incomes policy were fulfilled only in the Netherlands in the 1950s. The necessary mechanisms were set in motion during the period of national unity following the war. At that time, the Economic and Social Council was created, representing employers, workers and other economic interests. This was a consultative body covering the whole range of economic policy, and its judgment on the economic situation and possible size of wage increases was given great weight by the government. Wage increases were agreed centrally by employers and workers in the Foundation of Labour, and had to be approved by the Government Board of Mediators. In return for co-operation in the wage field, the government maintained price controls for a number of years, and prospective price increases by entrepreneurs had to be notified to govern-

---

[1] See the report of the O.E.E.C. Group of Experts, *The Problem of Rising Prices*, Paris, May 1961. This analysis of the failure of policy stimulated a good many governments to define their attitude to this problem more clearly. This expert report was followed by an intergovernmental report which recommended a more direct pursuit of price stability than had hitherto been the case. See O.E.C.D., *Policies for Price Stability*, November 1962.

ment agencies which kept a watchful eye on profit levels. The Netherlands is the most open of the European economies, and there is a great public awareness of the effect of wage increases on the international competitive position of the country. At one stage, the Dutch unions went so far as to accept a wage cut of 5 per cent as their contribution to the solution of the balance-of-payments difficulties of the Korean crisis in 1951, and there was no further general round of wage increases until 1954, when they were raised twice by a total of 13 per cent to stimulate demand and reduce the payments surplus. There was a coherent connection between incomes policy and fiscal policy. On several occasions, the government agreed to wage increases specifically designed to compensate for its policy changes, e.g., for increased pension contributions in 1957, or the abolition of rent controls and milk subsidies in 1959.

In Norway and Sweden there was no incomes policy but wage bargaining is highly centralized, and there was sufficient sense of responsibility by both employers' and workers' organizations so that wage inflation proceeded no faster than in other countries. In Switzerland pent-up post-war demand was small and could be met by imports. It was not therefore a source of inflationary pressure, nor was there any devaluation in 1949, so that there was a much better price atmosphere than in other countries. The large influx of foreign labor reduced the pressure for an increase in wage rates as Swiss workers moved out of the lower-paid jobs and raised their income by moving into white collar or professional occupations. Denmark suffered a good deal from cost and demand inflation in the fifties, and her growth was impeded by serious payments difficulties. Belgium and Italy had higher unemployment than the other European countries in the 1950s, and avoided wage pressure because of the weak bargaining position of unions.

In France the inflation of the 1950s was largely due to excess demand. Cost pressures from labor were not a major problem. Government influence on wages is larger in France than in most other countries. The legal minimum wage (S.M.I.G.) and indexation of wages played a leading role because of the prevalence of inflation and the weakness of the unions. Only two and a half million wage and salary earners in France are in unions, as compared with 8·5 million in the United Kingdom, and 7·5 million in Germany. During the inflationary period from 1955 to 1957 wage increases were combatted by manipulation of subsidies to keep the cost-of-living index from rising, as had been the practice in many countries in the early post-war years. At the end of 1958, an important part of the stabilization program was the abolition of wage indexation (i.e. a legal link between wage rates and the cost-of-living index) and the refusal of wage increases in the nationalized industries in a period when workers' living standards were being reduced by rising prices. This policy was, of course, possible only because of the rather extreme political circumstances at that time. In 1962 the government tried to set up a more normal procedure for wage restraint. It initiated an incomes policy and began an annual round of consultations with unions and employers on the non-inflationary scope for wage increases.

In Germany the problem of controlling inflation was more easily solved than in most other countries because of the psychological shock administered by the currency reform, the weak position of the trade unions which was enhanced by unemployment and the flow of refugees, and the fact that productivity was rising so fast. But success was not due entirely to luck. The authorities managed to avoid having the same degree of excess demand as most other countries by enforcing a restrictive monetary policy quickly when inflation seemed to loom. However, they did not take measures to restrain demand in the building sector, and this was a leading source of inflationary pressure. In the early 1950s the German policy of demand restraint probably led to more unemployment than was necessary, but for most of the decade the inadequate level of home demand was compensated by excessive foreign demand and an export surplus which amounted to about 3 per cent of G.N.P. There was, however, some direct intervention in the price field. There were unilateral tariff reductions in 1956 and 1957, an early removal of quantitative restrictions, and the revaluation of 1961. Dr. Erhard made constant and violent public attacks on firms that raised prices, and reprisals were threatened in the form of increased import facilities. This threat was carried out in 1961 when the car manufacturers raised prices and tariffs were cut. In 1960 the Bundesbank made a lengthy public statement, setting out what was considered a non-inflationary rate of wage settlement. These measures did not amount to an incomes policy, and in recent years the pressure of full employment and the slackening pace of productivity increase have produced price rises which were not too bitterly contested by the authorities who saw this as one means of reducing the payments surplus.

In the United Kingdom cost inflation was a worse problem than in most other countries. In the first place, the United Kingdom payments position was very vulnerable because of the weak reserve position. Unions in the United Kingdom are fairly powerful, but the central trade union body, the T.U.C., had no influence on the pace of wage claims, and there was a tendency for competitive leapfrogging wage pressure from different unions. Government anti-inflationary policy was largely a matter of repressing demand. For most of the 1950s the Conservative government was reluctant to put up any direct opposition to the pace of wage claims, and any such pressure was bound to be given political overtones by the memory of the 1926 General Strike. There was the further embarrassment of the nationalized industries. Some of the key wage settlements were made in these industries, particularly in the railways, and on several occasions the government increased wages in these industries by amounts which obviously were bigger than they could afford, or out of line with what was nationally desirable. This was usually done to avert strikes. The government also resorted to independent arbitration to settle its difficulties, although the arbitrators were seldom given clear criteria for their decisions.

There was widespread criticism of government deflationary policies in 1957, which were introduced at a time of slack demand, but after a round of large wage increases and in a period of payments weakness. The government therefore created a three-man Council on Prices, Productivity and Incomes to give advice on the problem of inflation, and it published its first report in February 1958. This report carried little weight with the unions or employers, and the government used little except exhortation to carry out its suggestions. There were four reports of the Council between 1958 and 1961 and its membership was completely changed over this period. The last report recommended a number of policy measures to enforce an incomes policy which should deal with both profits and incomes. It suggested that profit margins should be cut by action against retail price maintenance and reduction of tariffs. It rejected the idea of price control, but recommended that the government keep a watching brief over price rises. For wages and salaries it suggested that the government should give guidance on the overall rate of increase for the economy as a whole.

At the time this report was published in July 1961, the government was again engaged in a major exercise designed to curb inflation and demand, and to check the payments deficit. For the first time these measures included a direct attack on cost inflation. Among the measures adopted was the wage 'pause'. The Chancellor declared that all income payments controlled by the government would be frozen at their existing level for a period. This was in fact done, and some of the regular arbitration decisions were overruled in pursuance of this policy. The policy was modified before the April 1962 budget, and a White Paper on incomes policies was issued suggesting that an appropriate rate of wage increase would be about 2–2·5 per cent a year. There was also an attempt to restrain wage settlements in nationalized industries. The previous Commission was replaced by a National Incomes Commission in July 1962. However, the unions refused to co-operate in this body, which is now a set of arbitrators to which cases of difficulty can be referred. The authorities therefore have still to find a mechanism for an incomes policy.

In the United States, fear of inflation was much stronger than in the United Kingdom, even though the balance of payments was not a disturbing problem for most of the 1950s. It was the fear of inflation that lay behind a good deal of the conservatism of fiscal policy and the move to tight money immediately after the 1958 recession. However, anti-inflationary policy was not used to check the excess demand in 1955, particularly in automobiles where consumer durable restraint would have been most appropriate.

The Kennedy administration has tried to tackle the problem of cost inflation directly, and has been highly conscious of the payments consequences of inflation. One of the first acts of the administration was to form a Labor-Management Advisory Council so that the main bargaining parties could brief themselves better on the economic situation and Presidential views. In October 1961, the President urged both the employers and the unions who were making a new wage agreement in the steel industry to take cognizance of the national interest. The unions in fact signed a moderate wage agreement, but shortly thereafter all the main steel companies simultaneously raised their prices. The administration responded with an immediate threat of anti-trust action and a television campaign against the price increases. The steel companies then rescinded the price increases. Thus, for the time being, the administration is attaining success in the policy of keeping wage increases in line with productivity.[1] It is doubtful whether this policy goal can continue to be sustained by such dramatic means or in conditions of fuller employment.

Conclusions on the Control of Prices

It is clearly more difficult for governments to carry out an incomes policy than it is to control demand. It is a much more delicate matter politically because it touches more closely on other fundamental problems of social equity and freedom to bargain. It also involves difficult jurisdictional decisions between different categories of workers. Because it is more political, the solutions adopted will vary a great deal between countries.

It has been suggested in some quarters that creeping inflation of the post-war type is good for growth as it keeps expectations buoyant and favors investment rather than consumption. Opposed to this is the argument that any steady inflationary movement will inevitably gather momentum and lead to a collapse of the financial mechanism and a fall in output. Both of these theories are too simple. There is no evidence that inflation is particularly good for growth, and the

[1] The policy was set out in the *Annual Report of the Council of Economic Advisers*, January 1962, p. 185ff.

fastest-growing countries of the 1950s, Germany and Italy, had the lowest price increases. It is also true that creeping inflation has continued for a long time without breaking into a gallop. There is no doubt, however, that inflation is a nuisance, and where it becomes endemic, as it has in France, it has led to misallocation of resources and a good deal of social bitterness which are a hindrance to both growth and welfare. No matter how easy it may seem on paper to gear social institutions to offset the bad effects of inflation, the devices adopted seldom do so satisfactorily and they nearly always accelerate the inflationary process. This was certainly the case with the French attempts at wage indexation. However, the major threat of creeping inflation to growth is not internal but external. In countries which depend on trade in highly substitutable industrial products, it is easy to lose export markets if one's costs and prices rise faster than those in neighbouring countries. Loss of export markets means balance-of-payments difficulties which may have to be solved by deflation. There is plenty of evidence from the 1950s that countries with competitive exports have grown fast, and those with less competitive exports have grown slowly. For a number of reasons described in the next chapter, the only satisfactory means of achieving external competitiveness in our present payments system is via an incomes policy.

In the course of the 1950s the only one of our group of countries to have an incomes policy was the Netherlands. The relatively successful experience of Germany and Italy was due to some extent to circumstances which are disappearing, though Germany had more of a policy than most countries. Sometimes it is assumed that Dutch policy was not successful because prices rose there too, but it was never Dutch policy to keep prices stable. In a world where other countries' prices were rising, the Dutch were mainly concerned to preserve their international competitive position.[1] They recognized the duty of surplus countries to take a little inflation now and again to avoid hurting their neighbours. It would be more legitimate to criticize the Dutch on the grounds that they were not able to avoid cyclical swings in competitiveness. At periods, Dutch prices were excessively low, and an embarrassing payments surplus developed. In attempting to compensate for this they swung too far in the opposite direction in 1957–58. Thus, even with their rather extensive apparatus for an incomes policy the Dutch did not achieve full

[1] The necessity for symmetry in incomes policies is pointed out in the report of an intergovernmental O.E.C.D. Committee, *Policies for Price Stability*, Paris, 1962. 'If a country's incomes policy has resulted in it becoming an island of low costs in a world of high and rising costs, the growth of wage increases in excess of the growth of productivity, i.e. acceptance of some cost inflation, may be the most expedient policy.'

control. Dutch policy involved close consultation between the main economic interests of the country on the general economic situation and on government policy; a centralized bargaining procedure; fiscal measures—both taxes and subsidies; and price controls. The degree of effort required for a successful incomes policy is therefore substantial, and will not necessarily lead to price stability.

In the interest of both price stability and economic growth it would be desirable for other countries to consider establishing consultative bodies of the type of the Economic and Social Council in the Netherlands. There is such a council in France, and a recently established Economic Council in Denmark. Such bodies may come into conflict with existing parliamentary institutions, and it is sometimes difficult to decide who should properly represent the interests of trade unions, employers, farmers or consumers, particularly if the existing central bodies representing these organizations happen to be weak or inarticulate. However, the experience of such a consultative process breeds a sense of responsibility and sophistication about economic problems which is invaluable to governments with difficult decisions to make. Furthermore, such centralized and articulate discussion of economic policy will force the participants to improve their own organization and to think more clearly about their own problems. This would clearly be an asset in a country like the United Kingdom where the professional staff of both the unions and the employers is meagre.

Apart from such a consultative body on general economic policy, there may or may not be need for direct government intervention in the labor market or in the process of price formation. No such intervention has taken place in Norway and Sweden where the price rise has been about the same as in the Netherlands. The degree of intervention needed will depend very largely on the social traditions and atmosphere of the country concerned. The problem seems easier in the smaller countries, both because people are more conscious of the external payments position and because their social cohesion is usually greater than in the large countries.

FOSTERING THE GROWTH OF OUTPUT POTENTIAL

Thus far we have described the role of government in promoting levels of demand that make full and steady use of available resources and in avoiding the inflationary pressures that distort resource allocation and threaten the maintenance of high demand through payments difficulties. The successful pursuit of such policies will itself contribute very substantially to economic growth, not only because it avoids waste of resources and increases efficiency, but because it produces better expectations of growth and a genuine reduction in investment risks which will lead entrepreneurs to push up the rate of investment. In addition to this, governments have also sought to improve the output potential of the economy more directly. The most important of such measures has been the attempt to raise the share of resources going to investment, but other means have also proved useful, including efforts to make the flow of capital or labor easier, to promote productivity growth, to facilitate the allocative efficiency of markets, to break particular bottlenecks, or to correct distortions in the economy. In a few cases 'planning' was used in the 1950s to help foster growth, and it has become increasingly popular in the last year or so (see section on 'Planning' in this chapter).

Education and Research
Governments affect the output potential by their spending on human and intellectual resources. Expenditure on education and health is fundamental to the maintenance of growth. It is significant that Italy which has the lowest productivity level in our group also has the highest illiteracy rate and that the United States which is at the top in productivity has much the highest proportion of graduates from higher education. Furthermore, if we look outside our group, we find a fairly close relation between living standards and education levels, and the most rapidly advancing industrial countries, the U.S.S.R. and Japan, devote a large share of resources to education. This is partly due to the fact that education is an item of consumption which often gives more satisfaction than material goods. However, it is clear that education is an investment in human resources which is vital to economic growth. The study of the relation between education and economic growth is in its infancy and is not considered here, largely because of inadequate data. Broadly speaking, it may be concluded that in the 1950s governments made little attempt to gear their educational spending to the growth needs of the economy. Nor is there any evidence that the educational effort bore much relation to the growth rate of the economy. In the longer run, however, the supply potential of the economy will inevitably be influenced strongly by this type of government spending. The neglect of this aspect of policy was therefore a deficiency of both the fast- and slow-growing countries in the 1950s, and does not explain differences in their growth performance. It is probably true that the steady influx of highly qualified refugees into Germany was a factor stimulating the supply potential there.

It is not easy to evaluate the contribution of government-sponsored research to economic growth. Much of this is of a military character which pushes hard (and usually in secret) at the remote frontiers of knowledge and whose value for productive purposes is therefore often limited or only of very long-term significance. Such spending was in fact highest in the two slow-growing countries, the United States and the United Kingdom. The economic results were probably poorest in the United Kingdom where a great deal was spent on atomic energy and aircraft research. On the other hand, scientific research which raises the production potential usually becomes common property rather quickly, so that its impact tends to be felt by the world as a whole rather than being confined to the country doing the research.

Incentives to Corporate Investment

Governments have modified the flow of investment and savings in several different ways: by taxes and subsidies on the private sector, control of financial intermediaries, their own saving, and the investment policies of public enterprise.

High levels of taxation are not in themselves a hindrance to investment. Their impact depends on the distribution of the tax burden and the expectations of future taxes. High levels of corporate tax combined with generous depreciation allowances may well stimulate investment. The major source of finance for investment in all the economies considered is corporate profits and depreciation allowances. It is therefore useful to see how taxation affects the flow of these funds and the incentive to invest.

In all European countries the corporate tax burden is lower than in the United States. This is partly because of lower tax rates but mostly because of bigger depreciation allowances. The rate of U.S. tax on profits is 52 per cent, and distributed profits are again subject to income tax in the hands of the dividend recipient. In the United Kingdom profits tax now amounts to 15 per cent and income tax of about 39 per cent is levied on companies but not retaxed in the hands of recipients (in other countries dividends are usually taxed again to some degree in the hands of the recipient). In Germany undistributed profits are taxed at 51 per cent and distributed at 15 per cent. In France profits are taxed at 50 per cent, but there are reduced rates of tax on investments related to the Plan. In the Netherlands the tax is 47 per cent, in Denmark 44 per cent, and in Sweden 40 per cent. In Belgium the tax progresses gradually to 40 per cent on corporate income exceeding $200,000. In Norway the tax is 30 per cent, in Italy about 16·5 per cent, and in Switzerland it is progressive up to 8 per cent.[1]

In the course of the 1950s there was frequent variation in corporate tax rates in the United Kingdom as a counter-cyclical device

---

[1] The situation as described here and in succeeding paragraphs is largely that of 1962. Details of tax rates and depreciation allowances are from *Taxation in Western Europe 1962*, Federation of British Industries, London, June 1962.

to influence investment. These frequent changes were unsuccessful in their anti-cyclical impact as they worked rather slowly, and their impact on growth was also bad since they upset entrepreneurial expectations. In Germany there was also some switch in the emphasis of corporate taxation in the mid-1950s. Here, however, the authorities were largely concerned with long-term objectives. In the late 1940s and the first half of the 1950s the extensive German tax incentives for saving and investment contributed considerably to creating the momentum of growth. Once this had been achieved, the authorities tried to remove some of the incidental distortions they had created, and they switched their emphasis to an attempt to build up the capital market.

In the years from 1948 to 1954, the German government gave very substantial investment subsidies and tax-free status to investment in the iron and steel, coal, electricity and shipbuilding industries and in housing. Until 1956 undistributed profits in Germany were taxed at a lower rate to foster investment, but they have since been taxed more highly than distributed profits in order to encourage the creation of a capital market. Tax privileges were granted for certain kinds of savings—housing bonds, shipbuilding loans and equalization of war damage—and the government has also subsidized certain other kinds of saving. Accelerated depreciation was allowed on war-damaged plant and machinery, residential property and industrial, commercial and agricultural plants, while a large number of short-lived assets were allowed to be written off in the year of purchase.

Tax rates do not give the full story of tax burdens and incentives because the basis on which corporate income is calculated varies considerably. There are variations in the degree to which companies are required to keep proper accounts of their expenditures, in method of stock valuation and in the tax treatment of losses. In Italy and France there is probably a greater degree of tax evasion than in most countries, and probably less in the United States than elsewhere. In the Netherlands, the United Kingdom and the United States taxable income is confined to trading profits minus depreciation, but in several continental countries it includes net capital gains. In some cases these gains are not counted if they are reinvested (Denmark) or the tax on gains is reduced to take account of price increases as in France.

Depreciation on investment is a tax-free element of cost which is allowed against gross profits. Depreciation allowances have an important impact on tax liability as they are usually well over half of gross profit. In most cases depreciation allowances cover all investment, but the United Kingdom does not allow depreciation on commercial buildings. In the United States depreciation allowances are limited to the original cost of the asset, but in most European

K

ıntries the allowance is larger. The Netherlands, Germany and aly have all allowed revaluation of assets at some stage in the post-war period, and this is a permanent feature of French allowances. In the United Kingdom, Belgium, the Netherlands and some Swiss cantons, there have been tax-free investment allowances on different types of new investment. In Sweden, tax-free reserves of up to 40 per cent of profits can be accumulated as business cycle equalization reserves. These are partially frozen as deposits with the central bank, and are released together with a further tax bonus when the government wants to foster investment. Firms are free to spend such reserves at other times if they choose, but they are then subject to tax. Tax-free reserves of various kinds have also existed in Denmark, the Netherlands and Norway, and in the early 1950s tax inducements were substantial in Germany under the Investitionshilfegesetz.

The normal tax life for equipment on the continent is about ten years, but in Sweden it is half this, while in the United Kingdom it is about twenty-seven years. Accelerated depreciation is an important investment incentive because it provides more funds to firms which are almost certain to be used for investment. It reduces the risk of investment and makes borrowing easier because a higher proportion of earnings is freed from tax in the earlier, high-profit, years of an asset's life. Acceleration of depreciation means that the firm will have a smaller allowance later, but in the meantime it can earn a return on the funds released from tax. In effect, therefore, accelerated depreciation is an interest-free loan. This is particularly useful if prices are rising steadily, for the real value of the depreciation allowance will fall if it is spread out over a long period. If the firm is expanding, it will be using the extra funds for investment and have a constantly increasing stream of depreciation allowances.

It is difficult to give any exact comparison of the impact of differing depreciation allowances, but some impression of the inter-country variation can be derived from U.S. estimates[1] showing the degree of write-off on fifteen-year equipment in the first three service years of its life. At the beginning of 1961 this amounted to about 35 per cent in the United States and Germany, but was over 70 per cent in the United Kingdom and Sweden, over 60 per cent in Italy, and just under 50 per cent in France. In the earlier part of the 1950s German depreciation provisions were more generous and American and British provisions less so.[2] Recently, U.S. tax provisions have been changed to stimulate investment. There was a tax credit (an investment allowance) of 7 per cent on the cost of new productive equip-

[1] See 'Tax Depreciation Here and Abroad', *Capital Goods Review*, No. 44, January 1961, Machinery and Allied Products Institute, Washington, D.C.

[2] See George Terborgh, 'The Tax Depreciation Problem,' *Capital Goods Review*, No. 34, June 1958, Washington, D.C.

ment in the Revenue Act of 1962, and administrative action was taken at the same time to allow new depreciation techniques. It has been estimated that these two provisions will produce a tax saving of $2·5 billion a year for corporations. This is about 10 per cent of corporate taxes or about 5 per cent of the cash flow (i.e. gross profits minus taxes and dividend distributions) of corporations.

While it is not possible to summarize briefly the impact of corporate taxation, some idea of its relative burden may be obtained by looking at the column of Table IV-6 which shows the proportion of G.N.P. taken in corporate taxes. It should be interpreted with caution as the importance of the corporate form of ownership varies between countries. It is higher in the United States than in Europe and higher in the United Kingdom than on the continent. On the other hand, the rate of pre-tax profit of corporations was probably much higher in Europe than in the United States. With these reservations, it appears that the corporate tax burden has been much heavier in North America than in Europe.

Tax treatment of investment may have contributed to growth in Europe, and a reduction of the corporate tax burden may well help to create a faster growth momentum in the United States and the United Kingdom, just as it did in Germany. However, it can hardly be claimed that tax policy had major responsibility for the investment boom of post-war years, though it has certainly increased the role of self-finance. In most countries, corporate tax rates were lower in pre-war years than they are now, but this did not bring high investment. It is also true that Belgian taxes on corporations have been lighter than in some countries with higher investment. High investment was achieved in the 1950s largely because entrepreneurs had buoyant expectations of markets and profits. For this, governments could claim responsibility in other ways.

Tax Inducements to Personal Savings
Personal savings were low in the first half of the 1950s, but rose rapidly in the middle of the decade. In Germany these private savings have been as high as 10 per cent of G.N.P. The revival of personal savings was a spontaneous reversion to pre-war habits after a long period of abnormally pent-up consumer demand. However, private savings have also been affected by tax policy. Savings are biggest in the higher-income groups, and taxation of such incomes is much lower in Italy, France, Belgium and Switzerland than it is in other countries. A number of governments have given tax privileges or subsidies to savings. These were most important in Germany,[1] but were also substantial in other countries. Governments promote institutional private saving by granting tax privileges to life insurance

[1] See Henry C. Wallich, *op. cit.*, pp. 160-2.

and mortgage companies who can then make more tempting offers to savers. Many tax incentives affect the form in which people save rather than the amount, but there is little doubt that the German incentives for housing finance helped to ensure that a high level of housing demand could be satisfied at the same time as high levels of productive investment. The British system of direct building and letting of houses at subsidized rents probably had an opposite effect.

Government Influence on the Pattern of Private Investment
Some of the tax privileges given by governments are discriminatory and affect the sectoral distribution of investment. This is true of the German and French tax privileges, and also of the accelerated depreciation provisions in several countries. The country which exercises most control over the allocation of private savings is France. This arises not only because of discriminatory tax treatment and control over access to the capital market, but also because most of the large financial intermediaries belong to the state. The largest of these is the Caisse des Dépôts et Consignations, which handles the investment of social security funds and the large post-office savings accounts as well as being a compulsory depository for trustee funds. This is run by Mr. Bloch-Lainé, a leading planning theoretician, and its funds are used to support the aims of the plan. Its annual investments in 1961 amounted to $787 million, and its assets to $8·7 billion.[1] Also important are the Crédit Foncier, mainly engaged in housing finance, the Crédit National and the Crédit

TABLE IV–8
SOURCES OF GROSS DOMESTIC SAVING IN 1957
AS A PROPORTION OF G.N.P.

	General Government	Corporate Enterprise	of which depreciation	Households	Total
Belgium	1·3	10·3	9·8	8·6	20·2
Denmark	4·5	8·1	6·5	7·4	20·0
France	2·4	10·8	8·7	4·6	17·9
Germany	7·2	10·1	8·2	9·8	27·1
Italy	2·2		8·9		21·2
Netherlands	5·6	13·7	8·7	7·3	26·6
Norway	8·1		10·0		29·9
Sweden	5·2	11·4		5·6	22·2
United Kingdom	2·2	11·5	7·1	3·6	17·3
Canada[a]	3·4	15·5		4·1	23·0
United States	2·9[b]	10·3		5·3	18·4

[a] Includes stock appreciation.
[b] Includes public corporations.

Source: U.N. Yearbook of National Accounts Statistics, 1960.

[1] See the sixteenth annual report of the *Conseil National de Credit*, pp. 124 and 182.

Agricole. In Norway and Sweden, the government also exercises substantial control over private savings by directing banks and insurance companies as to the allocation of their funds. By contrast, the control of other governments over non-bank financial institutions is weak.

TABLE IV–9

OVERALL SURPLUS OR DEFICIT OF GOVERNMENT, ENTERPRISES
AND HOUSEHOLDS IN 1957 AS A PROPORTION OF G.N.P.

	General Government[a]	Public and Private Enterprises[b]	Households[c]	Foreign Balance
Belgium	−0·5	−1·1	3·4	1·8
Denmark	2·4	−6·1	4·5	0·9
France	0·3	−2·9	0·0	−2·6
Germany	4·6	−6·7	4·9	2·8
Italy	−0·2			−1·2
Netherlands	1·4	−5·1	2·1	−1·6
Norway	5·2			0·3
Sweden	1·7	−2·4	0·5	−0·3
United Kingdom[d]	0·7	−1·1	0·8	1·0
Canada	−0·5	−3·8	−0·3	−4·4
United States[d]	0·1[e]	−0·3	1·2	0·8

[a] General government saving minus general government investment.

[b] Saving of enterprises minus fixed non-residential investment of enterprises and investment in inventories.

[c] Saving of households minus residential investment.

[d] Figures of the United Kingdom and the United States do not add to zero because of statistical discrepancy in original data.

[e] Includes public enterprise.

Source: Tables IV–5 and IV–8.

Government Saving and Investment

The savings and investment effort of European governments is greater than that of the United States. If government saving is defined as the excess of revenue over current expenditures (including social security funds but excluding revenues from government enterprise) we find that in the period 1952–58 the government accounted for a quarter of total saving in Germany, Norway and Sweden. Only in Belgium, where government savings were negative, was the share of government in savings lower than in the United States.

Government savings are primarily used to finance public works and housing, some are put into nationalized industries, which tend to run at a deficit, and a little goes to private industry. In some countries, particularly Germany, government savings have also been required to finance a large increase in foreign exchange reserves. European governments needed a bigger surplus than the United States because of their heavier investment responsibilities and because of the more inflationary state of the European economies and their weaker capital markets, which made it necessary to supplement private savings to meet heavy investment demands. There was therefore a deliberate policy of budgeting for surplus in the early 1950s, the government share in savings being reduced somewhat as private savings revived. It is difficult to judge the extent to which government saving was at the expense of private saving, but in view of the high level of private saving in the countries with high government saving, the total effect of the government surpluses was almost certainly to increase the flow of funds for investment. These government surpluses are therefore in no sense to be interpreted as reflecting deflationary policies, but were directly linked with the desire to promote high rates of investment and affect its pattern.

Apart from their budgetary and quasi-budgetary measures, governments also affect the total savings and investment effort of the economy by their policy in nationalized industries. In general, the pricing policy of public enterprises made it necessary for them to seek external finance, and only in Italy did the public sector earn large profits. Nationalized industry affects the supply potential of the economy by its rate of investment. In this respect the continental nationalized industries helped growth more than those of the United Kingdom.

Nearly all governments provide some capital to the private sector directly. Some of this is to fill 'gaps' in the capital market for small or new firms. This is done in the United Kingdom, for instance, by the Finance Corporation for Industry and the Industrial and Commercial Finance Corporation. There is also provision in most countries for grants, loans or subsidies in connection with development of depressed regions or industries. Some of the government aid to investment is simply a preferential treatment for weak industries, such as agriculture and textiles, and in these cases often hinders rather than helps growth. Such aid to private industry is no more widespread in Europe than it is in the United States, and does not represent any basic difference in philosophy.

Other Measures Affecting the Allocation of Resources
The measures so far discussed are designed to affect the level of aggregate demand and income, and the level and distribution of investment. There are other weapons designed to deal with more specific problems which might impede growth. Productivity agencies, which helped spread knowledge of best-practice technique, were set up in all European countries in the 1950s. Labor market policy to promote mobility by giving retraining and movement grants was developed to some extent and was carried furthest in Sweden. Regional incentives to locate new industry in depressed areas were used in most countries, particularly in Belgium, France and Italy.

Not all government measures favor growth. Some types of intervention may hinder growth if markets are distorted to protect particular pressure groups, or incentives are reduced in the pursuit of social equality.

Planning

In the course of the 1950s, very few countries would have claimed to have had a growth policy in the sense of striving consciously for a given output goal. Two exceptions were France and Norway, which had official growth targets for most of the period and made consistent efforts to influence resource allocation in order to reach such targets. The Netherlands also had so-called plans with indicative forecasts for the guidance of policy, but they were not regarded as targets to be fulfilled by an active policy of allocating resources. Sweden, too, had quasi-official long-term forecasts of the Dutch type. At the time of the Marshall Plan in 1947–48, most European countries produced four-year plans showing how they expected to fit U.S. aid into their pattern of resource allocation. But the idea of planning was associated with controls and quickly went out of fashion. For most of the 1950s, nearly all countries placed the main emphasis of policy on dealing with short-term anti-cyclical problems of inflation, full employment or payments equilibrium, and very few Finance Ministers had any explicit idea of what the growth potential should be over a period of several years, or any strategy for achieving it. In most cases, demand was pushed to the stage where output appeared to be sticky, and apart from a general incentive to investment, there were few measures designed to increase the production potential. Insofar as policy has been responsible for growth, it has been a by-product of successful anti-cyclical efforts and the attempt to push up investment rates. It was only towards the end of the decade when the unusual achievements of the fast-growing countries came to be recognized, that the slow-growing countries began to feel the need for a comprehensive review of policy in the light of an assessment of growth potential.

The new awareness is now general: planning offices have been set up in Belgium, Italy and the United Kingdom, and the first ministerial council of O.E.C.D. recognized the need for long-term perspective by setting up a collective 50 per cent growth target for these countries for the 1960s. The latter-day popularity of planning has not spread to Germany. Here, there has been a coherent philosophy of development which was explicitly anti-planning, i.e. the theory of the social market economy. This has misled many observers into believing that the rapid German growth was a miracle or an accident, or that Germany had no policy. There was in fact a fiscal policy which provided stronger investment incentives than in most countries. While no target of potential growth was set forth, there was a very careful attempt to promote demand, and in the latter part of the 1950s this policy was pushed to the limit the economy could stand without inflation.

Although lack of planning was no obstacle to German growth in the circumstances of the 1950s, in the United Kingdom the absence of a coherent official view as to growth potential was probably a considerable hindrance to growth. In the first place, the government was forced willy-nilly to allocate a substantial part of investment resources through its ownership of nationalized industries. These were not run on the same lines as private enterprise, and a considerable part of them were competing with each other or with oil imports. That there was little serious analysis of the energy problem is revealed by official miscalculation of the impact of the closure of the Suez Canal. Furthermore, many of the anti-cyclical fiscal weapons used in the United Kingdom hit expanding industries like consumer durables or had harmful effects on investment. Similarly the view taken of export prospects was always excessively pessimistic in the light of world market trends, and not enough attention was given to the real problem of competitiveness and to the size of capital balance which should be aimed at. Only the most cursory assessment was given to long-term growth prospects, as in the casual reference by the Chancellor of the Exchequer, Mr. R. A. Butler, to doubling the standard of living in twenty-five years in his speech to the Conservative Party Conference in 1954.

The country in which planning was pushed furthest in the 1950s was France, but this does not mean that there was a sensible growth policy. French planning started in 1946 as a series of targets for basic industries and only developed gradually into a coherent and detailed set of forecasts for the economy as a whole, with intensive discussion of all its aspects by entrepreneurs, trade unionists, nationalized industries, the Finance Ministry and other government departments.

For most of the 1950s, French planning was carried out against the background of extremely inflationary policies by a series of weak governments. Budgets were always in large deficit and government military spending was high. There were certainly no long-term objectives in budgetary policy or any link between fiscal policy and the objectives of the plan. As a result, there were two major devaluations, a much bigger price inflation than elsewhere and a constant balance-of-payments crisis which was only handled by massive foreign aid and running the reserves down to zero. In the course of the 1950s, France ran up E.P.U. debts of $1·5 billion and received U.S. aid of $6·5 billion. This happened in spite of the fact that French dependence on foreign trade is smaller than that of any other European country, and its export position bolstered by an almost completely protected market in the French franc area. France also used quantitative restrictions to protect its payments long after such restraints had been abandoned elsewhere. It is doubtful whether any other country could have pursued such policies without inducing retaliation. Resource allocation was also badly distorted by price and rent controls. The combination of price distortions and heavy protection induced an extremely restrictionist attitude on the part of entrepreneurs and kept the rate of investment below that in most other countries.

There is no doubt that the Plan played a leading role in promoting growth in this chaotic situation. In particular, it succeeded in creating an adequate infrastructure of energy, transport and heavy industry, so that there was scope for faster growth on a sounder basis in the Fifth Republic. It also ensured that the large nationalized sector was run efficiently by people who had a clear idea of what their long-range goals should be. However, it would be a mistake to take French planning or its sanctions as a model for other countries in a less desperate situation. The French planners had at their disposal a large apparatus of direct controls over the location of new investment, and had substantial control over access to funds in the capital market or via specialized financial institutions. They also exercised direct influence in allocating resources and used discriminatory fiscal and monetary devices in carrying out the Plan.[1] Administrative practice in France is highly centralized, interventionist and discriminatory. Some of these sanctions have now diminished as the pressure on the economy has lessened and it has become more open.

The function of 'planning' in normal circumstances is (1) to give the government an articulated perspective view so that it can do its other jobs such as demand management or the formulation of social policy in the light of long-term as well as short-term considerations; (2) to help it make rational decisions in its investment and pricing policy in the public sector; (3) to provide the private sector with what M. Pierre Massé, the present chief of French planning, has called 'generalized market research'. The hope is that this will also enhance the performance of the private sector by strengthening its expectations. In this sense of a perspective for a coherent and integrated long-term policy, planning in France is only just beginning.

THE PROCESS OF POLICY FORMULATION

In a modern economy where the state intervenes in so many ways and where entrepreneurial and wage earner attitudes to growth are

[1] See Economic Planning in France, P.E.P., London, August 1961, p. 228. 'Firms are unlikely to disregard the advice of the planning authorities unless they believe they will not need the state's financial backing during the period of the Plan.'

important, it is important that public policy be properly understood and supported. In most countries institutional and political arrangements have not reflected the changes in the nature and scope of economic management, so that public and parliamentary reaction to economic developments and policy is not as sophisticated or responsible as it should be. The parliamentary arrangements and access of politicians to information are usually inadequate for the highly complex problems involved. All economic issues are political to some extent, particularly the choice of policy weapons, but this should not obscure the fact that a large range of problems are of a more or less technical economic character. Furthermore, most governments have had little to hide, and the reluctance to face more extensive discussion is usually because of pressure on the time of ministers or civil servants.

Most of the major policy changes of the 1950s were an honest adjustment to market forces and not electoral tricks. In modern conditions a political opposition needs access to a good deal of the information now usually reserved to governments if it is to formulate a responsible alternative line of policy and keep the government on its toes on the right issues. Parliamentary procedure normally concentrates the main economic debate dramatically on the budget, which reflects political and social issues as well as economic ones, and arouses unnecessary passions over rather technical questions of economic management which could more properly form the subject of a semi-continuous examination in parliamentary committee. The civil service would of course have to be expanded somewhat to service such a committee and one or two more ministerial posts would need to be created, but it should be well worth the investment.

Even more important is the need to improve public understanding of policy directly. In many cases governments are driven into seemingly desperate situations in which they try to reach the public in sporadic appeals for price restraint or exhortations to export or invest which are often in lieu of a policy. It is because of lack of public sympathy that governments have given considerable emphasis to automatic stabilizers as a substitute for discretionary policy, or have tried to fob off their responsibilities on central bankers or have explained policy in deliberately mystical or metaphorical terms. This type of approach is unlikely to be effective, because a lack of understanding or sympathy for government policy on the part of ordinary people and businessmen will only increase uncertainty and lower investment incentives. If governments wish to follow a fully rounded growth policy which entails the management of demand and the price level, as well as perspective planning to achieve full growth potential, they will almost certainly need some forum outside parliament where the main organized interests affected—employers, workers, farmers and consumers—can engage in articulate discussion of the issues and be properly briefed on the state and prospects of the economy. Such a body existed in the 1950s in the Conseil Economique et Social in France and in the Economic and Social Council in the Netherlands. They deal with general economic policy and not with wages policy alone. In addition, there is obvious scope for extending the amount of articulate written analysis put out by the fiscal or monetary authorities themselves in some countries. For instance, the United Kingdom was following as active a monetary policy as Germany in the 1950s but had no written commentary on its actions. The Bundesbank, on the other hand, had an extensive analytical and statistical monthly report in both German and English, and this clarity on policy aims probably contributed to the greater success of the German monetary authorities.

CONCLUSIONS

After this extensive discussion of the role of government in the economy, we should now be in a position to define what constitutes an economic growth policy, to judge the extent to which governments have had such a policy and to assess their degree of success.

A growth policy is not concerned exclusively with long-term issues. The trend and the cycle are closely linked, and a growth policy is implicit in the essential day-to-day management of the economy. A growth policy in this sense includes responsibility for active management of the overall level of demand and prices to ensure that resources are fully used. It also implies an articulate effort to define the potential of the economy and to see that resource allocation, particularly investment, is adequate to reach this. These ends are complex and cannot be achieved by getting a tax structure that automatically provides built-in growth or built-in stability. Policy will have to be pretty continuously active, although the need for intervention will vary between countries with different problems and institutions.

In the course of the 1950s very few governments deployed the full range of policies for growth. Nearly all European countries sustained a buoyant level of demand. In few cases did they refrain from using any of the necessary policy weapons for this, although they sometimes acted too late to restrain excess demand in booms. In the United States, on the other hand, policy was lacking in this respect. Most governments did not have an adequate policy for keeping incomes in line with production, and although most of them are now trying to tackle this problem more directly, few have yet laid a firm basis for policy action. Sometimes this problem was tackled with the wrong weapons. The failure to check inflation, and use of the wrong weapons, was a major handicap to growth in the United Kingdom. Success in this field in the 1950s was only relative, and was more often due to luck than to policy. Most European governments managed to promote investment in the course of the 1950s, with Germany and Norway putting forth the most determined efforts. In the United States, on the contrary, the tax structure was a deterrent to investment. The major reason for high investment in the European countries in the 1950s was the buoyant and stable level of demand rather than the incentives directly aimed at investment. The responsiveness of investment to this demand stimulus was particularly favorable in Europe for the reasons set forth in Chapters II and III, and it may well be that greater emphasis on fiscal incentives to investment will be needed in future as Europe approaches closer to the technological frontier on which the United States operates.

Apart from the promotion of investment, there are other ways in which governments can help raise the production potential, e.g., the formulation of education policy in terms of growth needs and the creation of a perspective plan. Neither of these was widely used in the 1950s, nor was there enough of an effort to educate the public as to the needs of policy.

In attempting to assess the success of policy, it is necessary to have some idea of the growth potential of different countries and of any special difficulties they faced. Some idea of growth potential has been provided by the analysis of the preceding three chapters, but it is, of course, hazardous to estimate what growth might have been with better policy. The most obvious evidence of failure to achieve growth potential is the existence of unemployed resources. On this ground it seems that the United States and Canada did not achieve success.

The rate of productivity growth is another test of performance. We have given reasons for thinking that the productivity achievements of some countries, such as Germany, France and Italy, were due to special factors, and have also suggested that the productivity growth potential of European countries is better than that of the United States. To go further than this and pick on a particular rate as a yardstick of course involves some guesswork, but, after so much statistical analysis, we should be willing to venture a judgment. For European countries an average productivity growth rate of less than 3 per cent a year can probably be taken as evidence of deficient policy. By this criterion policy was inadequate in Belgium, Denmark and the United Kingdom, and in view of the special factors favoring productivity growth, it was deficient in France as well. For the United States and Canada it is difficult to fix a norm, but by the standards of the early 1950s, their productivity performance from 1955 onwards was very poor.

Did any of these countries have to face particular difficulties in carrying out policy? The United Kingdom had great difficulties on external account, which are examined more fully in the next chapter. Canada, too, had special problems because of her extreme dependence on the United States. In France there were special political difficulties, but these were compensated to a large extent by massive foreign assistance. They were not insuperable, and some of the fast-growing countries also had special problems—this was certainly true of Germany. To treat the performance of the slow-growing countries as a failure of policy does not imply that growth policy in the fast-growing countries was adequate even if their growth potential was fully utilized. In a group of highly interdependent economies, growth policy must take account of its repercussions on other countries. German growth in the 1950s was accompanied by a chronic payments surplus. This was a major source of disequilibrium in the world economy and was one of the reasons why the slow-growing countries had payments difficulties that prevented them from reaching their full growth potential.

CHAPTER V

THE INTERNATIONAL
ENVIRONMENT

The countries we are considering are highly interdependent. Mutual trade in goods and services is very big and there is a large flow of capital, ideas and techniques between them. In all of these respects their ties have been strengthened in the post-war period, and the trade and payments barriers erected in the 1930s and during the war have been steadily removed. As a result, the domestic growth policies of individual countries have had a strong external effect. Buoyant demand at home has meant buoyant export markets for other countries. Increased trade has contributed substantially to the increase in productivity, both because countries have been able to specialize more on the things they do best and because pressure of competition has been increased. This group of countries has been more closely bound politically in the post-war period than at any time in the past and this is, of course, a major reason why economic cooperation between them has been closer than ever before.

The existence of this favorable international environment was a necessary condition for rapid growth in such open economies. Nevertheless, the need to balance external payments continued to be felt as a constraint on growth in several countries, and posed policy problems which could not be adequately dealt with by the instruments described in Chapter IV. It is, therefore, necessary to analyze how international economic policy has affected growth and contributed to payments equilibrium in the post-war period. It will be clear from this analysis that a fully rounded growth policy in such an interdependent group of countries must include a properly managed international payments system which minimizes the risks of economic expansion and irons out payments disequilibria without inducing recessions.

The Structure of the World Economy

The external relations of the countries we are examining do not, of course, form a closed circle. They are affected by and affect developments elsewhere in the world. It can be seen from Table V–1 that these countries produce about 56 per cent of world income and

TABLE V–1
STRUCTURE OF THE WORLD ECONOMY IN 1960

	Per Cent of World Total			
	Industrial Europe	North America	Sino-Soviet Bloc	Rest of World
Population	8·6	6·8	34·6	50
Real G.N.P.	25	31	22	22
Average *per capita* income as per cent of world average	292	458	64	43
Exports	38	21	12	29
Imports	39	16	12	33
Industrial production	24	35	28	13
Agricultural production	15	21	32	32

Source: The first five rows are derived from my article 'Growth and Fluctuation in the World Economy 1870–1960', *Banca Nazionale del Lavoro Quarterly Review*, June 1962, the sixth row is derived from various issues of the U.N. *Monthly Bulletin of Statistics*, and the last row is derived from figures supplied by M. Louis Goreux of F.A.O.

an even bigger share of world industrial output in spite of having only 15 per cent of world population. The *per capita* income of industrial Europe is lower than that in North America, but all our countries are wealthy in comparison with the rest of the world.

Because of their great wealth, these countries are dominant in world trade. Their share is about 60 per cent, with Europe accounting for about two-thirds of this and North America about a third. North America has a large trade surplus, and Europe has a large surplus on invisible account. These surpluses enable these countries to finance large international capital exports, virtually all of which emanate from the group. These countries also account for about 75 per cent of world reserves of gold and foreign exchange (excluding those of the Sino-Soviet bloc).

The underdeveloped countries are dependent on the industrial countries for export earnings, and international trade is as important a part of their income as it is in industrialized countries. Because the underdeveloped countries are poor, they generally do not have large foreign exchange reserves and they usually spend on imports all they receive in export earnings. They are too small, individually, to have much of a world impact on their own, and any of their fluctuations having purely domestic origins are not too likely to be synchronized in time, since their trade, capital and psychological interrelations are much smaller than those they have with industrial countries. For these reasons, they are at the receiving end rather than the generating end of world economic cycles. They do, of course, re-transmit any destabilizing influences they receive. When their exports or capital receipts fall off, their lack of reserves forces them to cut imports quickly.

The developed countries have a very heterogeneous range of export products and a very flexible industrial structure. They suffer less from trade fluctuations than the underdeveloped countries, which depend on a narrow range of primary commodities for their exports. The industrial countries between them are, therefore, responsible for setting the world economic climate (except for the rather autarkic Communist bloc) and for the international transmission of growth and cyclical influences. The major external economic influences they receive are transmitted from each other, usually in a direct way, but sometimes via the rest of the world.

The Nature of the Interdependence of Industrial Countries

The industrial countries have many economic ties with the outside world, but in nearly all of these relations they are the dominant rather than the dependent partners. The acceleration of their post-war growth owes little to the actions of the outside world. Between them the industrial countries have been masters of their own economic destiny. We must now examine the nature of their interdependence. We can start with the relations between the United States and Europe.

Because the economy of the United States is as large as that of the whole of industrial Europe, it is often assumed to be the dominant factor in the world economy. That it has a much greater influence than any other individual country is true, but its total world trade, and hence its influence, is much smaller than that of Europe as a whole. Even in the bilateral trade between Europe and the United States, the United States is not dominant. European exports to the United States are only about 8 per cent of Europe's total exports, or less than 2 per cent of European G.N.P. Belgium and Switzerland are extreme cases where exports to the United States amount to 3·2 per cent and 2·6 per cent of G.N.P., respectively. Europe takes a quarter of U.S. exports or about 1·1 per cent of U.S. G.N.P.

The influence of the United States as a destabilizing force is also often exaggerated. In spite of the greater fluctuations in U.S. internal activity U.S. imports have fluctuated less than those of Europe in the post-war period, and U.S. exports have suffered more from European trade fluctuation than vice versa. It is true that this post-war behavior of the U.S. economy is somewhat new. Historically, the U.S. economy has been more volatile than the European, and until the second world war its import fluctuations were greater than those of Europe. However, it has always tended to transmit its internal fluctuations to a smaller degree relative to its G.N.P. fluctuations than was the case in Europe. By contrast with the dampening of U.S. import fluctuations, the post-war volatility of U.S. exports has been much higher relative to both G.N.P. and import fluctuations than it was prior to the war.[1] The United States has always had very volatile exports, but it is now even more susceptible to cycles transmitted by other countries than it used to be.

The relation of the United States to the European economy for most of the past decade has been symbiotic, and neither side can be said to have been the dependent partner in the economic sense. In contrast to the 1929–33 crisis when the whole world cycle was synchronized and the major country responsible for transmitting the depressing influence was the United States, there is now no clear originator of world trade cycles. The cycle in European countries has usually been fairly closely in phase, both in timing and intensity, but no single European country is the lynchpin. In fact, there appears to be a distinctly European 'conjuncture' in both trade and income. There has been little long-term relation between European and U.S. growth rates or in the timing, frequency and amplitude of fluctuations. Since 1950 the United States has had three business recessions, none of which has had a serious impact on European payments or more than a minor impact on European demand and output. The most severe was in 1958 and coincided with an extremely mild recession in Europe, but the U.S. recession contributed to it rather than caused it. If we turn from the cycle to the trend, we find that the main impact on Europe of slower U.S. growth in the 1950s has not been any direct deflationary influence but the transmission of depressing price influences to primary product markets, which has improved Europe's terms of trade with third countries and, if anything, fostered European growth.

Although the slow growth and relatively slow development of U.S. imports were a weakness in its contribution to world growth in the 1950s (particularly as compared to the dynamic role it played in earlier periods), the U.S. government offset this to a great extent by promoting the outflow of capital, particularly official capital. This massive post-war outflow of capital was made possible only by enormous U.S. gold reserves, which enabled the United States to ignore the balance-of-payments consequences.

Capital flows between the United States and Europe have had a significant effect on growth and stability not only by contributing to balance-of-payments equilibrium and to investment but because they reinforce the psychological links in business decisions between the areas, and are a major element in the two-way flow of technological knowledge. The direction of the capital flows has varied consider-

---

[1] For a more detailed analysis of the character of trade fluctuations, see my 'Growth and Fluctuation in the World Economy, 1870–1960', *Banca Nazionale del Lavoro Quarterly Review*, June 1962. The change in U.S. exports is also noted by Ilse Mintz, *American Exports During Business Cycles 1879–1958*, National Bureau of Economic Research, 1961, pp. 11 and 21.

ably. The overall creditor-debtor position, taking both short- and long-term capital into account, is now in favor of Europe. Before 1913 there were large movements of European capital to both the United States and Canada. During the first world war and in the 1920s this flow was reversed, European assets in the United States were reduced and the United States lent a great deal to Europe. In the 1930s there was a withdrawal of U.S. capital from Europe, and a considerable European capital flight to the United States. In the second world war, the pattern of the first was repeated. From 1946 to 1958 U.S. aid and government loans to Europe amounted net to $25 billion. During this period there were small flows of private capital in both directions with a net recorded flow from the United States of $200 million but with an unrecorded flow to the United States.

Since 1958 the situation has changed. The United States has become a net recipient of government capital from Europe because of European repayment and prepayment of debt accumulated in the Marshall Plan period. On the other hand, United States private capital has been increasingly drawn to Europe. The convertibility of European currencies and the strength of European gold and exchange reserves have reduced the risk for U.S. investors, and U.S. capital has become responsive to the higher interest rates and profits. The creation of the Common Market and the removal of the differential war risks have also strengthened the attraction of investment in Europe. These influences have re-created a transatlantic market in private capital of a type unknown for forty years. In this new situation short-term capital has shown itself capable of disturbing both the United States and Europe. Hence, on capital account as well as current, there is no evidence that the European relationship is one of dependence on the United States.

It is clear that the United States does not dominate the European countries economically, though it did so in the cataclysm of 1929–33 and in the Marshall Plan period of reconstruction. The role of the United States is greatest as a capital exporter, as the major reserve currency and the biggest single producer of many raw materials and agricultural products. U.S. internal prices have an important bearing on prices received in the rest of the world, even though these U.S. products may not enter international trade.

So much for the U.S. But what of the relations between European countries? Do the big countries dominate the small ones? In fact, in the trade and payments relations between European countries no individual country is dominant. The four big countries do not have nearly the influence over their smaller trading partners that one might expect. None of the smaller countries except Ireland is really heavily dependent on a large country for its export markets. Apart

TABLE V-2
STRUCTURE OF EXPORT MARKETS IN 1960

From/to	France	Germany	Italy	United Kingdom	Other Industrial Europe	United States	Canada	Sino-Soviet Group	Other Third Countries	World
										Percentage of Each Country's Total Exports
Austria	1·7	26·8	16·6	2·8	14·5	4·4	0·6	14·8	17·6	100·0
Belgium	10·4	15·8	3·1	5·6	31·0	9·5	1·1	3·7	19·9	100·0
Denmark	1·5	18·7	4·6	26·4	18·4	9·1	0·7	3·9	16·6	100·0
France	—	13·7	5·8	5·1	19·0	5·8	0·8	4·0	45·8	100·0
Germany	8·8	—	5·9	4·5	37·7	7·9	1·1	4·7	29·4	100·0
Ireland	0·9	3·1	1·0	74·0	2·6	7·3	0·8	0·1	10·2	100·0
Italy	7·6	16·5	—	6·9	19·0	10·6	1·1	5·8	32·6	100·0
Netherlands	5·9	22·6	3·2	11·0	27·0	4·9	0·7	1·7	23·1	100·0
Norway	2·6	13·7	3·5	22·6	26·4	6·9	0·4	4·8	19·1	100·0
Sweden	3·9	15·2	3·3	16·0	27·5	6·4	0·8	4·8	22·1	100·0
Switzerland	6·7	18·4	8·2	5·8	16·8	10·0	1·7	3·7	28·7	100·0
United Kingdom	2·6	4·9	2·5	—	18·5	9·3	6·0	3·5	52·7	100·0
United States	2·8	5·2	3·2	6·9	9·8	—	18·0	0·9	53·2	100·0
Canada	1·4	3·1	1·2	17·2	5·0	56·6	—	0·8	14·7	100·0

Source: A. Maddison, op. cit.

from Ireland, the heaviest dependence is that of Austria and the Netherlands, which send about a quarter of their exports to Germany, and Denmark and Norway send about the same proportion to the United Kingdom. The main impression one gets from Table V–2 is that the European trade pattern is surprisingly dispersed. It is true that the smaller countries are more dependent on trade than the larger ones, and insofar as trade is more volatile than income, they might be expected to have a more volatile income than the larger countries. There is, in fact, no evidence of this in the record of fluctuations. To some extent it may be due to better economic policy, but it is partly due to their heavier import dependence on goods which are amongst the more volatile components of demand— capital goods and consumer durables. As their economies are more heavily geared to foreign trade, general economic policy weapons have a bigger leverage on their foreign balance than in big countries. Their greater dependence has also habituated the public to the need for corrective policy in times of payments difficulty, and has made it politically easier to follow such policies.

In the 1870–1913 period there were substantial intra-European capital flows, but these were greatly reduced in the inter-war period in favor of European-American flows. Now that the United States is no longer a uniquely secure haven for investment, there has been a revival of intra-European flows. The private capital flow within Europe is large and is likely to grow much farther as the process of European integration proceeds. It is noteworthy that the small countries—Switzerland and Holland—have played the leading role in these capital movements, and there is again no evidence of dominance by the large countries.

In spite of Europe's successful record of growth and stability in the 1950s, its trade has remained quite volatile, and more so relative to its domestic activity than U.S. trade. European imports are more volatile than exports, and have been just as volatile as they were before 1913 (see Table V–3). European trade has, therefore, become a relatively more destabilizing force in the world economy, and the problem of external balance remains one of the key problems of smooth economic growth. The large size of fluctuations in trade relative to those in income indicate clearly that these fluctuations in trade have been a major contributor to instability.

The greater relative post-war sensitivity of imports in Europe is probably due partly to the operation of the economies closer to capacity, which has given entrepreneurs a greater incentive to vary stocks. This demand pressure was largely absent in the United States, and the United States has also become much more of a marginal producer than it was. Raw material fluctuations hit U.S. producers more than they hit U.S. imports. Increased European

TABLE V–3
EXPERIENCE OF RECESSION IN TRADE
Maximum Cyclical Percentage Fall in Dollar Value from Peak to Trough

	Value of Exports			Value of Imports		
	1890–1913	1921–38	1948–60	1890–1913	1921–38	1948–60
Austria	8·2	68·2	6·2	4·3	64·5	19·7
Belgium	14·0	53·5	14·7	14·4	54·5	11·9
Denmark	5·2	52·9	0·7	8·3	55·0	4·9
France	18·0	64·1	7·6	22·0	48·7	16·8
Germany	11·2	57·4	0·0	12·4	67·1	1·7
Ireland		64·0	6·5		50·2	18·7
Italy	11·2	56·5	15·8	14·9	63·2	12·5
Netherlands	2·6	57·4	0·0	10·7	52·6	12·9
Norway	10·9	49·2	17·9	10·4	56·8	11·9
Sweden	10·1	64·2	16·9	12·6	55·4	19·9
Switzerland	11·8	62·0	0·0	13·6	33·7	24·2
United Kingdom	18·2	64·0	8·6	15·4	57·9	14·5
Canada	5·3	67·9	6·5	12·5	71·4	5·6
United States	12·3	69·4	19·1	18·7	70·1	6·2
Western Europe	11·1	59·7	0·6	7·5	56·8	6·8
Third Countries	15·6	60·6	8·2	15·7	61·9	5·7
World	8·8	61·7	3·4	8·0	60·9	5·2

Source: A. Maddison, 'Growth and Fluctuation in the World Economy', op. cit.

import sensitivity in the early 1950s may also have had something to do with expectations concerning import controls. This is true of the 1952 fluctuations, which in every European country were the most severe of the post-war period. It is true, of course, that the 1952 recession arose from the special circumstances of the Korean war. Nevertheless, this crisis was allowed to have a much bigger impact on trade than on output. Post-war import movements have been strongly influenced by deliberate policy measures to correct balance-of-payments disequilibria. Governments have now abandoned the use of import controls as an anti-cyclical device and demand pressures are less excessive than in the early 1950s, so that import fluctuations tended to become milder in the later 1950s.

Trade, Trade Policy and Economic Growth

The outstanding feature of the international economy since the war has been the restoration of a system of relatively free trade between the major industrial countries. Progress has been gradual rather than dramatic. There has been a steady reduction in quantitative restrictions and tariffs through a series of *ad hoc* arrangements. There was some temporary back-sliding, mainly by France, but the move towards liberalism has been strongly sustained. This development in trading policy was concentrated on the industrial countries. The rest of the world did not pursue policies of trade liberalization.

However, this has not mattered much to the growth or stability of the industrial countries as the volume of trade with these other areas has depended largely on the size of their export earnings, and the temporary reinforcement of restrictions by one or another under-developed country has never been large enough to exert a significant deflationary shock.

As a result, world trade has grown faster than world income. The external influences affecting the industrial countries were almost never deflationary in the 1950s. Payments deficits were due largely to the pressure of domestic demand on imports rather than to falling exports. When exports were falling or stagnant the cause was usually rising prices and declining competitiveness and not deficient external demand. It is noteworthy that the fastest-growing countries, in terms of output, tended to be those with the most rapid increase in exports. As Table V–4 shows, between 1950 and 1960 German exports increased in volume by an average of 16 per cent per annum, Italian exports by 12 per cent, Dutch by 10 per cent and French by 7 per cent. By contrast, British exports rose 2 per cent and U.S. exports 5 per cent per annum.

TABLE V–4
RATE OF CHANGE IN THE VOLUME OF EXPORTS

	Average Annual Percentage Growth		
	1890–1913	1913–50	1950–60
Belgium	3·5	0·2	7·7
France	2·8	1·1	7·2
Germany	5·1	−2·5	15·8
Italy		1·4	11·8
Netherlands	4·6	1·2	10·0
Sweden	3·8ᵃ	1·9	5·5
Switzerland		0·3	7·8ᵇ
United Kingdom	2·1	0·2	1·9
Western Europe	3·2	0·1	7·0
Canada	6·5	3·3	3·8
United States	3·8	2·3	5·0
Third Countries	3·5	1·8	6·4
World	3·5	1·3	6·4

ᵃ 1893–1913.   ᵇ 1950–1959.

Source: A. Maddison, op. cit.

In some continental European countries the rise in exports was the most dynamic factor in demand, and the large and continuing pay-ments surpluses in Germany are evidence of a substantial trans-mission of demand from other countries. There is little doubt that the opening up of the economies to trade was a stimulus to growth, both in fostering high levels of demand and in stimulating produc-tivity. Because of stagnant exports it was difficult to stimulate British growth, and the attempt to rectify the balance-of-payments consequences further impeded growth. The continental countries received even bigger stimuli than they transmitted, as their exports rose faster than imports, but the rise in their imports was large in all cases and all these countries contributed something to the general ambience of growth.

We should now examine the role of commercial policy in stimulating trade. In the immediate post-war years European trade was conducted largely on the basis of bilateral agreements and imports were rationed by a system of controls. This meant that each country had to balance its trade with each of its trading partners individually. Such a system was very inefficient; it arose because of the inadequacy of foreign exchange reserves and the enormous pent-up demand for imported goods. The failure of the U.K. convertibility experiment of 1947 demonstrated that controls on imports of dollar goods were required in Europe, but it was also obvious from the success of the sterling area and the franc area that even within a regime of controls, extremes of bilateralism could be avoided and trade freed on a regional discriminatory basis.

The freeing of European trade was made possible by Marshall Plan aid. The United States not only provided finance for a higher level of imports but made it a condition of its aid that the European countries should remove the mass of bilateral trade barriers which had developed in the 1930s and during the war. This was done by means of a code of trade liberalization for the member countries of the Organisation for European Economic Co-operation, which agreed to establish gradually increasing targets for trade liberalization. There was also a code providing for gradual liberalization of capital movements and invisible payments. At the same time the payments arrangements of European countries were liberalized by the establishment of the European Payments Union. Liberalization was extended on a discriminatory European basis (but including European imports from the sterling and franc area) over a number of years from 1948 to 1956. During this period, when Europe was recovering its competitiveness, the United States tolerated European discrimination against dollar goods without retaliation. As a result, European countries increased their exchange reserves greatly and hence were able to restore a viable payments system in conditions of trade freedom.

In the period from 1956 to 1960 European trade discrimination against dollar goods was gradually eliminated, and the discrimination against Asiatic textiles relaxed. As a result, non-agricultural quantitative restrictions have virtually disappeared in Western Europe, although they still exist for oil, coal and agricultural products. The last time trade restrictions were used to protect the balance of payments was by France in 1957–58.

So much for quantitative restrictions, but what happened to tariffs? Progress in reducing or binding tariffs was gradual up to 1956. Some tariff reduction was carried out on a world-wide basis within the G.A.T.T., but because of the most-favoured-nation clause it was regarded as a rather sharp bargaining operation without any particular onus on the economically strong to take the lead as was the case in O.E.E.C. arrangements to cut quantitative restrictions. Various efforts were made towards European tariff integration in the early post-war years, but the only successful exercise was the creation of the small Benelux customs union and the European Coal and Steel Community.

In 1956 the Treaty of Rome was signed by Belgium, France, Germany, Italy, Luxemburg and the Netherlands, which proposed to set up a customs union. This spurred the other European countries to the effort to form an O.E.E.C. Free Trade Area. However, these efforts broke down in December 1958 on the eve of the creation of the Common Market. In an attempt to continue the momentum of the idea, a limited European Free Trade Area (E.F.T.A.) was created in 1959 by seven of the European countries outside the Common Market—Austria, Denmark, Norway, Portugal, Sweden, Switzerland and the United Kingdom. But the Common Market countries had little interest in joining this, and the United Kingdom applied for membership in the Common Market in July 1961. The other E.F.T.A. countries followed suit in 1962. These negotiations failed in February 1963, and the outlook for a unified European trading system is now rather bleak.

There is little doubt that the Common Market gave great impetus to the process of tariff reduction. Within its area internal tariffs have been reduced by half and are likely to be abolished in the next four years. Furthermore, it has been generally accepted policy within the Common Market to accelerate trade freedom in accordance with the strength of the balance of payments and the rate of growth of the economies. E.F.T.A. internal tariff cuts have generally matched the pace of those in the Common Market. There was also a general reduction of tariffs in industrial countries by 20 per cent in the 'Dillon round' of negotiations in G.A.T.T. in 1962. The whole tariff question has been given a new urgency by the speed of the Common Market integration. As a result, the U.S. Congress passed the Trade Expansion Act in the summer of 1962 which gave the President powers to cut tariffs by half or to eliminate tariffs in which the United States and its negotiating partners do 80 per cent or more of world trade.

Thus the process of tariff reduction in the Common Market has operated in the same way as the O.E.E.C. Code of Trade Liberalization operated to remove quantitative restrictions. It is achieving a discriminatory liberalization followed by a liberalization *vis-à-vis* the world as a whole. There is, of course, a difference in that the ultimate goal of the Common Market is not free trade, and there is no indication of how far the reduction of external tariffs will go. If it is to continue to be a growth-stimulating instrument, however, the external tariffs will have to be pretty low. The creation of a new discriminatory trading group that is so large in relation to world trade is obviously of a different order from the kind of grouping for which the G.A.T.T. rules were made and which require of a new customs union simply that its external tariff be something like the average of previously existing rates of its members. The consummation of the Common Market at its present external tariff levels may seriously distort world resource allocation. Although there are dangers in this new creation, one can hardly doubt its dynamic influence so far, nor is there any good reason to doubt its future creative role. The Common Market goes a good deal further than a trading arrangement, and there is no reason why it should need any external tariffs at all to preserve its unity.

Thus the liberalization of trade has so far been a very positive stimulus to high growth of demand and better allocation of resources. Apart from the widening of trade opportunities, the new code of behavior in trade matters has also been of fundamental importance. The lack of retaliatory measures helped to ensure that no country's growth prospects were hurt by sudden deflationary shocks. The mitigation of this risk was a potent stimulus to investment and growth and to expansionary internal policies. Nevertheless it should be recognized that the achievement in the tariff field has not been nearly as great as was hoped, that present arrangements mean increasing discrimination, that tariff reductions have seldom been used by surplus countries as a means of promoting payments equilibrium and that the industrial countries have not created a unified and effective forum for joint discussion of tariff policy as they did within O.E.E.C. for quantitative restrictions.

Capital Movements as a Stabilizing and Destabilizing Force
In the inter-war period, international capital movements had played a largely destabilizing role in world payments. They were nearly all private, and short-term movements were predominant. Because of the shakiness of financial institutions, fear of recession, fear of exchange rate changes and, in the late thirties, fear of war, short-term capital was highly volatile. U.S. capital was repatriated from Europe on a large scale at the outbreak of the Great Depression. The German current account and reparation payments had been heavily dependent on large U.S. capital flows, and the withdrawal of U.S. capital created payments difficulties which were tackled by

deflationary policies. There were also destabilizing flows within Europe. There was serious exchange rate disequilibrium between major European currencies, particularly sterling and the franc which were respectively overvalued and undervalued when they were stabilized in 1925 and 1926. The effects were seen in the late 1920s in growing French reserves and short-term claims on London, but the attempt to live with this payments situation was also reflected in severe deflation and unemployment in the United Kingdom and boom conditions in France. In this situation, the major recession in U.S. imports and the sudden reflux of U.S. capital from Europe caused both external and internal financial collapse in central Europe, and set off a withdrawal of French funds from London. There were government attempts to provide some modicum of international liquidity to palliate the problem but these were miserably inadequate. On the private level there was a breakdown of the international mercantile credit mechanism in 1931, and the United Kingdom also closed the London capital market to foreign borrowers in 1931 and 1932.

The attempt of the United Kingdom to achieve better equilibrium by abandoning a fixed gold parity and devaluing in 1931 was followed by a round of competitive devaluations inaugurated by the United States in 1933. The French were fairly immune to the United Kingdom devaluation, but they suffered in consequence of their delay in following the United States. After this, the international payments system collapsed. Trade had also been restricted by commercial policy. The United States increased its tariffs in 1930 and was followed by the United Kingdom in 1932. World trade, income and liquidity were rebuilt gradually in the 1930s on a protectionist and discriminatory basis, mainly by the efforts of the European countries. The system of reparations and government debt payments was abandoned with enforced U.S. consent. In the late thirties there was a strong flow of private capital to the United States because of war fears.[1]

After this experience there was naturally a great reluctance in Europe to return to freedom of capital movements in the post-war period. Restriction of capital movement was agreed to be a desirable transitional measure in the articles of the I.M.F. formulated during the war, and these so-called transitional measures of restraint in fact lasted until the end of 1958 in Europe.

During the 1950s, therefore, international capital movements were dominated by the United States, and most of the U.S. flow consisted of government funds. This flow of American capital played a major

[1] For a description of this period, see *International Currency Experience*, League of Nations, 1944, and Hal B. Lary and Associates, *The United States in the World Economy*, U.S. Department of Commerce, 1943.

role in the restoration of the world economy. After the initial mistake of premature termination of lend-lease and some temporary hesitation, the United States went into peacetime foreign aid on a large scale in 1947, and has continued ever since. Considering the fact that the U.S. government has greater difficulty in getting money out of Congress than European governments have in their parliaments, the U.S. record is a major triumph of statesmanship over expediency and is in stark contrast with its policy in 1929–33. American aid enabled European governments to adopt much more expansionary programs of recovery than would have otherwise been possible. It set a momentum of growth which was continued in the 1950s. U.S. military spending also made a major contribution to European exchange receipts so that the U.S. government's direct role in payments was very large indeed.

The role of these U.S. capital movements in stimulating growth has not been so much as a supplement to investment resources or as a conveyance for new production techniques, but as a stabilizing and sustaining element in world payments which allowed most countries to exploit their growth potential fully without external restraints or deflationary shocks.

Apart from these stabilizing flows there were some destabilizing short-term private capital flows in the 1950s, most of whose adverse effect was concentrated on the United Kingdom. However, the scope for such moves was limited in most major financial centres by substantial capital controls and inconvertibility of currencies. A good deal of the speculative movement consisted of leads and lags in normal commercial payments, or involved Swiss funds. The United States was a free market, but U.S. investors were not significantly involved in currency speculation as nearly all European currencies seemed weak compared with the dollar.

Since the end of 1958 this situation has changed completely. There had been a gradual freeing of European capital movements before then, but the establishment of convertibility for European currencies marked a clear watershed. European countries increased their exchange reserves from $10 billion in 1950 to $20 billion in 1958 and felt able to establish non-resident convertibility for their currencies in December 1958. In the four years that followed, official European reserves rose by another $7 billion, there was a considerable freeing of exchange control for residents, and the foreign exchange holdings of European commercial banks also increased substantially. The new strength of European currencies and the decrease in the strength of U.S. official reserves helped change the attitude of U.S. private investors towards currency risks. In the winter of 1960–61 there was a very large outflow of short-term capital from the United States to Europe amounting to about $3 billion, and there was a substantial flurry in the London gold market in November 1960 which temporarily raised the dollar price of gold from $35 to $40 an ounce. This marked the end of a quarter century in which the dollar had had unquestioned strength. Apart from speculative movements there has been a large flow of U.S. short-term funds to the new 'Eurodollar' market, partly because European interest rates are higher than U.S. rates. The disparity has been wide enough in fact to make it worthwhile to invest short-term U.S. funds in Europe even when 'forward cover', i.e. an option to repurchase dollars at a given exchange rate, is taken out.

This new volatility of U.S. short-term funds and the enlarged facilities for European short-term capital movements have been the major problem of convertibility. There is now a freedom for capital movements which goes beyond what was envisaged at Bretton Woods, although the situation is not, of course, as free on the European side as it was in the 1920s. Apart from the speculation against the dollar in 1960–61, there were large-scale flows in the first half of 1961 after the revaluation of the German mark which had a seriously disturbing effect for the United Kingdom. Since then speculative flows have been smaller, but to some extent this has been due to official policy, which has been very active in devising new techniques of intervention in exchange markets, in providing compensatory official capital movements, and in harmonizing interest rate policies. There has been no attempt to meet these new problems by a tightening of exchange controls in deficit countries, although some of the measures taken by surplus countries to discourage capital inflows could virtually be regarded as controls.

Convertibility has also changed the situation for long-term private capital flows. The rapid growth of European production and profits has made Europe highly attractive for U.S. portfolio investment in equities, and European bond rates are also substantially higher than those in the United States. Direct U.S. investment has been stimulated both by high European profits and by the need to retain or establish footholds within the preferential tariff area created by the Common Market and E.F.T.A. Such a flow from the United States also represents a backlog of missed opportunities in the past. As the funds are coming from the wealthiest country to countries with a lower productivity level, it can be regarded as a rational redistribution of resources. But there are much poorer countries than those in Europe to which U.S. capital might be better directed, and the payments consequences are not so desirable for the United States. It is also arguable that the outflow is partly due to the slackness in U.S. demand; with higher domestic demand, investment and profit opportunities would be better in the United States, and a policy of higher interest rates could be pursued which would contribute further to curb the incentive to foreign investment. In order to deal with these problems the United States has made changes in its corporate taxes designed both to increase the attractiveness of home investment and to decrease the special tax incentives to foreign investment.

It is obvious that the new freedom for capital movements has not been an unmixed blessing. To some extent it is a necessary concomitant of freedom for trade. However, it puts a considerable strain on the payments system, and will require an extension of the weapons of international economic policy. It will also require a closer harmonization of national monetary policies, and a continuous strengthening of international liquidity arrangements.

International Liquidity and Payments Arrangements
If individual countries have shaky financial institutions or a weak currency system their economic expansion is subject to considerable risk. A financial breakdown will interrupt business relations severely and exert an extreme deflationary effect on activity. Fortunately, most industrial countries have achieved a reasonably sound internal financial structure which makes such risks remote enough so that internal speculation about them has virtually disappeared. In the international field, too, a sound financial system is necessary. This was one of the obvious lessons of the inter-war period when the collapse of international payments arrangements led to retaliatory restrictions on trade and an extreme deflation of production, employment and incomes.

An international payments mechanism requires a commonly agreed unit for settling accounts and an agreed set of policy instruments for curing payments disequilibria. Unless there were such an understanding, retaliatory practices would abound. A third requirement of the international payments system is liquidity. Each country should have some individual margin of liquid funds which can be used to meet regular seasonal or cyclical swings in its payments, and give it time to allow corrective policy measures to work without having to resort to deflationary policies. As a supplement to national foreign exchange reserves there must be some mutual provision of credit or international reserves to deal with situations of extreme pressure for which national reserves are inadequate. These three requirements are not independent. The amount of national or international liquidity required will depend on the nature of the payments unit and the policy weapons used to achieve equilibrium.

Present-day liquidity is relatively very much larger in relation to world trade than in the period before the first world war because governments are not willing nowadays to solve payments problems by seriously deflationary policies and because there are bigger speculative movements now. Speculation is bigger because there are now three units of settlement—gold, dollars and sterling—instead of one, and there is much more uncertainty of their future value in relation to each other than there was in 1913 after several decades of stable exchange rates.

In the post-war period the major means of settling payments between countries have been gold or one of the two key currencies, i.e. dollars or sterling. The addition to the world's monetary gold stock depends on the output of gold and the movement of private hoards. Monetary gold stocks increased by about three-quarters of a billion dollars a year in the 1950s. The role of sterling has been largely confined to the sterling area; reserve holdings of this currency did not expand and it was not convertible for most of the period, but the dollar became increasingly used as a reserve currency.

The post-war period has been one of fixed exchange rates. There was a major round of devaluations in 1949, but since then changes in the major currencies have been very few—two devaluations of the franc and a revaluation of the German mark and the guilder. However, speculation on exchange rate changes has unfortunately been frequent, and has been a major cause of payments disturbance. One of the reasons for this has been the weak reserve position of sterling, but it was also due to the fact that exchange rate changes were to some degree considered as a legitimate instrument of policy, and changes were in fact frequently urged upon governments. Furthermore, there were rather prolonged payments problems for all of the major countries, and for a good deal of the period European currencies were not fully convertible for non-residents and, therefore, less attractive than dollars. The timing of the move to convertibility was also a matter under active discussion for several years before it happened.

In the early post-war years the payments difficulties of most European countries were similar. They nearly all had low reserves and intense demand pressure. Most of them had heavy deficits financed by U.S. aid, and protected their payments by extensive exchange controls and quantitative restrictions. The International Monetary Fund had been created in 1947 to provide a pool of international liquidity of $7 billion which was designed to supplement individual country currency reserves. However, the only currency which was worth borrowing at that time was dollars, which represented about a quarter of the I.M.F. assets and this was quite inadequate to European needs. The immediate impact of the creation of the I.M.F. was to reduce European reserves by the extent of the initial subscriptions which cost Europe about $0·4 billion at a time when total European reserves were only about $10 billion. The I.M.F. played little role in the payments mechanism of major industrial countries and did not provide liquidity to European countries in difficulty until the end of 1956. In the 1950s, European liquidity needs were met by the outflow of massive U.S. aid and by the European Payments Union.

TABLE V–5
CHANGES IN WORLD LIQUIDITY, 1950–62

$ billion at or between ends of period

| | Reserves of Gold and Foreign Exchange | | | Change in Reserves | |
	1950	1958	1962	1950-58	1958-62
U.S.	22·82	20·58	16·16	−2·24	−4·42
Canada	1·77	1·95	2·55	0·18	0·60
Germany	0·27	5·73	6·45	5·46	0·72
France	0·79	1·05	3·61	0·26	2·56
Italy	0·60	2·08	3·44	1·48	1·36
U.K.	3·67	3·11	2·81	−0·56	−0·30
Other O.E.C.D.	4·47[a]	7·96	10·84	3·49	2·88
Total European O.E.C.D.[b]	9·80	19·93	27·15	10·13	7·22
of which:					
gold	6·85	12·78	18·53	5·93	5·75
foreign exchange	2·95	7·15	8·62	4·20	1·47
Other countries except Sino-Soviet	14·12	14·85	15·84	0·73	0·99
I.M.F. holdings	7·02	8·27	14·59	1·25	6·32
of which:					
gold[c]	1·47	1·53	3·00	0·06	1·47
U.S. dollars	1·30	0·79	3·06	−0·51	2·27
Sterling	1·36	1·62	1·45	0·26	−0·17
Other major currencies[d]	1·22	1·82	2·54	0·60	1·72
Other currencies	1·65	2·51	4·55	0·86	2·04
World, excluding Sino-Soviet bloc	55·53	65·58	76·32	10·05	10·74

[a] Figure for Spain roughly estimated.
[b] Excluding Iceland, Ireland and Luxembourg; the breakdown for Denmark into gold and foreign exchange is estimated.
[c] Including holdings of U.S. securities acquired by the Fund with a gold repurchase guarantee. The amounts involved were:
1950—zero
1958—$200 million
1962—$800 million
[d] Currencies of the following countries: Belgium, Canada, France, Germany, Italy, Japan, Netherlands and Sweden.

Source: International Financial Statistics, January 1951, May 1961 and September 1963.

Regional payments arrangements were set up in Europe through the creation of the European Payments Union within O.E.E.C. in 1950. This was an arrangement which eliminated bilateralism in

European payments. It differed from the I.M.F. in that it set up a clearing mechanism by which member countries settled their accounts with each other, and it created automatic credit up to certain limits in these settlements. If at the end of a month a country was in deficit with its fellow E.P.U. members, it would get automatic credit. By contrast, governments could only get funds from the I.M.F. by a formal request to borrow from a fixed pool of liquidity. In the E.P.U. the credit was created automatically by the surplus countries. The automatic credit element was diminished from 60 to 25 per cent over the life of the E.P.U. There were upper limits on each country's debt or credit quota, but there were large *ad hoc* supplements to these, chiefly by Germany in favor of France. When it was wound up at the end of 1958, the outstanding E.P.U. credit which needed to be consolidated was about $1·6 billion and the total of the balances cleared through E.P.U. during its eight and a half years' life was $46·4 billion.[1] The E.P.U. was a powerful mechanism which helped to make a reality of international co-operation and to ensure a non-retaliatory policy of enlightened self-interest. As a result, the O.E.E.C. became a place where governments turned to discuss their mutual payments problems. Their basic policy objectives were always expansionary, and they exercised a wise collective restraint in preventing the premature establishment of convertibility on the pattern followed after the first world war.

The European Payments Union was abolished at the end of 1958 at the time of the move to convertibility. By this time European exchange reserves were $20 billion, or double the level they were at when E.P.U. was established. E.P.U. was replaced by the European Monetary Agreement (E.M.A.), whose main function has been to provide an exchange guarantee which has been useful in fostering bilateral credit arrangements between central banks. It did not provide automatic credit and its limited resources have not been used for lending to industrialized countries but for the benefit of less-developed European countries.

The I.M.F. became an active source of liquidity to the industrial countries in 1956 during the Suez crisis when it lent large amounts to the United Kingdom and France. Its new vigor led to an agreement to increase quotas by 50 per cent in 1958. At the same time, the new convertibility of European currencies meant that the lending power of the I.M.F. had been further strengthened because it became worthwhile for borrowers to take currencies other than dollars, and of course the I.M.F. encouraged them to do so. The I.M.F. made a major loan of $1·5 billion to the United Kingdom in July 1961. This loan was made in several different currencies. This I.M.F. loan

[1] See *European Payments Union*, Final Report of the Managing Board, O.E.E.C., Paris, 1959.

to the United Kingdom was, in fact, a consolidation operation which enabled the United Kingdom to repay a number of special bilateral credit agreements between the Bank of England and European central banks made at the Bank for International Settlements in Basle in the spring of 1961. This Basle agreement had provided support of about $900 million, which was necessary because of the speculation against sterling following the revaluation of the German mark and the guilder. This new type of cooperative action by central banks has been continued in several fields since then to the benefit of both the United Kingdom and the United States and is a very useful and discreet form of augmenting international liquidity. The United States now has a series of swap arrangements with European central banks which give it an assured borrowing potential of about $1·1 billion. The United Kingdom has not made such formal arrangements but prefers to borrow by *ad hoc* agreement in time of strain.

International liquidity arrangements were further strengthened in 1962 by an agreement by the industrial European countries, Canada, Japan and the United States, to provide the I.M.F. with supplementary resources in the form of standby facilities of $6 billion. The rationale behind a standby arrangement rather than a general extension of I.M.F. quotas is that it concentrates the increased liquidity on those currencies which are, in fact, likely to be used. It also avoids the political difficulties of altering voting strengths within the I.M.F. These standby credits are not shown in Table V–5. These new arrangements are of a character which would make it feasible to make a substantial loan to the United States. The United States has never made a drawing on the I.M.F., but its payments have been helped on occasion in a disguised form by I.M.F. switching of its funds from gold to dollars in the form of U.S. treasury bills and notes which carry an exchange guarantee. In July 1963, the United States made arrangements for its first standby credit from the I.M.F. for an amount of $500 million.

In the past two or three years there has, therefore, been a very great strengthening of world liquidity arrangements, and there is an obvious willingness to go further than explicit written commitments would warrant. The changed situation in which the overwhelming reserve strength of the United States has ended and that of continental Europe greatly increased has also led to substantial changes in the management of the international payments system. A regular monetary committee of the main European countries, the United States and Canada was created within the Organisation for Economic Cooperation and Development (O.E.C.D.) in 1961. O.E.C.D. is the successor body to O.E.E.C.; it includes the United States and Canada as full members, and has become the main focus for the

M

monetary and payments strategy of the industrial countries. There is also regular consultation in the I.M.F., the Basle meetings of central bankers, the monetary committee of the Common Market and the Managing Board of E.M.A. Thus, in the new conditions of convertibility, international payments problems are subject to a good deal of articulate economic management.

In the period since convertibility, the industrial countries have attempted to co-ordinate monetary policies to offset destabilizing capital flows. Some success has been achieved in harmonizing interest rate policy, there have been a number of bilateral credit arrangements for operations affecting the U.S. dollar, and there have been a number of large debt prepayments by European countries to the U.S. Payments arrangements of this group of countries have developed steadily towards greater liberalization and interdependence but are under constant surveillance by a process of continuous and professional economic diplomacy. The arrangements have been flexible and designed to avoid deflationary effects, and there has been a pragmatic emphasis on regional arrangements. These countries are the main source of international liquidity and if they are in difficulty the credit cannot come from outside the group. There is, therefore, little point in treating their liquidity problems on a worldwide basis. They are also committed to a non-retaliatory code of behavior in their use of policy weapons which is not followed by the less-developed countries. It is for this reason that transatlantic regional arrangements are likely to be a continuing and necessary feature of the world payments system. Furthermore, the limited number of countries involved means that the leading officials can keep in regular personal contact by virtue of jet travel. They can set out their views fully and frankly in an articulate joint policy review and avoid the kind of tragic misjudgments of the 1930s. All of the major industrial countries have experienced payments difficulties in the past decade or so and have been helped by international credit. There is a growing emphasis on and willingness to use international liquidity arrangements. This has been done quietly and discreetly in in a way designed to build confidence.

In spite of these improvements in liquidity arrangements in the past few years it has nevertheless been widely suggested that international liquidity is inadequate and there have been a number of proposals for widening the scope of the I.M.F. to deal with the problem. The leading protagonist in this discussion is Robert Triffin.[1] Triffin's suggestion would give the I.M.F. the power to create credit automatically in favor of deficit countries at the expense of surplus ones. Countries would keep their reserves in the form of deposits with the I.M.F.

[1] See his *Gold and the Dollar Crisis*, Yale University Press, New Haven, 1961.

There are, of course, considerable advantages in increasing the degree of automaticity in international liquidity arrangements. It would contribute substantially to improving confidence. There would not be the same incentive to panic selling of a currency with substantial automatic access to supplementary reserves. Confidence would also be strengthened by the fact that there would be only one trategic reserve unit instead of three as at present. There are, however, difficulties in moving towards such a system. There would be much less reason for governments to hold short-term dollar and sterling reserves so that both the United Kingdom and the United States would have to repay these holdings over a period of time. There are political difficulties in transferring so much power to an international institution. The degree of extra liquidity which can be created depends ultimately on the willingness of surplus countries, and such credit has generally tended to be given more generously on a bilateral basis than through an international institution. It would be difficult to ensure that it was able to enforce sanctions for appropriate corrective policy action on the part of deficit or surplus countries. It might even prove more conservative in meeting liquidity needs of deficit countries than is the case under the present system. The main value of the reform of the I.M.F. proposed by Triffin is not its liquidity-creating aspect but its contribution to confidence. Triffin's rather dramatic emphasis on the liquidity aspect of the international payments problem concentrates on mathematical calculations of future world liquidity needs in relation to the growth of world trade. The spectre conjured up by this money Malthusiasm is not realistic. Except in the United Kingdom the problems of the 1950s were not due to inadequate liquidity but to inadequate policy adjustments and to the fact that the supplementary liquidity already available was not automatic enough. The adequacy of liquidity arrangements cannot be judged in relation to the size of world trade, but depends on the kind of payments problems experienced, and the sanctions used to deal with them. If better policy weapons were used and there were a higher degree of automaticity in credit arrangements, the world might well manage with less liquidity.

An alternative suggestion made by some analysts who have emphasized the liquidity problem is the revaluation of gold. However, such a move would destroy confidence in the present reserve currencies. The reduced willingness to hold these currencies as reserves would offset a good deal of the gain in liquidity occurring from the increased value of gold. It would also strengthen greatly the feeling of insecurity. If revaluation of gold had once been used as a means of increasing world liquidity, a repetition would be constantly expected.

Payments Problems

In the early post-war years nearly all payments problems in Europe were those of excess demand. This reflected not only general demand pressure but all sorts of specific bottlenecks due to wartime backlogs. To have tried to achieve equilibrium without controls would have led to a lower level of activity. This period ended in 1952, though there was great caution in removing these controls.

In the 1950s several countries had temporary cyclical payments problems. These were experienced even in such a well-managed economy as the Netherlands. There were also brief speculative difficulties arising from political events such as the Suez crisis. But there were some more persistent problems of disequilibrium in the bigger countries.

France. France had continuous difficulties up to the end of 1958 because she followed an inflationary domestic policy. These policies were possible only because of massive foreign aid received by France. France tried devaluation twice in the 1950s. The second devaluation, in 1958, worked, but only because of strong policy measures to repress its inflationary consequences including a substantial cut in real wages. The 1958 devaluation was so successful that the French have since been able to repay most of their large debts, have had a big reserve increase, and their payments surplus has become embarrassingly large.

Germany. Germany had a persistent payments surplus from 1951 onwards, averaging 3 per cent of G.N.P. In the first few years when unemployment was high, it could be argued that this was due to inadequate demand, but as the surplus persisted in a period of very full employment, it became more apparent that it was due to a highly competitive situation and better domestic defenses against inflation than those of other countries. Germany took a number of policy measures to raise imports such as reduction of tariffs and removal of quantitative restrictions, and there was also a 5 per cent revaluation of the mark in 1961. None of these measures was very successful in reducing the surplus. There were also occasions in the course of the 1950s when German monetary policy had a perverse effect on payments. Measures to check domestic demand by raising interest rates attracted a good deal of foreign capital which was only partially checked by a number of discriminatory controls governing commercial bank terms for foreign deposits, and encouragements to banks to lend abroad.

The United Kingdom. The United Kingdom suffered from recurrent payments difficulties in the 1950s which were generally tackled by restrictive monetary policies, and sometimes by restrictive fiscal policy. Some of these difficulties were due to excess demand, particularly in 1951 and 1955. There was also a somewhat weak competitive position as evidenced by the fact that the increase in exports lagged below the increase in domestic demand at a time when other European countries had the reverse experience. A major problem peculiar to the United Kingdom was the recurrent speculation against sterling induced by a position where liquid short-term sterling debts (official and private) amounted to about $10 billion and reserves were usually below $3 billion. These speculative pressures arose in 1947, 1949, 1951, 1955, 1956–57 and 1961.

The two major shortcomings of British policy as it affected foreign payments in the 1950s were the attempt to tackle rising prices simply by checking demand, and a miscalculation as to the potential role of sterling. The United Kingdom authorities never attempted to scale down the sterling liabilities in the way that was done, for example, for German liabilities in the London debt agreements of 1952. The United Kingdom operated no capital controls on sterling area investment from the United Kingdom, and restrained United Kingdom companies and local authorities from borrowing abroad. It did not use fiscal policy to influence the flow of capital abroad. A different policy in these respects might have helped bolster the liquidity position of the United Kingdom and reduced the dangerous exposure to speculative movements. Instead there was a premature and prolonged official hankering for convertibility from 1952 to 1955 which was received coolly by other countries. Official British ideas about sterling seemed overambitious to many foreigners and created a feeling that there might be a need for devaluation. The official consideration of floating rates in the mid-fifties was also harmful to confidence and created the feeling in other countries that the value of sterling might fall. The United Kingdom also displayed some reluctance to broaden international liquidity arrangements because of the fear that they might diminish the role of sterling as a reserve currency, whereas the United Kingdom was in fact likely to be the major beneficiary of such arrangements. Unfortunately, some of the reaction against official policy has been to suggest that sterling should contract out of being a reserve currency. This would, of course, worsen the payments position of the United Kingdom as it would have either to repay debt on a large scale or to default on it. The policy should rather have been to preserve sterling's limited role as the reserve currency for the sterling area, while gradually fostering the move towards greater international liquidity. This is, in fact, the direction for policy which was indicated by the Radcliffe Report in 1961, and there has been a change in policy in this direction since then, first reflected by the suggestions of the British Chancellor of the

Exchequer, Mr. Reginald Maudling, at the 1962 meetings of the I.M.F.

The United States. The post-war payments system worked well for most countries, because of the peculiar position of the United States. The continental countries were able to run surpluses for years on end without anyone else except the United Kingdom suffering greatly, largely because the United States was running the corresponding deficit (or at least financing it). The United States could absorb the other countries' surpluses because of its formidable liquidity position.

Throughout the 1950s the United States ran a substantial trade surplus, but this was more than matched by the outflow on capital and military account. The result was a continuous increase in U.S. short-term liabilities, which rose from $7 billion in 1950 to $20 billion in 1962. At the same time, the U.S. gold stock fell from $23 billion to $16 billion. During most of the 1950s the increase in U.S. liabilities was an equilibrating movement and helped to produce a more healthy distribution of world liquidity. But from 1958 the annual deficits of the United States became much larger and its liquidity position deteriorated more rapidly.

This process did not force the United States into deflation as payments difficulties did the United Kingdom. The United States could afford to weaken its net reserve position by $20 billion. Payments questions were not felt to be a restraint on U.S. domestic policy until 1961. Even now, they are much less of a restraint than in the United Kingdom because the liquidity ratio of the United States is still three times better than that of the United Kingdom and it has a much greater bargaining power due partly to the fact that a bigger proportion of its foreign payments are governmental and partly to its greater political and economic strength. In future, however, the U.S. payments problems will interfere with domestic policy as in other countries, and in many ways the United States is less well equipped with policy weapons to manage its payments situation than are European countries.

We have already suggested the measures needed internally to foster U.S. growth. Some of these measures, particularly a more active policy to foster demand, would worsen the payments problem by raising imports. On the other hand, faster U.S. technical change might well increase exports, and faster growth would make the profit prospect of the United States much better for investors, and would enable the government to raise interest rates, which is probably an essential step to avoid too wide a disparity with European countries. If this disparity in the profit situation continues, there will be a strong and increasing drain of private U.S. investment to Europe.

The United States has, of course, already applied a series of measures designed to correct its payments disequilibrium. These were first applied in 1960, and have included a reduction in government overseas spending, tying of such spending to U.S. goods, changes in taxes which reduce the incentive to foreign investment, measures to foster international liquidity and reduce speculation, an export drive backed by increased export credit facilities, and an increased effort to promote price stability. So far, these measures have not succeeded in reducing the deficit to a tolerable level for long-term equilibrium. Given the rather persistent character of the U.S. deficit, it will probably not be easy to remove it.

At the very least, the United States must reduce its overall deficit to the level of the early 1950s, and it may well need to reach an overall balance. The move to such a position represents serious problems for the United States and has serious long-run implications for other countries in terms of the growth of world liquidity.

We have seen that the United States has been much more conservative than European countries in promoting an active policy to maintain adequate demand, and there is a danger that this tendency will be reinforced by the new external constraints. The other danger is that the United States might be tempted by some desperate remedy such as trade restrictions, devaluation or floating exchange rates.

The very size of the United States makes its adjustment a matter of importance for the rest of the world and reinforces the urgency of action by the surplus countries. The new discrimination against U.S. goods which is being created by the Common Market makes it the more necessary for this group to have low tariffs for balance-of-payments reasons. The biggest countries have the most persistent payments problems, partly because trade is less important in their economies. General policy measures have a smaller payments leverage than in small countries. This is true, *a fortiori*, of the United States. As Lary puts it, there is 'a greater sluggishness in making adjustments compared with countries whose economies are more closely geared to international trade'.[1] All the more reason for countries which benefited from Marshall aid to adjust their tariff policy in a helpful direction. European countries should also take more U.S. farm products. This would help the U.S. payments balance and release European manpower for more productive employment. Europe should also have freer trade with the less-developed world as this would help the United States indirectly.

Several general points emerge from this experience. Within the framework of the present payments system it is difficult for the major countries to achieve the right degree of price competitiveness.

[1] Hal B. Lary, *The United States as World Trader and Banker*, National Bureau of Economic Research, New York, 1963.

They can no longer do this by taking serious deflationary measures, they cannot cut wages as they tried to do in the 1920s, and specific measures affecting trade such as import controls or exchange rate changes are so upsetting to the system that they have almost been outlawed. The big countries have only just begun to fill this policy vacuum by an incomes policy. The result has been that payments deficits or surpluses have tended to be persistent. The surplus countries did not do enough to reduce their surpluses and the deficit countries did not take the steps necessary to increase their competitiveness. Imports and exports are very sensitive to changes in domestic demand pressure, but in the case of highly substitutable manufactured goods, a country's trading performance also depends heavily on its price competitiveness.[1]

The present payments system is subject to very large speculative capital movements. The relaxation of exchange controls has greatly increased the speculative ability of European countries, and a series of events has changed the attitude of dollar holders and made them willing to speculate against that currency. Thus far speculative movements have not broken the post-war payments system and there have been no unnecessary or retaliatory exchange rate changes. Measures have been developed for checking these speculative flows, but some of them have been very costly in terms of output, particularly in the United Kingdom.

The third major weakness of the system is not a general problem of liquidity but the special problem of the United Kingdom. That country has suffered a good deal from inadequate liquidity, for it was often forced into deflationary measures by purely speculative movements. Greater liquidity would not merely have helped to offset these pressures at lower cost in terms of output, it would have prevented most of the speculation from occurring. There is no evidence that other countries suffered from a lack of liquidity in the 1950s; the fault was rather the inadequacy of policy measures. More liquidity would simply have meant a persistence of problems for a longer period. In fact, deficit countries other than the United Kingdom have always been able to borrow to the extent necessary to overcome their problems without deflation.

The fourth problem, and one for the future, is the decline of the U.S. dominance as a key currency country. The liquidity problem of the future arises from the fact that the United States can hardly increase its short-term indebtedness much further without landing in the same unenviable position from which the United Kingdom has suffered for almost two decades. The increase in U.S. indebtedness was the major source of increased liquidity in other countries in the

[1] See M. FG. Scott, *A Study of United Kingdom Imports*, Cambridge University Press, London, 1963, for a detailed analysis of this point.

1950s, and if U.S. payments are to be balanced in future, this liquidity source will dry up.

Policy Weapons for External Equilibrium

Many of the policy weapons required to meet payments difficulties have already been described in Chapter IV, for external disequilibrium is in many respects simply an extra symptom of internal disequilibrium. In the post-war period a good many payments difficulties reflected excess demand pressure or price inflation, or both. Among the industrial countries, structural problems were not serious for the external balance. Sometimes, however, the payments trouble was unrelated, or not directly related, to domestic disequilibrium. This was the case with speculative capital movements, which were a frequent cause of embarrassment in the United Kingdom and affected other countries too, including the United States. The payments difficulties of Germany in having a large and chronic surplus were similarly not so much due to domestic disequilibrium as to the fact that domestic policy was more successful in Germany than in most other countries. The United States was the only major case in the post-war period of a common pre-war situation—a country in substantial external deficit at a time of internal recession. Thus there were cases of conflict between domestic and foreign economic policy considerations. Even where there was no basic conflict, the internal and the external policy decision differed in urgency, because the ultimate constraint of solvability was more pressing in the foreign balance, particularly if reserves were low. There is, of course, a difference in the urgency of the external constraint between deficit and surplus countries, though both can quite properly be regarded as being in disequilibrium. The foreign balance, therefore, was a question which raised some conflicts in growth policy, if only because of timing considerations, and corrective action was sometimes more severe than would have been warranted by domestic considerations alone. Given this situation, it is natural that countries should seek to strengthen their capacity to secure equilibrium by taking policy measures whose specific effect is concentrated on the foreign balance.

Before the first world war, if a country was in payments difficulties, the equilibrating mechanism was to raise the rate of interest and to deflate domestic activity. This was assumed to cut import demand and wage rates, as wages were then flexible in a downward direction. It also attracted gold. No thought was given to changing exchange rates, and the major currencies were firmly attached to gold for several decades. The major source of international liquidity was borrowing in the London market. Because of the basic confidence in exchange rates and the willingness to take deflationary measures, currency speculation was unknown, although in those days financial institutions were weaker than they are now and there were plenty of purely financial panics. But here again the British financial structure was far sounder than most others and the international economy was firmly anchored to sterling. However, the basic conflicts between payments equilibrium and growth were resolved in favor of the former.

An attempt was made to reintroduce this system after a chaotic period of floating exchange rates following the first world war. In the United Kingdom, the policy was supplemented by an organized attempt to reduce wages which led to the general strike of 1926 and was not very successful. In the 1920s confidence was vulnerable to political crisis, financial institutions were still unsound, there were two alternative reserve currencies instead of one. There were no international liquidity arrangements, no regular channels of economic diplomacy except by *ad hoc* conference, and there was a lack of mutual confidence and a willingness to use beggar-your-neighbor weapons.

The collapse of the international financial system in 1929–33 brought a whole series of experiments designed to deal with the specific problem of the external balance while attempting to follow expansionary domestic policies. The weapons introduced were exchange control on capital movements, quantitative restrictions on imports, devaluation, inconvertible currencies, blocked accounts, multiple exchange rate manipulation, export subsidies, discriminatory tariff and trading blocs. The remedies were desperate because the conflict between external and internal policy requirements was acute. There was a fall in export markets at a time of massive unemployment. The right policy for each country was expansion. Not all followed this path, but those that did feared that their imports would rise too fast. They tried to ensure against this by these special devices. The trouble with such devices is that they hurt neighboring countries, which are then forced to retaliate. As a result of these autarkic and uncoordinated moves, the export problem was worsened for each country. Countries could not break this circle of external deflationary pressures because of lack of mutual trust and unwillingness to provide each other with credit. It was, of course, recognized that such a system was deflationary and uneconomic, and world trade was rebuilt somewhat in the 1930s in discriminatory blocs like the sterling area. In fact, the economic growth of some European countries was fairly substantial in spite of this, and there was a recovery of employment in the autarkic countries, but productivity growth suffered.

The feeling that these special policy weapons of the 1930s should be retained in some managed way for at least a transitional period was very strong in the early post-war years. Nevertheless, there has been a steady move back towards liberalism in international economic policy. This has been of a pragmatic kind which has generally recognized the need for a managed international payments system. In a world of expanding demand and generally full employment there has not been as acute a conflict between the internal and external needs of policy, and these specific weapons have been gradually abandoned. A new code of international behavior was gradually established in which such weapons are not used by the advanced industrial countries. As a consequence a remarkable feature of the post-war period has been the lack of retaliatory measures. The basic fact of interdependence was recognized as inevitable, and countries realized that pursuit of beggar-your-neighbor policies could only narrow and distort this relationship of interdependence but could never eliminate it.

But if these weapons are abandoned, how is equilibrium to be achieved? A major feature of the 1950s was the inadequate use of an incomes policy. Very few governments made the political effort necessary to sell such a policy, although in such an open system, quickly responsive to price competition, it is clear that an incomes policy can be very effective. The main onus in an incomes policy is on the deficit countries. Within limits, a surplus country should be willing to take a little price inflation as its contribution to payments equilibrium. But the momentum of price inflation is difficult to judge and its psychological impact bad, so that too much cannot be hoped from surplus countries in this respect.

An incomes policy can therefore carry more of the burden than it did in the 1950s, but some supplementary special-purpose weapons are still required. What are the permissible special policy weapons whose impact is concentrated on payments equilibrium? We have already dismissed import controls as incompatible with the present payments system. They are clumsy, involve great risks of retaliation, and induce speculation. But what about exchange rate changes? In fact, devaluation is not an option which the two key currency countries can use without putting the world payments system at risk, and they have no guarantee that such a move would improve their own competitive position. As neither the United Kingdom nor the United States has a strong payments position, an exchange move by one of them would force the other in the same direction. Other countries would almost certainly follow such a move, both in order to preserve the value of their exchange reserves and to maintain their competitiveness in a situation where such a major trader had changed his prices. In any case, if devaluation is to work effectively in increasing competitiveness, it needs to be accompanied by such drastic measures to curb the inflationary consequences of higher import prices that these measures alone are usually enough to meet the problem, unless the competitive position is out of kilter by a very substantial amount. Apart from the French devaluation of 1958, which worked only because it was accompanied by a severe incomes policy and where excessive disequilibrium had been allowed to occur because other countries had been too generous in supplying credit, there was little satisfaction with the exchange rate moves of the 1950s. Exchange rate variations are not, therefore, a valid method for curing international disequilibrium for large trading countries. Harmonization of incomes policies with a little inflation in the surplus countries is much more useful.

Apart from changes in exchange rates there has also been some advocacy of floating rates. At one time, in 1954–55, flexible exchange rates seemed to gain official favor in the United Kingdom. There was fairly general opposition to this device in other countries and the discussion provoked speculation against sterling. This was another case of wishful hankering after the will-o-the-wisp of automatic devices, which springs from a desire to abandon the heavy responsibility of formulating policy. It would be a step in the dark which might destroy many things carefully built up in the past decade. The international payments mechanism needs a stable unit of account so that traders are not saddled with unnecessary risks. The adoption of flexible exchange rates would produce instability harmful to investment and profit expectations, would accelerate inflationary pressures, and could well lead to retaliatory trade restrictions. A system of floating exchange rates would destroy confidence in the key currencies and put an end to the gold exchange standard. This would mean reverting to gold as a means of settlement. It is extremely unlikely that in such a system there would be enough mutual confidence to build up the world's liquidity resources by mutual credit facilities.

In the long run, a system of payments without substantial controls can hardly continue to exist unless there is confidence in the stability of exchange rates. Given the range of other policy weapons available to achieve equilibrium and the supreme importance of confidence, there is no reason why the present structure of rates should not be regarded as more or less permanently frozen. The desirability of stability might well be publicly stressed by narrowing the range within which existing exchange rates are allowed to fluctuate.

If import controls and exchange rate changes cannot be used, a good deal of the burden of adjustment must lie with incomes policy. There are some other weapons which cannot carry a heavy burden, but can play a useful auxiliary role. One equilibrating weapon used in the 1950s which was consistent with the liberal code of policy behavior was the unilateral reduction of tariffs by the countries in payments surplus. In a world moving towards freer trade on a multilateral basis, it is desirable for the surplus countries to accelerate the process by provisional unilateral tariff reductions which can later be consolidated. This process by which surplus countries take the lead was applied with respect to quotas by most European countries in the 1950s. Tariff reduction was practiced by Germany in 1956 and 1957 and, for motor cars, again in 1961. Italy and Austria have made minor use of this device. The only deficit country to have used the reverse weapon of a temporary tariff surcharge was Canada in May 1962. It is a pity that greater use has not been made of tariff reduction by surplus countries. Since 1958 it has been pleaded that the scope for such action has been eliminated now that the continental countries have put their tariff policy in a common mould. However, such a reduction in tariffs for balance-of-payments reasons would be particularly appropriate for the Common Market as a whole. For this reason it would be useful to try to break away from the concept of tariff reduction as a bargaining process with more or less equal cuts being expected of both surplus and deficit countries. There is no doubt of the political difficulty of such a change of emphasis. On the other hand, the tariff issue is the most dangerous point of division in international economic policy in the West, and it is vital to the maintenance of the spirit of co-operation that this conflict should be minimized. From the point of view of world economic growth, the best way of dealing with this problem is to emphasize the effort for lower tariffs all round.

There has been no real experiment in applying fiscal policy weapons directly to the foreign balance, largely because it would be at variance with G.A.T.T. rules. Nevertheless, use of a temporary but low rate of general import tax or export rebate is something which might well prove beneficial. It would certainly have a less distorting effect than direct controls, and if its duration were known to be definitely limited, its immediate impact would be even stronger. The drawback of such measures is, of course, that they might be treated as equivalent to devaluation and lead to speculative capital movements.

Stronger arguments can be advanced for using fiscal measures to influence capital movements. Moves in this direction have been taken in the United States, which in earlier years stimulated private capital exports by reducing rates of corporate tax on foreign investment and exempting undistributed and non-repatriated foreign earnings from tax. This system was reversed in 1962 in the interest of payments equilibrium and in 1963 a tax on the purchase of foreign securities was introduced. Changes in tax on foreign earnings were also made in Canada in 1961, but for political rather than economic reasons. The tax incentives to private investors can be affected not only by changes in tax law but also by temporary withdrawal of the terms of double taxation agreements. Temporary tax measures relating to private investment can have a particularly important impact if they affect the repatriation of capital as well as the current flow of savings.

Attempts have also been made to foster compensatory capital movements by bank rate changes. In general, the more dramatic changes of this nature have succeeded because they were accompanied by some other measures of self-mortification. They did, however, ensure that the money rolled in *ex post*. The more mundane but continuous co-ordination of bank rate policy and forward markets of the past year or so has had greater success. There is scope for further experiment in creating specially high interest rates for foreign depositors in the deficit countries, instead of moving the whole domestic rate structure to help remedy the foreign balance. The United Kingdom began to experiment in this respect in 1963.

Other kinds of monetary action affecting private capital movements could be developed. In France, Germany, Italy and Switzerland, the authorities have used rather far-reaching methods to influence commercial bank foreign currency holdings. The French banks were obliged to repatriate foreign reserves during the 1957 *ratissage* operations, and the Italian banks were forbidden to borrow abroad in 1961. The German and Swiss authorities have similarly imposed special reserve requirements for foreign deposits and have fixed interest rate ceilings on such deposits. If all central banks, including those in deficit countries, were to be equally strict, some of the speculative pressure would be mitigated, although it is, of course, easier for surplus countries to use such measures than for deficit countries.

There are a variety of measures involving technical intervention and mutual support in the gold and foreign exchange markets and the forward exchange markets which can help check speculation and which have been used increasingly in the past few years.

The degree of convertibility for residents varies with the strength of the payments situation, but the U.S. position here is quite different from that in any European country in that there are no controls over private capital at all. The same is true of the United Kingdom *vis-a-vis* the sterling area. Even in Switzerland, where there are no exchange controls, the authorities can exercise a control over foreign issues in the capital market, and the U.S. and U.K. authorities might also usefully exercise more control over resident capital movements.

Governments could also use each other's capital markets to a greater extent than they do. Issues by central or local authorities in each other's capital markets might have a useful stabilizing role, they would be a useful technical move in the process of integration, and would help to educate public opinion to the idea of a managed international economy. The possibility of such foreign issues would have been useful to U.K. local authorities, who could have borrowed more cheaply by issuing bonds on foreign capital markets in 1961–62 than by borrowing short-term foreign capital on deposit account once it had come into the United Kingdom.

There is even greater scope for government compensatory finance by direct deals between governments. European government debt to the United States is about $8 billion, and accelerated repayment of this has already helped equilibrium in the past three or four years. Governments can also issue their securities to each other directly with an exchange guarantee. The U.S. government has done this and has even issued foreign currency bonds to other governments. There is also scope for negotiation on the payments burden of defense or aid commitments. Measures can be taken to 'tie' such payments which are not entirely outside the rules of the game.

In such an open system there is a limit to the possibility of using particular expedients affecting capital flows to achieve equilibrium. Countries with well-organized capital markets, convertible currencies, equal political risks, and a growingly sophisticated and international group of investors can hardly coexist without friction if their interest rate structures or profit possibilities differ widely. In the United States, for instance, the government bond rate is about 4 per cent and in Europe it is generally about 6 per cent. Short-term interest rates are also higher in Europe than in the United States. It is desirable that the interest rate differential be narrowed if equilibrium is to be achieved. European rates may well come down somewhat, but as the basic profit situation in Europe is better, there are difficulties in getting the rate down very far, so that U.S. rates will probably have to rise somewhat. This, of course, raises a conflict with U.S. policy of stimulating growth by relatively low interest rates, and it provides yet another reason for developing U.S. fiscal policy as a means for stimulating growth. It was already clear in Europe in the 1950s that the particular policy-mix appropriate to maintain fast growth must necessarily be affected by external payments considerations. In Germany the neglect of this had adverse results (high interest rates did not repress domestic inflation, but worsened the payments surplus).

Shortage of liquidity was not a major problem of the 1950s except in the United Kingdom and increased liquidity cannot in itself provide a panacea for world payments problems. It is, nevertheless, a necessary ingredient for a payments system which allows countries to reach their growth potential. The post-war policy objectives and code of behavior require a high degree of liquidity in order to give corrective action time to take effect and to offset speculative moves which will inevitably occur. The new international arrangements for liquidity have been very substantial, and the growing tendency for countries to give exchange guarantees for mutual support facilities probably ensures that more will be forthcoming when needed. However, the efficacy of liquidity arrangements depends not only on their size but on their speed and certainty. Some degree of automatic credit would be highly useful in this respect. In the case of the United Kingdom, policy should aim to limit the net capital outflow until the reserve position is substantially stronger than in the 1950s. In other countries there is little evidence that the present level of national reserves is inadequate, Indeed it is excessive in some cases, particularly in Germany.

If such a system is to continue to function with growing possibility of short-term capital movements, it will require continuous co-ordination of policy between central banks, a willingness to give immediate credit to choke off speculation at the beginning, and a mutual trust as to the basic soundness of policy in the major industrial countries. It will not be possible to farm out the problem of managing this system to an independent institution, but the logic of the system implies a need to strengthen international co-operation in certain fields, and particularly in trade policy.

Conclusions

The post-war payments mechanism has worked reasonably well for most industrial countries, and there has been a greater degree of success in meeting payments difficulties than in pre-war years. All the major countries have had payments difficulties and are tolerant of each other's problems. There are, of course, problems in living in a world in which the most direct methods of dealing with the payments problem are ruled out because they hurt one's neighbours more than oneself, but there is the great consolation that one's neighbours are helpful and not retaliatory. In any open system, there are bound to be very difficult problems in achieving equilibrium, and there is no possibility of opting out of interdependence.

The regime of convertibility with fixed exchange rates, liberal trading policies and a non-retaliatory code of behavior has been very favorable to economic growth. It has shown a capacity for adjustment and change which has proved extremely pragmatic. There is no point in scrapping this system for the completely unknown risks of floating exchange rates. However, some major problems remain which require further policy evolution in order for countries to reach their full growth potential. These include the strengthening of domestic policy weapons for growth and their closer harmonization, and new approaches specifically adapted to problems of external equilibrium, such as the use of tariffs for balance-of-payments problems in surplus countries, an application of fiscal policy to the capital balance, and a more specialized use of monetary instruments to affect capital flows. Greater automaticity in world liquidity arrangements would help to strengthen confidence. The United Kingdom in particular needs to take measures to strengthen its capital balance and liquidity position. Finally, it will be necessary for the surplus countries to do more to achieve equilibrium. Otherwise there is the danger that the system will always exercise a deflationary restraint on the countries in deficit. This kind of vicious circle is bound to be broken in the long run by some breach of the rules which will put the whole system at risk.

It is particularly necessary that international policy goals should be properly defined and then carried out by quiet diplomacy. In the long run a consistent adherence to a responsible code of behavior will in itself eliminate one of the major dangers of the system, i.e., speculative confidence crises. For this the political solidarity of these countries is essential.

APPENDIX A

OUTPUT

The output figures refer, wherever possible, to gross domestic product. For several countries the only available pre-war figures are for net product, i.e., they exclude depreciation, or they refer to national product rather than domestic, i.e., they include income from abroad. In none of these cases is this likely to affect the measurement of growth rates appreciably over long periods. In the United Kingdom, where income from abroad has been largest and has varied most, e.g., 9·4 per cent of G.N.P. in 1913 and 0·7 per cent in 1960, we have a G.D.P. series throughout.

We have attempted to select figures which are as comparable as possible, and in a number of cases adjustments were made to existing estimates to bring them as close as possible to the definition of total output used in the O.E.E.C. standardized system of national accounts.[1] This was done for Italy, Norway, Sweden and the United States. The figures we have used for pre-war years for Belgium, France and Switzerland are based on less intensive research than for the other countries, and are therefore presumably subject to greater error. The figures are presented for individual years for the convenience of those who may wish to rebase them, but the pre-war year-to-year movements are in most cases subject to too wide a range of error to be treated as significant.

The figures are adjusted, where necessary, to eliminate the effect of territorial changes. The impact of boundary changes is summarized in the following table. It was assumed that the impact of boundary changes on income was the same as that on population, unless there was a separate estimate available of the income effect.

A major problem in long-term comparisons of output trends is the correction for price changes. The choice of different periods as a

[1] Cf. *A Standardised System of National Accounts*, O.E.E.C., Paris, January 1959, for the standard definitions. The magnitude of the adjustments made in practice by the O.E.E.C. in order to achieve a standardization of the data ordinarily presented in national sources can be judged by consulting pp. 107–71 of *Statistics of National Product and Expenditure*, No. 2, O.E.E.C., Paris, 1957. The O.E.E.C. has also attempted to foster standard techniques for adjusting national accounts for price changes; cf. Richard Stone, *Quantity and Price Indexes in National Accounts*, O.E.E.C., Paris, 1956.

TABLE A-1
IMPACT OF BOUNDARY CHANGES[a] ON POPULATION
AND INCOME, 1870–1960

Ratio of Old to New Area

	1913–25[b]		1938–50[c]		1950–60[d]	
	Population	G.N.P.	Population	G.N.P.	Population	G.N.P.
Belgium	99·3	99·3	100·0	100·0	100·0	100·0
Denmark	94·4	94·4	100·0	100·0	100·0	100·0
France	95·4	95·4	100·0	100·0	100·0	100·0
Germany	111·0	108·3	172·2	170·5	100·0	100·0
Italy	95·8	96·9	101·5	101·5	100·0	100·0
United Kingdom	107·3	107·3	100·0	100·0	100·0	100·0
Canada	100·0	100·0	97·4	98·7	100·0	100·0
United States	100·0	100·0	100·0	100·0	99·5	99·5

[a] This table does not give coefficients for all the adjustments we have made, e.g. the successive switches of the Saar from Germany to France. It refers to changes in political boundaries of long standing. For the impact of boundary changes on customs areas, see A. Maddison, 'Growth and Fluctuation in the World Economy 1870–1960', *Banca Nazionale del Lavoro Quarterly Review*, June 1962.

[b] All the ratios are for 1913. For Germany, France and Italy, the changes are those resulting from the war. The figure for Belgium includes the acquisition of Eupen and Malmedy in 1925. The Danish change is due to the South Schleswig plebiscite in 1920. The U.K. change is due to the independence of Ireland.

[c] For Germany the ratio is that of the pre-war Reich (including the Saar but excluding Austria and Sudetenland) to the area of the Federal Republic including the Saar (and excluding West Berlin). The ratio refers to 1939 for population and 1936 for income. The ratio for Italy refers to 1938, the ratio for Canada to 1949 (acquisition of Newfoundland).

[d] Change due to accession of Hawaii and Alaska as states in 1960. The G.N.P. of Alaska and Hawaii was about $2·5 billion in 1960 as compared with U.S. G.N.P. of $504 billion. However, about $1·5 billion of the G.N.P. of these two states was already included in U.S. G.N.P. so that the explicit addition to U.S. G.N.P. was only 0·2 per cent.

weighting base can affect quantitative developments significantly. Generally, the prices of an earlier year will give a higher increase in output than those of a later year, because of the tendency to consume more of those items whose relative price falls. In fact, each of the series is made up of a number of separate price or weighting links, and there is little that can be done by the lone investigator to unscramble the weighting systems for different countries to make them uniform, though it would certainly be worth making an inter-country comparison of long-term changes in relative prices. In the following notes, the series are sometimes described as being in the 'prices of 1913, 1929', etc., but this usually means simply that the constant value figures have been based on that year, and not that the series are weighted by the price relationships of a given year throughout. There is no reason to believe that there is any systematic tendency for the figures of particular countries to be biased upwards or downwards relative to the other countries.[1] The figures for different countries are therefore subject to the same type of deficiency, and as our concern is with relative rather than absolute errors, the estimates can be treated with a fair degree of confidence for our purpose.

The figures for 1938–60 for all countries are derived from various O.E.E.C. and O.E.C.D. publications. They refer to G.N.P. in all cases, except the United Kingdom where G.D.P. is available. The 1938–50 figures can be found in *General Statistics*, O.E.E.C., May 1960, or in the O.E.E.C., *Eleventh Annual Economic Review, Europe and the World Economy*, Paris, April 1960, p. 116, and the 1950–60 figures are generally from the September 1962 O.E.C.D. Bulletin, *General Statistics*. For years before 1938, the sources are outlined in the individual country notes below:

Belgium
Figures for 1913, 1929, 1938 and 1948 for gross domestic product derived from C. Carbonnelle, 'Recherches sur l'Evolution de la Production en Belgique de 1900 à 1957', *Cahiers Economiques de Bruxelles*, No. 3, April 1959, p. 353. Movement from 1870 to 1913 in net domestic product from Colin Clark, *Conditions of Economic Progress*, 3rd edition, Macmillan, London, 1957, pp. 101-2. 1870 is an interpolation of Clark's figures for 1846 and 1895.

Denmark
1870–1938, G.D.P. at factor cost from K. Bjerke and N. Ussing, *Studier over Danmarks Nationalprodukt, 1870–1950*, Copenhagen, 1958. These figures were adjusted to eliminate the effect of the cession of North Schleswig in 1920.

France
1870–1913, net domestic product from Colin Clark, *op. cit.*, pp. 124-5. 1913–38, net national product from I. Svennilson, *Growth and Stagnation in the European Economy*, E.C.E., Geneva, 1954, p. 233.

The figures for France are not very satisfactory. For the period before 1913, there are a large number of national income estimates for various years. Colin Clark derived figures for selected years from

---

[1] We are assuming that the weights chosen will, in practice, tend to lie between the extremes which would be yielded by initial year and end year weights. In the only case where the weighting basis is quite explicit, i.e. for the United States, the weights are a number of separate links, each of which is cross-weighted between the initial and end years, i.e. a Marshall-Edgeworth type of index.

these estimates. His figures agree fairly well with those of F. Perroux 'Prise de Vues sur la Croissance de l'Economie Française 1780–1950', *Income and Wealth*, Series V, London, 1955, p. 69, who gives decade averages for the nineteenth century. Clark shows a 72 per cent increase from 1870 to 1900, and Perroux an increase of 65 per cent (taking 1870 and 1900 as center points of his averages for the adjacent decades). The movement over the whole of this period also checks fairly well with the figures on the commodity producing sectors in J. Marczewski, 'Some Aspects of the Economic Growth of France 1660–1958', *Economic Development and Cultural Change*, Vol. IX, No. 3, April 1961, p. 376.

For the inter-war period there are two main series by Froment and Gavanier and Dugé de Bernonville. Svennilson used the former, but for the link with 1913 used Clark, *op. cit.*, second edition, who used Dugé.

There is an estimate for 1901–53 by A. Sauvy in a report on national income to the Conseil Economique, *Journal Officiel*, 7 April 1954. This gives a movement from 1901 to 1913 of 35·6 per cent, whereas our source gives 13·8 per cent. For the 1913–38 period, Sauvy gives figures a little higher than our source. However, Sauvy gives no source and presents *per capita* estimates which are inconsistent with his total income estimates.

Germany

1870–1913, net national product. Figures of national income at current prices for individual years are given by W. G. Hoffmann and J. H. Müller, *Das Deutsche Volkseinkommen, 1851–1957*, Tübingen, 1959, pp. 39–40. These were reduced to constant prices by use of the price index of A. Jacobs and H. Richter, 'Die Grosshandelspreise in Deutschland von 1792 bis 1934', *Sonderheft des Instituts für Konjunkturforschung*, No. 37, Berlin, 1935. This is the price index used by Hoffmann and Müller to deflate their own figures, which they present in constant prices only for quinquennia, cf. *op. cit.*, p. 14. They have, however, reweighted the price index, and smoothed it by taking a seven-year moving average. In fact, the figures cited by Hoffmann and Müller for the movement in real product from 1871–75 to 1911–13 differ only fractionally from our figures, i.e., 1871–75 is 30·5 per cent instead of our 30·2 per cent of 1911–13. Hoffmann's figures show a faster rise than the old estimates of the German Statistical Office, cited by Ferdinand Grünig, 'Die Anfänge der Volkswirtschaftlichen Gesamtrechnung in Deutschland', *Beiträge zur empirischen Konjunturforschung*, Berlin, 1950, p. 77. This is partly due to improved coverage in the Hoffmann estimates, and partly to use of a different deflator. 1913–25, net national product, Hoffmann's current price figures, pp. 40 and 56, deflated by the cost of living index as he suggests. The latter is derived from Grünig, *op. cit.*, from whom we have also taken the territorial adjustment. 1925–38, gross national product from *Statistisches Jahrbuch für die Bundesrepublik Deutschland 1961*, p. 544. These figures are for the territory of the Bundesrepublik (excluding the Saar). They show a bigger increase for this period than do Hoffmann's figures. The value series for G.N.P. show a rise of 42·4 per cent between 1925 and 1938, whereas Hoffmann shows a rise of only 37·4 per cent for national income, in spite of the fact that he includes the Saar from 1935 onwards. Hoffmann's figures move in the same way as the old Reichsamt figures quoted by Grünig. The new official series seems to be higher because of wider coverage of war production in the 1930s.

Italy
1870–1938, gross national product from *Annali di Statistica*, Serie VIII, Volume 9, Instituto Centrale di Statistica, Rome, 1957. We have increased the estimates to include certain government purchases of goods and services which are treated in the Italian study as intermediate products, in order to conform with the O.E.E.C. standardized system. The figures refer to the present Italian territory.

Netherlands
1900–1938, net national product at factor cost from *Het Nationale Inkomen van Nederland 1921–39*, Centraal Bureau Voor de Statistiek, Utrecht, 1948.

Norway
1900–1938, gross domestic product at market prices from *National Accounts, 1920–1929*, No. XI, 143, Central Bureau of Statistics, Oslo, 1953. These estimates were adjusted to eliminate repair and maintenance expenditures. The adjustment was a reduction of the original figures of gross investment by a third. Figures for the individual years 1871, 1877 and 1887 were linked to the foregoing estimates via 1905. They are from J. Bjerke, 'Some Aspects of Long-Term Economic Growth in Norway since 1865', paper presented to the Portoroz meeting of the International Association for Research in Income and Wealth, August 1959, p. 27. The figures for these years refer to G.D.P. including repair and maintenance.

Sweden
1870, 1880, 1890 and 1900, gross domestic product at market prices (excluding inventories). Constant price figures are given in *Sveriges Nationalprodukt 1861–1951*, p. 43, Konjunkturinstitutet, Stockholm, 1956. The figures include a rising proportion of repair and maintenance, and we have eliminated this by reducing the constant price

figures by the ratio of repair and maintenance to G.D.P. in current prices. Table I, in *op. cit.*, shows G.D.P. and capital formation in current prices, and repair and maintenance is assumed to be 30 per cent of the original figures for gross investment. The figures for 1870, 1880 and 1890 were raised by 5 per cent because of the under-estimate of investment before 1896 (see *op. cit.*, p. 41). This adjust-ment assumes that investment was about the same proportion of G.D.P. before 1896 as it was in the decade following.

1900–38, gross domestic product (excluding inventories). The year-to-year movements are derived from Östen Johansson, 'Economic Growth and Structure in Sweden', paper presented to the 1959 meeting of the International Association for Research in Income and Wealth. However, he shows a rise of 32·4 per cent from 1910 to 1923 as compared with the 13·3 per cent increase shown by the Konjunkturinstitutet. The latter series has been preferred to make this link, as Johansson's use of consumer price deflators probably does not take adequate account of wartime price rises. For 1921–38, Johansson's figures show a similar movement to those of the Konjunkturinstitutet for the years where the latter are available, i.e., 1923, 1929 and 1939. For 1938–60, we have used O.E.E.C. and O.E.C.D. figures. O.E.E.C. gives figures for the average of the years 1938-39 and it was assumed that the movement in these two years was as shown by Johansson.

Switzerland
1890–1938, net domestic product from Colin Clark, *op. cit.*, pp. 188–9. These figures seem to be close to the estimate of the Schweizerisches Institut für Aussenwirtschafts und Marktforschung, which are presented graphically by F. Kneschaurek, 'Probleme der langfristigen Marktprognose', *Aussenwirtschaft*, December 1959, p. 336.

United Kingdom
1870–1938, gross domestic product from James B. Jefferys and Dorothy Walters, 'National Income and Expenditure of the U.K., 1870–1952', *Income and Wealth*, Series V, Bowes and Bowes, London, 1955. These figures refer to gross national product in 1912-13 market prices. Investment was deflated by the capital goods price index of Table XVI in *op. cit.*, pp. 39–40, and the rest of G.N.P. by the consumer goods and services price index, *op. cit.*, pp. 39–40. Gross domestic product was estimated from these figures by deducting net income from abroad from Colin Clark, *op. cit.*, pp. 137–41. The link between 1913 and 1924 was made after an upward adjustment of 7·3 per cent to allow for the exclusion of Southern Ireland. 1938–48, G.D.P. from *Statistics of National*

Product and Expenditure, No. 2, O.E.E.C., 1957. 1948–60, average of the two alternative figures for G.D.P. given in O.E.C.D., *General Statistics*. The figures for 1870–1938 are based on the national income estimates. Jefferys and Walters cite an alternative estimate based on expenditure, to which they give less credence, which would show a somewhat smaller rate of increase from 1870–1913 and would make little difference for the 1913–38 movement. A more recent estimate of national income at current prices by C. H. Feinstein, 'Income and Investment in the United Kingdom, 1856–1914', *Economic Journal*, June 1961, gives a lower figure for national income throughout but does not appear to make much difference to the long-term rate of growth. Feinstein's figures show 1870 money income as 41·3 per cent of 1913, as compared with Jefferys and Walters 39·8 per cent. For 1938–60, two G.D.P. figures are available as there is a discrepancy between the series deflated from the expenditure side and the output side. We have used the expenditure series.

Canada

1870–1926, gross national product from O. J. Firestone, *Canada's Economic Development 1867–1953*, London, 1958, p. 276. 1926–38, G.N.P. from *National Accounts Income and Expenditure 1926–56*, Dominion Bureau of Statistics, Ottawa, p. 36. It would have been desirable to adjust the Canadian figures to a G.D.P. basis, because dividend and interest payments have been significant and have varied over time. No continuous series appeared to be available.

United States

1889–1938, gross domestic product (Dept. of Commerce concept) from John W. Kendrick, *Productivity Trends in the United States*, National Bureau of Economic Research, Princeton, 1961, pp. 298–300. For the period 1913–38 they have been adjusted upwards to include depreciation on government property, from Raymond W. Goldsmith, *A Study of Saving in the United States*, Princeton, 1955, Vol. I, pp. 993, 1023, 1045 and 1063. This is a minor adjustment, amounting to 0·5 per cent of G.N.P. in 1913, and reaching a peak of 2·0 per cent in 1933. For 1889–1913, no adjustment was made as the ratio was under 0·5 per cent. For 1869–1889, unpublished G.N.P. estimates have been made by Simon Kuznets, which have been adjusted by Kendrick to a Department of Commerce concept. There is some doubt about these figures, particularly for the 1870s when they exaggerate growth because of the understatement of output in the 1869 census. Kendrick therefore presents these figures only as decade averages for 1869–78 and 1879–88. Kuznets presents his own figures annually only as five-year moving averages, in *Capital in the American Economy*, National Bureau of Economic Research,

TABLE A–2
MOVEMENT IN TOTAL VOLUME OF OUTPUT (1913 = 100)

	Belgium	Denmark	France	Germany (F.R.)	Italy	Netherlands	Norway	Sweden	Switzerland	United Kingdom	Canada	United States (constant territory)
1870	31·8	25·8	51·1	30·0ᵃ	54·8		40·9ᵃ	28·5		39·1	20·2	16·9ᵃ
1880		33·4	57·5	38·7	60·2			37·3		45·1	29·6	
1890		45·1	72·2	51·3	62·6			45·0	58·0	69·1	38·0	41·5
1900		62·7	87·9	68·4	70·4	75·0	72·0	62·3		85·8	49·9	60·4
1901		64·5		73·0	76·8	73·4	74·3	63·6		85·5	54·8	67·2
1902		65·1		76·1	73·6	78·1	75·4	61·5		86·6	58·8	67·9
1903		70·1		78·9	80·0	79·7	75·0	68·5		84·2	60·5	71·2
1904		72·1		81·1	79·1	79·7	74·9	69·2		84·7	61·6	70·3
1905		74·7		80·3	83·3	81·3	75·6	69·9		88·0	66·3	75·5
1906		76·1		81·8	83·5	84·4	77·7	78·4		91·7	70·1	84·2
1907		79·8		82·0	88·6	85·9	80·6	78·5		93·1	70·4	85·5
1908		79·5		89·9	89·7	85·9	82·8	79·1		89·5	73·4	78·5
1909		80·3		91·6	92·3	89·1	84·7	80·6		91·3	81·7	88·1
1910		84·0		95·1	87·5	89·1	88·8	85·8		93·7	83·3	89·0
1911		89·3		96·0	96·7	92·2	90·7	89·1		95·7	90·5	91·9
1912		95·5		92·2	96·2	98·4	94·6	87·3		99·3	92·2	96·2
1913	100·0	100·0	100·0	100·0	100·0	100·0	100·0	100·0	100·0	100·0	100·0	100·0
1920			77·6		106·6	117·2	122·4				103·7	114·5
1921		97·1	71·8		108·9	123·4	110·1				94·3	112·0
1922		103·9	88·2		113·4	128·1	123·1				101·9	118·3
1923		117·7	95·3		116·6	132·8	126·9	97·3			108·3	133·8
1924		120·4	110·6		117·2	137·5	126·4	100·6	119·2	112·1	108·1	138·0
1925		117·2	110·6	90·3	122·1	143·8	131·8	103·6	127·8	113·4	112·8	141·3
1926		120·9	116·5	92·9	122·9	151·6	133·2	108·0	134·2	114·4	122·7	150·6
1927		125·1	111·8	102·1	122·1	156·3	139·2	113·0	141·5	124·5	133·9	152·2
1928		130·1	118·8	106·7	130·4	164·1	136·8	113·3	149·3	126·5	146·4	154·0

ᵃ 1871.

TABLE A–2 (contd.)
MOVEMENT IN TOTAL VOLUME OF OUTPUT (1913 = 100)

	Belgium	Denmark	France	Germany (F.R.)	Italy	Netherlands	Norway	Sweden	Switzerland	United Kingdom	Canada	United States (constant territory)
1929	127·8	134·1	130·6	106·2	132·9	168·8	156·1	122·8	154·5	128·7	146·7	163·4
1930	125·2	140·0	129·4	104·9	125·7	168·8	168·1	127·0	153·6	128·6	140·6	149·1
1931		142·3	123·5	96·7	127·4	157·8	154·9	114·8	147·2	130·0	122·6	140·8
1932		139·5	115·3	89·5	132·7	153·1	165·0	110·0	142·2	131·3	110·1	120·9
1933		141·5	115·3	94·9	132·0	150·0	169·0	115·2	149·2	139·3	103·0	117·7
1934		146·9	112·9	103·4	131·0	148·4	172·6	125·7	149·2	144·0	115·4	128·0
1935		150·4	108·2	112·8	144·1	151·6	181·7	131·8	148·9	149·3	124·4	144·7
1936		154·9	107·1	122·5	145·3	159·4	191·7	139·8	149·4	155·2	129·9	159·7
1937		160·1	110·6	136·4	154·2	171·9	198·2	149·0	156·5	155·8	142·8	172·6
1938	122·0	160·5	109·4	149·9	153·8	170·3	202·8	154·6	162·6	158·3	143·7	163·3
1948	135·0	189·7	107·7	110·9	143·4	194·0	248·2	201·1	204·1	177·3	250·5	269·6
1949	139·1	198·7	120·9	128·9	151·0	209·2	252·4	213·6	192·3	182·8	257·6	269·3
1950	146·0	216·1	130·3	157·8	161·8	216·8	265·8	225·0	205·1	189·7	278·7	293·0
1951	154·4	215·8	138·2	173·8	174·1	222·9	274·6	224·0	217·9	196·3	295·5	312·7
1952	153·0	218·6	141·7	188·3	179·1	227·5	285·2	230·3	222·8	195·8	319·2	325·9
1953	159·2	232·3	146·0	202·4	192·7	247·5	296·6	238·5	235·7	204·0	331·5	339·4
1954	166·5	230·2	153·1	217·5	202·5	264·9	309·8	254·0	254·4	212·0	321·6	334·0
1955	171·7	230·6	162·0	242·5	216·1	285·6	317·0	263·4	270·2	218·8	349·5	360·9
1956	178·0	245·2	170·1	259·2	225·1	296·9	332·5	271·7	285·0	224·6	379·8	367·6
1957	182·5	258·9	180·3	273·2	239·3	304·3	339·4	282·3	295·8	228·0	384·5	375·0
1958	179·3	265·5	183·4	282·1	249·8	305·8	338·7	285·0	301·7	227·3	389·5	369·2
1959	185·9	280·3	187·8	301·0	268·9	324·2	351·9	298·8	316·5	234·3	401·0	394·0
1960	193·7	298·7	199·8	327·4	287·9	350·7	373·4	311·0	337·3	244·3	408·8	403·1
1961	201·4	312·5	208·8	344·5	310·9	359·6	392·2	330·5	367·0	248·8	416·0	410·9

Princeton, 1961, p. 563. Kuznets quotes estimates that the 1869 census understated output by 5–13 per cent, but it has been suggested that the understatement may have been as high as 18–22 per cent. Cf. Milton Friedman, 'Monetary Data and National Income Estimates', *Economic Development and Cultural Change* (Kuznets's birthday edition), April 1961, pp. 274, 281. We have therefore estimated 1871 by raising the published Kuznets figure (Variant III concept of G.N.P.) by 15 per cent.

APPENDIX B

POPULATION

All figures are adjusted to refer to constant territory as described for G.N.P., and refer to mid-year.

For 1950–60 the figures for all countries are from *Manpower Statistics 1950–1960*, O.E.C.D., 1961, with revisions supplied by the O.E.C.D. Secretariat.

Belgium

1870–1950, derived from *Annuaire Statistique de la Belgique* (1955 and 1960), adjusted to a mid-year basis. Corrected to exclude the effect of the cession by Germany of Eupen and Malmedy in 1925, which added 0·81 per cent to population.

Denmark

K. Bjerke, 'The National Product of Denmark 1870–1952', *Income and Wealth*, Series V, 1870–1950, p. 151. Corrected to exclude the effect of the incorporation of North Schleswig in 1920 which added 5·8 per cent to population.

France

1870–1950, *Annuaire Statistique de la France 1956* (partie rétrospective), pp. 8–9. The figures are adjusted to exclude the effect of the return of Alsace-Lorraine.

Germany

1870–1913, W. G. Hoffmann, *op. cit.*, pp. 39–40. 1913–38, Svennilson, *op. cit.*, p. 236. 1938–50 link from O.E.E.C., *General Statistics*.

Italy

1870–1950, *Annuario Statistico Italiano*, 1955, p. 369. Figures refer to population living within present boundaries, adjusted to a mid-year basis. The 1950–60 figures also refer to present-in-area population.

TABLE B-1
POPULATION (1913 = 100)

	Belgium	Denmark	France	Germany (F.R.)[a]	Italy	Netherlands	Norway	Sweden	Switzerland	United Kingdom	Canada	United States (constant territory)
1870	66·5	63·3	92·7	61·2[a]	75·4	58·4	70·9	74·1	68·5	68·5	47·2	41·0
1880	72·3	69·8	94·2	67·3	80·1	65·4	78·4	81·3	73·1	75·9	55·4	51·7
1890	79·5	76·9	96·5	73·5	85·8	73·9	81·6	85·1	77·4	82·0	62·0	64·9
1900	87·6	85·8	97·8	83·7	91·8	83·4	91·1	91·0	85·4	90·2	68·9	78·3
1901	88·7	86·9	98·0	84·9	92·3	84·7	92·2	91·7	86·5	91·0	70·0	79·8
1902	90·0	87·9	98·2	86·2	92·8	86·1	93·0	92·3	87·6	91·8	71·8	81·4
1903	91·3	88·9	98·4	87·5	93·2	87·4	93·5	92·7	88·7	92·6	74·0	82·9
1904	92·4	89·9	98·5	88·8	93·7	88·8	93·9	93·2	88·9	93·5	76·2	84·5
1905	93·6	90·9	98·6	90·1	94·2	90·1	94·4	93·9	91·0	94·3	77·9	86·2
1906	94·7	91·9	98·7	91·3	94·6	91·4	94·8	94·6	92·1	95·1	80·8	87·9
1907	95·7	93·0	98·7	92·6	95·2	92·6	95·2	95·3	93·3	96·0	84·1	89·5
1908	96·7	94·2	99·0	93·9	95·7	93·9	95·9	96·1	94·4	96·8	86·5	91·2
1909	97·5	95·4	99·1	95·1	96·8	94·8	96·7	97·0	95·5	97·6	88·9	93·1
1910	97·8	96·6	99·4	96·4	97·7	95·7	97·2	97·8	96·7	98·5	91·5	95·0
1911	98·0	97·8	99·6	97·6	98·6	97·1	98·1	98·6	97·7	99·3	94·0	96·5
1912	99·0	98·9	99·7	98·8	99·5	98·4	99·0	99·3	98·8	99·7	96·8	98·0
1913	100·0	100·0	100·0	100·0	100·0	100·0	100·0	100·0	100·0	100·0	100·0	100·0
1920	98·5	108·1	93·5	100·9	102·1	111·0	107·7	104·5	100·3			109·5
1921	97·9	109·5	94·1	102·0	102·9	112·6	109·0	105·5	100·3		114·0	111·6
1922	98·8	107·4	94·5	102·6	103·9	114·5	110·1	106·2	100·3		115·4	113·2
1923	99·6	111·9	95·6	103·2	104·7	116·4	110·9	106·7	100·5		116·9	115·1
1924	100·5	113·0	96·6	103·9	105·5	118·2	111·5	107·1	100·8	105·2	118·7	117·4
1925	101·5	114·2	97·3	104·7	106·4	119·9	112·2	107·5	101·2	105·4	120·7	119·1
1926	102·3	115·1	98·6	105·4	107·3	121·6	112·9	107·9	101·8	105·9	122·9	120·7

[a] 1871.

TABLE B-1 (contd.)
POPULATION (1913 = 100)

	Belgium	Denmark	France	Germany (F.R.)	Italy	Netherlands	Norway	Sweden	Switzerland	United Kingdom	Canada	United States (constant territory)
1927	103·1	115·8	98·1	106·1	108·3	123·3	113·4	108·2	102·4	106·2	125·4	122·4
1928	103·9	116·6	98·4	106·7	109·3	125·0	113·8	108·5	103·2	106·7	127·9	123·9
1929	104·8	117·3	98·8	107·3	110·3	126·6	114·2	108·7	104·1	106·9	130·3	125·2
1930	105·3	118·1	99·7	107·8	111·2	128·3	114·7	109·1	104·8	107·3	132·5	126·7
1931	106·0	119·0	100·3	108·4	112·2	130·2	115·4	109·4	105·6	107·8	134·5	127·7
1932	106·8	120·1	100·3	108·9	113·1	132·2	116·1	109·9	106·2	108·4	136·1	128·5
1933	107·4	121·1	100·4	109·4	114·1	134·1	116·8	110·3	106·7	108·9	137·6	129·3
1934	107·8	122·2	100·6	110·0	115·0	135·8	117·4	110·7	107·1	109·2	138·9	130·1
1935	108·1	123·2	100·5	110·8	116·0	137·3	118·1	111·0	107·5	109·7	140·3	131·0
1936	108·5	124·1	100·5	111·6	116·9	138·6	118·6	111·4	107·9	110·2	141·5	131·8
1937	108·9	125·0	100·5	112·4	117·7	139·9	119·3	111·7	108·2	110·7	142·8	132·6
1938	109·2	125·9	100·6	113·4	118·6	141·3	120·0	112·0	108·5	111·2	144·3	133·7
1950	112·7	142·4	100·0	136·6	128·6	164·6	133·5	124·8	121·5	117·8	171·8	156·0
1951	113·2	143·5	100·8	138·1	129·8	167·1	134·7	125·8	122·9	118·4	175·6	158·8
1952	113·9	144·5	101·5	138·9	130·7	168·9	136·0	126·8	124·6	118·8	181·1	161·5
1953	114·5	145·7	102·2	140·3	131·2	170·9	137·5	127·5	126·2	119·1	186·1	164·1
1954	115·0	147·0	103·0	141·8	131·9	172·8	138·8	128·3	127·5	119·6	191·6	167·1
1955	115·7	148·1	103·7	143·2	132·7	175·0	140·2	129·2	128·8	119·9	196·7	170·0
1956	116·4	149·0	104·6	144·9	133·3	177·3	141·5	130·2	130·4	120·4	201·5	173·0
1957	117·2	149·7	105·7	146·8	133·8	179·4	142·8	131·0	132·4	120·9	207·9	176·1
1958	118·1	150·7	106·9	148·8	134·6	182·0	144·2	131·9	134·2	121·4	213·5	178·9
1959	118·7	151·7	108·1	150·7	135·2	184·7	145·4	132·7	135·6	122·1	218·5	182·1
1960	119·4	152·8	109·2	152·3	136·3	187·0	146·7	133·2	138·5	123·0	223·2	185·0

Netherlands

1870, derived from *The Aging of Populations and Its Economic and Social Implications*, U.N., New York, 1956. 1880–1938, Svennilson, *op. cit.*, p. 236.

Norway

1870–1900, J. Bjerke, *op. cit.*, p. 17. 1900–38, Svennilson, *op. cit.*, p. 236.

Sweden

1870, *The Aging of Populations and Its Economic and Social Implications*, U.N., New York, 1956. 1880–1938, Svennilson, *op. cit.*, p. 236.

Switzerland

1870–1959, derived from *Annuaire Statistique de la Suisse*, 1961, adjusted to a mid-year basis where necessary. 1960 from O.E.C.D., *Manpower Statistics*.

United Kingdom

82nd Statistical Abstract for the U.K., 1939, pp. 4 and 5, gives decennial (April) figures for the census years and for mid-years for 1913 and 1924–37. Our index for 1870–1913 is based on interpolation of the census figures adjusted to a mid-year basis. The link between 1913 and 1924 is made after excluding the effect of the loss of Southern Ireland. 1938–51 derived from the *Annual Abstract of Statistics*. 1951–60 from O.E.C.D., *Manpower Statistics*.

Canada

1870–1950, O. J. Firestone, *op. cit.*, pp. 240–1. The figures have been adjusted to exclude Newfoundland.

United States

1870–1950, *Historical Statistics of the United States, Colonial Times to 1957*, U.S. Dept. of Commerce, 1960, p. 7. The figures for 1959 and 1960 are adjusted to exclude Hawaii and Alaska.

APPENDIX C

POPULATION OF WORKING AGE
(Aged 15–64 Inclusive)

All figures refer to constant territory and to mid-year.

For most countries the percentage of population aged 15–64 is given in *The Aging of Population and Its Economic and Social Implications*, United Nations, New York, 1956, for census years between 1870 and 1950. For inter-censal years, these percentages were interpolated. The percentages were then applied to our figures for total population. The publication cited does not give figures for the United Kingdom but only for Great Britain. U.K. percentages for census years are from the *82nd Statistical Abstract* and the *1958 Annual Abstract*. The U.N. source does not cover Canada and the United States before 1900. For Canada, for 1870–1900, the figures are derived from O. J. Firestone, *op. cit.*, p. 57, adjusted to include females. For the United States, the figures for 1870–1900 are from *Historical Statistics of the United States, 1789–1945*, p. 28. For France, the U.N. figures were supplemented by the figures in the *Annuaire Statistique 1956* (partie rétrospective), p. 2. For 1950–60, the movements in the population of working age for all countries were derived from O.E.C.D., *Manpower Statistics*. This source gives figures for Italy for the age group 14–65, and these were adjusted.

TABLE C-1
POPULATION OF WORKING AGE (1913=100)

	Belgium	Denmark	France	Germany (F.R.)	Italy	Netherlands	Norway	Sweden	Switzerland	United Kingdom	Canada	United States
1870	63·3	63·9	92·3	59·4a	77·2	59·3	72·0a	74·0	67·5	62·6	40·8	37·9a
1880	67·1	69·7	93·2	63·9	83·0	64·7	80·1	82·6	71·5	69·3	50·2	47·6
1890	74·7	74·4	95·6	69·7	87·3	72·4	79·6	82·9	75·1	76·4	58·4	61·8
1900	84·1	84·5	97·7	80·0	91·1	82·0	89·0	88·9	84·4	87·5	66·9	75·7
1901	85·3	85·8	97·9	81·4	91·4	83·3	90·2	89·7	85·4	88·8	68·2	77·5
1902	86·7	86·8	98·0	82·7	91·8	84·7	90·9	90·4	86·5	89·7	70·2	79·4
1903	88·0	87·9	98·2	83·9	92·2	86·0	91·5	90·9	87·6	90·6	72·6	81·1
1904	89·3	88·9	98·4	85·3	92·7	87·4	92·0	91·5	88·7	91·7	74·9	82·9
1905	90·5	89·9	98·5	86·5	93·2	88·7	92·5	92·3	89·8	92·6	76·8	84·9
1906	91·7	91·0	98·6	87·9	93·6	90·0	93·0	93·0	90·9	93·7	79·9	86·8
1907	92·9	92·1	98·6	89·1	94·1	91·3	93·4	93·8	91·9	94·6	83·4	88·6
1908	94·0	93·3	98·8	90·5	94·6	92·6	94·1	94·7	93·0	95·5	86·1	90·7
1909	95·0	94·6	99·1	91·7	95·6	93·5	95·0	95·7	94·1	96·5	88·7	92·9
1910	95·3	95·8	99·4	93·1	96·5	94·7	95·5	96·6	95·2	97·5	91·7	95·1
1911	96·4	97·1	99·6	95·4	97·4	96·4	97·0	97·8	96·7	98·5	94·5	96·7
1912	98·2	98·5	99·8	97·6	98·9	98·1	98·4	98·9	98·3	99·3	97·0	98·2
1913	100·0	100·0	100·0	100·0	100·0	100·0	100·0	100·0	100·0	100·0	100·0	100·0
1920	104·3	110·9	97·5	105·7	104·8	113·7	112·1	107·5	103·9			109·5
1921	103·8	112·8	97·9	107·5	105·9	115·7	114·0	109·1	104·2		111·8	112·0
1922	104·8	111·2	99·2	108·8	106·9	118·0	115·7	110·5	104·5		113·5	113·7
1923	105·9	116·6	100·3	110·2	107·7	120·2	117·1	111·7	105·1		115·3	116·0
1924	107·0	118·4	101·2	111·6	108·5	122·4	118·3	112·7	105·9	109·7	117·6	118·7
1925	108·2	120·4	101·8	113·2	109·4	124·5	119·7	113·8	106·6	110·3	119·9	120·6
1926	109·2	122·0	101·9	114·1	110·4	126·6	121·0	114·9	107·6	111·1	122·5	122·6
1927	110·2	123·4	101·8	115·1	111·4	128·7	122·1	115·9	108·6	111·8	125·4	124·7
1928	111·2	125·0		115·9	112·4	130·8	123·1	116·8	109·8	112·6	128·4	126·7

a 1871.

O

TABLE C–1 (contd.)
POPULATION OF WORKING AGE (1913=100)

	Belgium	Denmark	France	Germany (F.R.)	Italy	Netherlands	Norway	Sweden	Switzerland	United Kingdom	Canada	United States
1929	112·3	126·4	102·1	116·8	113·4	132·8	124·2	117·7	111·2	113·2	131·2	128·2
1930	113·1	128·0	102·8	117·5	114·3	135·0	125·3	118·8	112·4	114·0	133·8	130·1
1931	113·7	129·7	103·2	118·3	115·3	137·4	126·4	119·9	113·3	114·8	136·2	131·7
1932	114·5	131·6	102·5	119·1	116·3	139·9	127·4	121·2	114·0	115·7	138·5	133·2
1933	115·0	133·5	101·9	119·8	117·2	142·4	128·5	122·4	114·7	116·5	140·7	134·6
1934	115·4	135·4	101·4	120·1	118·2	144·7	129·4	123·6	115·3	117·1	142·5	136·0
1935	115·7	137·3	100·7	120·6	119·2	146·7	130·4	124·7	115·9	117·9	144·6	137·6
1936	116·0	138·3	99·9	121·2	120·1	148·5	131·3	126·0	116·3	118·7	146·6	138·9
1937	116·4	139·3	99·1	121·7	121·5	150·4	132·3	127·1	116·8	119·5	148·4	140·4
1938	116·7	140·2	98·6	122·4	122·9	152·4	133·4	128·2	117·2	120·3	150·6	141·5
1950	118·5	149·1	100·1	145·3	140·0	172·7	152·2	136·6	127·0	122·7	172·5	159·7
1951	118·6	149·7	100·3	147·0		174·4	153·1	137·4	128·2	122·9	174·2	161·0
1952	118·9	150·3	100·4	148·5		175·6	153·6	138·0	129·6	122·9	178·4	162·3
1953	119·1	151·0	100·5	150·5		176·7	154·2	138·2	131·0	122·9	182·0	163·4
1954	119·2	151·9	100·7	153·1		178·2	154·8	138·6	131·8	123·0	186·1	164·5
1955	119·2	152·7	100·8	155·5		180·0	155·5	139·3	132·7	123·1	189·6	165·8
1956	119·1	153·3	101·0	158·1		181·7	156·2	140·2	134·2	123·0	193·0	167·2
1957	119·0	153·9	101·4	159·5		183·6	156·8	141·0	136·3	123·1	198·4	169·0
1958	119·0	155·2	102·0	161·1		185·7	157·7	142·2	138·2	123·4	202·9	171·0
1959	119·0	156·9	102·6	162·3		188·1	158·7	143·4	139·7	124·0	207·0	173·0
1960	119·0	158·8	103·1	163·3	149·7	190·1	160·3	144·7	140·3	124·6	211·0	174·0

APPENDIX D

LABOR FORCE

All figures refer to constant territory and to mid-year.

For 1870–1913, it was assumed that the labor force moved in step with the population of working age. For 1913–50, labor force activity rates (ratio of occupied population of all ages to total population aged 15–64) were derived from census data and inter-polated for inter-censal years. These activity rates were then applied to the figures for population of working age. 1960 census figures were available for very few countries at the time of writing, but for most countries O.E.C.D. annual estimates of the labor force are available from 1950 onwards, and these were linked to the last available census figures. In some cases, the O.E.C.D. labor force figures are not based on the same concept of activity as in the census, and we have therefore generally taken the O.E.C.D. figures only as an indication of *movements* in activity since 1950. The extent of the difference can be seen in Table D–1. For Switzerland, all the figures are derived from census material. The activity rates derived from the censuses are given below after the year to which they refer.

TABLE D–1
ACTIVITY RATES AS SHOWN BY O.E.C.D. AND BY THE
CENSUS IN 1950[a]

	Denmark	France	Germany	Italy	Netherlands	Norway	Sweden	U.K.	Canada
Census	74·5	73·5	68·9	63·8	61·2	64·2	66·5	69·4	61·4
O.E.C.D.	74·7	70·2	68·3	59·8	61·5	67·6	66·8	70·6	60·7

Note: In other countries there was either no difference between the two sources or we used the O.E.C.D. figures as an indication of absolute levels.

[a] In some cases the figures in this table are interpolations. Figures for the census years are given in the country notes below.

Belgium
Activity rates derived from *Annuaire Statistique*, 1960, pp. 38 and 48. 1910, 74·6 per cent; 1920, 63·2 per cent; 1930, 66·8 per cent. 1950–60 from O.E.C.D. *Manpower Statistics*.

Denmark
Activity rates derived from *International Statistical Yearbook*, 1927, League of Nations, for 1911, 74·7 per cent; 1921, 67·3 per cent; from I.L.O. *Yearbook 1938* for 1930, 68·6 per cent; from I.L.O. *Yearbook 1945–46* for 1940, 76·3 per cent; from I.L.O. *Yearbook 1957* for 1950, 74·5 per cent. These figures differ substantially from the estimates for 1870–1952 given by K. Bjerke, *op. cit.*, p. 151, which imply much higher but steadier activity rates, 1911, 82·6 per cent; 1921, 81·1 per cent; 1930, 81·4 per cent; 1940, 80·9 per cent; 1950, 77·2 per cent. But Bjerke's figures were derived by assuming that all persons of working age except married women were in the labor force; cf. Bjerke, p. 139. Movement from 1950–60 is derived from *Demographic Trends 1956–76 in Western Europe and in the United States*, O.E.E.C., 1961, with interpolation.

France
Activity rates derived from *Annuaire Statistique 1956* (partie rétrospective), p. 20. As there was considerable variation in the definition of female activity in agriculture from one census to another, we have adjusted the census figures for agricultural women on the assumption that women workers in agriculture were 68·5 per cent of male workers in agriculture for each census year. This is the average ratio for the census years from 1911 to 1954. Thus revised, the activity rates are: 1911, 82·9 per cent; 1921, 80·1 per cent; 1926, 77·4 per cent; 1931, 77·1 per cent; 1936, 75·2 per cent; 1946, 75·3 per cent; 1954, 71·9 per cent. Movement from 1950–60 derived from O.E.E.C., *Demographic Trends*.

Germany
Activity rates derived from *Statistisches Handbuch von Deutschland 1928–44*, 1949, München, p. 31, for 1907, 74·5 per cent; 1925, 75·2 per cent; 1933, 71·7 per cent; 1939, 74·8 per cent; from *Statistisches Jahrbuch fur die Bundesrepublik Deutschland, 1956*, p. 111, for 1950, 68·9 per cent. The adjusted rates derivable from Long, *op. cit.*, are steadier; 1907, 71·9 per cent; 1925, 72·3 per cent; 1933, 71·2 per cent; 1939, 72·7 per cent. 1950–60 movement derived from O.E.C.D., *Manpower Statistics*.

Italy
Activity rates derived from *Annuario Statistico Italiano*, 1955, p. 377, for 1911, 79·0 per cent; 1921, 76·7 per cent; 1931, 71·9 per cent; 1936, 70·7 per cent; 1951, 63·3 per cent. Movement from 1950 to 1954 derived from O.E.E.C., *Demographic Trends*; 1954–60 from O.E.C.D. *Manpower Statistics*, after deduction of workers employed

LABOR FORCE[a] (1913 = 100)

	Belgium	Denmark	France	Germany (F.R.)	Italy	Netherlands	Norway	Sweden	Switzerland	United Kingdom	Canada	United States
1913	100·0	100·0	100·0	100·0	100·0	100·0	100·0	100·0	100·0	100·0	100·0	100·0
1920	93·0	103·0		106·1	102·6	113·0	110·8	116·1	101·3	104·8		109·8
1921	93·1	103·6	94·9	108·0	103·4	114·8	112·5	117·3	101·2	105·5	109·8	112·2
1922	94·6	105·4	94·7	109·4	103·7	116·9	113·9	118·4	101·0	106·1	112·0	113·9
1923	96·0	107·6	95·3	110·8	103·9	118·9	115·0	119·2	101·1	106·8	113·7	116·1
1924	97·6	109·5	95·7	112·3	104·0	120·8	115·9	119·7	101·4	107·5	116·0	118·7
1925	99·2	111·6	95·8	114·0	104·2	122·7	117·0	120·4	101·7	108·1	118·6	120·4
1926	100·7	113·3	95·8	114·2	104·4	124·6	118·0	121·1	102·2	108·9	121·2	122·3
1927	102·1	114·8	95·7	114·5	104·7	126·4	118·8	121·6	102·7	109·6	124·4	124·4
1928	103·7	116·6	95·7	114·6	105·0	128·3	119·5	122·1	103·4	110·4	127·9	126·1
1929	105·2	118·1	95·8	114·8	105·2	130·0	120·3	122·5	104·2	111·0	131·3	127·5
1930	106·5	119·9	96·4	114·8	105·4	132·0	121·0	123·1	104·8	111·8	134·5	129·2
1931	106·4	122·8	96·7	114·9	105·6	134·3	122·0	123·5	105·4	112·6	137·5	130·7
1932	106·5	126·0	95·5	114·9	106·1	136·7	122·8	124·1	105·7	113·6	139·5	132·2
1933	106·3	129·3	94·5	114·9	106·6	139·1	123·8	124·6	106·0	114·4	141·6	133·7
1934	105·9	132·5	93·7	116·0	107·1	141·3	124·5	125·0	106·3	115·1	143·7	135·4
1935	105·5	135·8	92·6	117·4	107·6	143·3	125·4	125·3	106·4	115·9	145·8	137·1
1936	105·1	138·3	91·3	118·8	108·1	145·0	126·1	125·9	106·6	116·8	147·9	138·6
1937	104·7	140·8	90·2	120·2	108·6	146·8	127·0	126·2	106·6	117·7	149·9	140·1
1938	104·3	143·1	89·3	121·8	109·1	148·7	127·9	126·5	106·7	118·5	152·0	141·7
1950	100·9	151·7	89·6	134·1	113·7	162·9	144·4	132·3	116·3	120·6	167·9	167·0
1951	103·8	152·9	89·8	136·4		164·4	145·1	132·8	117·7	122·0	170·6	170·2
1952	103·2	154·1	90·0	138·5		166·0	144·8	133·4	119·2	122·3	174·4	171·7
1953	103·0	155·3	90·2	140·9		167·8	144·8	133·9	120·7	122·7	177·1	173·7
1954	103·3	156·6	90·5	144·3		171·2	145·6	134·4	121·8	124·3	180·5	174·8
1955	103·2	157·8	90·7	147·6		173·8	146·6	134·9	122·9	125·5	184·4	177·5
1956	103·0	159·0	91·1	150·3		176·6	146·6	135·9	124·5	126·5	189·9	181·5
1957	103·2	160·3	91·7	152·9		178·9	147·4	136·9	126·8	126·9	197·1	182·7
1958	103·2	161·6	92·1	154·3		179·5	147·1	137·9	128·9	126·3	201·1	183·9
1959	103·0	162·9	92·5	154·9		180·2	147·4	138·8	130·5	126·7	204·3	185·4
1960	102·8	164·1	92·9	156·2	128·5	182·0	148·2	139·8	131·4	128·2	209·9	187·6

a For the years before 1913 the labor force is assumed to move in the same way as population of working age.

outside Italy, as given in *L'Annuario di Statistiche del Lavoro e dell'Emigrazione.*

Netherlands
Activity rates derived from *International Statistical Yearbook*, 1927, League of Nations, for 1909, 65·2 per cent and 1920, 64·5 per cent; from *Statistical Yearbook of the Netherlands 1953–54*, for 1930, 63·4 per cent and 1947, 63·2 per cent. 1950–60 from O.E.C.D., *Manpower Statistics.* The 1950–60 figures are expressed in man-years.

Norway
Activity rates derived from *Statistisk Arbok 1957*, p. 20, for 1900, 69·1 per cent; 1920, 66·9 per cent; 1930, 65·4 per cent; 1950, 64·2 per cent. 1950–60 from O.E.C.D., *Manpower Statistics.*

Sweden
Activity rates derived from *International Statistical Yearbook*, 1927, League of Nations, for 1910, 66·5 per cent; 1920, 74·4 per cent; from I.L.O. *Yearbook 1938*, for 1930, 71·4 per cent; from *Statistisk Arsbok 1957*, p. 29, for 1940, 67·1 per cent and 1950, 66·5 per cent. 1950–60 movement derived from O.E.E.C., *Demographic Trends.*

Switzerland
Activity rates derived from *Annuaire Statistique de la Suisse*, 1961, for 1910, 75·5 per cent; 1920, 72·8 per cent; 1930, 69·7 per cent; 1941, 67·4 per cent; 1950, 68·4 per cent. The 1960 census figure of 70·0 per cent was taken from *La Vie Economique*, Berne, December 1961, pp. 508–9.

United Kingdom
Activity rates derived from *82nd Statistical Abstract for the U.K.*, p. XV, for 1911, 70·3 per cent; 1921, 68·5 per cent; 1931, 68·6 per cent; from the *Statistical Abstract for 1958*, for 1951, 69·4 per cent. Movement from 1950–60 from O.E.C.D., *Manpower Statistics.*

Canada
1913–31, unpublished estimates supplied by Prof. M. C. Urquhart to be published in *Historical Statistics of Canada.* 1931–50 from *Canadian Statistical Review, 1957 Supplement*, p. 26. Activity rates were: 1910, 63·4 per cent; 1920, 61 per cent; 1929, 62·2 per cent; 1930, 62·4 per cent; 1933, 62·4 per cent; 1950, 61·4 per cent; cf. Firestone, *op. cit.*, p. 58. 1950–60 from O.E.C.D., *Manpower Statistics.*

United States

1913–50 derived from *Historical Statistics* (1960 edition), p. 70. This gives a continuous series, from 1929 onwards, on the same definition used in the current population reports. It also gives figures for 1890–1950 for census years. For the years before 1929 the figures were derived by interpolating the census figures, but these were first adjusted upwards by 1·0565 to bring them into line with the series used for later years. Thus adjusted, the census activity rates were: 1900, 62·4 per cent; 1920, 63·0 per cent; 1930, 62·4 per cent. 1950–60 from O.E.C.D., *Manpower Statistics*.

APPENDIX E

UNEMPLOYMENT

Table E-1 shows unemployment as a proportion of the total labor force. These estimates are primarily intended to be used to derive estimates of long-term movements in employment in individual countries. They are adjusted to achieve as great a degree of comparability as possible, but use of the figures for inter-country comparisons of unemployment levels can only be made with caution and in the light of the difficulties noted below.

The coverage of the unemployment series published by different countries differs considerably. Table E-2 shows the size of the sample from which the regular unemployment figures are drawn. However, in most countries except Denmark and Sweden, the post-war series cover nearly all wage and salary earners, and these are the people most subject to unemployment risks.

The sample survey technique of recording used in the United States leads to a larger unemployment figure than would be recorded in the type of statistic used in most European countries. This is so, not only because it covers the whole labor force, but also because it is designed to catch all the marginal cases of unemployment. In the United Kingdom, for instance, married women, workers over retirement age, and juveniles seeking their first job are not entitled to unemployment benefits and have a smaller incentive to register as unemployed than adult males. Some workers are disqualified from benefits, e.g. by leaving their job voluntarily. Such categories of unemployed would be fully covered in the U.S. sample survey. In 1960, 21 per cent of British unemployed were married women and juveniles, whereas in the United States 32 per cent were in these groups.

It is not possible to find any neat or satisfactory way of standardizing the figures to achieve inter-country comparability. However, some idea of the degree to which the usual sources record unemployment can be gained from Table E-3, which compares the different national series with the unemployment recorded by the latest population census. We have assumed that the census coverage of unemployment is fairly comparable between countries, and we have therefore adjusted the regular series for most European countries upwards. In the United Kingdom the figure for registered unemployed in April 1951 was 1·2 per cent of the labor force (if we include those both wholly and temporarily unemployed), but the population census of the same date showed 2·2 per cent as unemployed. In Sweden the sample survey recently introduced showed an unemployment rate 1 per cent higher than insurance figures, and in France, too, the census showed unemployment 0·6 per cent higher than the registrations. In Canada, Germany and Switzerland the census showed unemployment only marginally higher than the regular series, and in Belgium, where unemployment insurance coverage is wider than elsewhere, the census figure was a little lower. The Italian sample surveys regularly show less unemployment than registration statistics, but there are special administrative reasons for for this discrepancy as noted below. In the United States the 1950 census showed unemployment 0·8 per cent lower than the sample survey, apparently because the census enumerators were less skilled in dealing with marginal cases than the people employed on the regular sample survey enquiry. Since then, the definition of unemployment in the sample survey has been widened even further, so that on present definitions the 1950 U.S. census appears to have understated unemployment by 1·1 per cent.

For pre-war years, the relation of census measures to the regular unemployment series appears to have been different. In 1931, for instance, the U.K. census recorded a smaller number of unemployed than the labor exchange registrations. The degree to which registrations reflect unemployment will depend on the level of unemployment. In the post-war years it has been fairly easy to get jobs, and people changing jobs seldom expect to be unemployed for any length of time. People have less incentive to register than in pre-war years, particularly if they are not entitled to unemployment benefits. In spite of the greater proportion of the post-war population covered by unemployment insurance, the post-war figures may well cover unemployment to a lesser extent than pre-war.[1]

Fortunately, there are long-term series available on a fairly consistent and continuous basis for most of the countries under review. In general, we have selected the measures with the widest possible coverage. In some cases, the sample of the labor force covered by the statistics has changed over time. This is a problem in the period 1913 to 1929 when the scope of unemployment insurance was being widened, but it is not a major difficulty for the 1929–38 period. Insofar as there is bias due to increased coverage, it will be felt in the same direction in all countries, and in any case the proportion of

[1] Cf. H. A. Turner, 'Employment Fluctuations, Labour Supply and Bargaining Power', *Manchester School*, May 1959, for a detailed analysis of the factors affecting the post-war labor market and their effect on unemployment measures.

the labor force which is most subject to the risk of unemployment, i.e. wage and salary earners, has also been increasing over time. For the 1913–29 period we have dealt with the problem of changing coverage by taking the movement in the rate of unemployment shown in the original source (suitably adjusted to link with our 1929 rate), instead of the absolute figure.

The basic sources for most countries were Walter Galenson and Arnold Zellner, 'International Comparison of Unemployment Rates' in *The Measurement and Behavior of Unemployment*, National Bureau of Economic Research, Princeton University Press, 1957, and the *Yearbook of Labour Statistics*, 1945–46, 1956 and 1961 editions, I.L.O., Geneva. These were generally used for the years 1913–28, 1929–36, 1937–52 and 1953–60 respectively.

Belgium
Unemployment insurance registrations. Absolute figures for 1950–60 from I.L.O., based on compulsory insurance scheme. These were linked with the figures of Galenson and Zellner for earlier years, which are based on voluntary insurance. 1913 figure is an extrapolation of the 1910 census figure.

Denmark
Trade union series raised by 50 per cent throughout. This adjustment assumes that the persons excluded from coverage had a lower unemployment risk than the trade unionists. 1929–60 from I.L.O., and 1913–28 from Galenson.

France
The annual series for France are all poor. For pre-war years we have stuck to the census data which are available for 1911, 1921, 1926, 1931 and 1936. We assumed the 1911 figure was valid for 1913, and 1938 was extrapolated from 1936 with the help of data on unemployment registrations. The 1950–60 movement is derived from registration figures of job applicants adjusted upwards by the difference in the unemployment rate shown by the 1954 census and that shown by 1954 registrations.

Germany
1929–60 from German unemployment office registrations, I.L.O. These seem to give a fairly complete coverage of the labor force, as shown by the 1960 microcensus. For 1913–29 the movement in unemployment rates was taken from Galenson's trade union figures.

Italy
1929–53 unemployment registrations from I.L.O. 1913 rate of unemployment assumed to be the same as in 1929. 1954–60, labor force

sample survey figure given in O.E.C.D., *Manpower Statistics*. For 1954–60 the unemployment registrations differ considerably in movement and absolute level from the labor force sample surveys, which show a lower figure. The registration figures are kept by local authorities whose grants from the Central authorities depend partly on the size of their unemployment. For this reason, unemployment is slow to disappear in the local government registers.

Netherlands
1931–38 unemployment registrations from I.L.O. 1950–60, unemployment from O.E.C.D., *Manpower Statistics*. These figures are somewhat higher than the registration series. 1913–31 movement in unemployment rates from Galenson's trade union figures.

Norway
Unemployment registrations and trade union figures are available from I.L.O. for 1929–60. The 1913–29 movement in trade union unemployment rates is available from Galenson. The Norwegian pre-war figures appear to cover a smaller sample of the labor force than in other countries. For our purpose, we do not need to use these figures as a series is available directly on employment.

Sweden
The figures for 1929–55 are trade union registrations from the I.L.O. From 1955–60 they are insured unemployed from the I.L.O. For 1913–29 the movement in unemployment rates is taken from Galenson's trade union figures. From the March 1936 unemployment census it appeared that unemployment was 2·2 times as large as reported by the trade unions; cf. Galenson and Zellner, *op. cit.*, p. 551. Therefore, the 1913–38 series have all been adjusted upwards by this factor. The Labour Market Board has recently been taking labor force sample surveys on the lines of the U.S. enquiries. In 1960 and 1961 the enquiries (for May and August) showed unemployment four and five times as large respectively as the registration figures. The difference was 1 per cent of the labor force in 1960. We can either raise the post-war unemployment rates by 1 per cent or use a proportionate adjustment. We have chosen the former course on the ground that the unemployment registrations probably cover the most volatile kinds of unemployment.

Switzerland
Unemployment registrations from *Annuaire Statistique de la Suisse*, 1946, p. 384, and 1961, p. 365. 1913 is an estimate.

United Kingdom
The 1929–60 figures are the registration series from I.L.O. and

TABLE E-1
UNEMPLOYMENT AS A PROPORTION OF THE LABOR FORCE

	Belgium	Denmark	France	Germany (F.R.)	Italy	Netherlands	Sweden	Switzerland	United Kingdom	Canada	United States
1913	3·1	2·0	1·0	1·9	1·7	1·5	1·1	1·0	1·8	3·0	4·3
1920		1·7		1·7		1·7	1·3		1·8		3·9
1921	6·1	5·1	2·5	1·2		2·6	6·4		9·6	5·8	11·4
1922	1·9	5·1		0·7		3·2	5·5		8·1	4·4	7·2
1923	0·6	3·3		4·5		3·3	2·9		6·6	3·2	3·0
1924	0·6	2·9		5·8		2·6	2·4		5·8	4·5	5·3
1925	0·9	3·9		3·0		2·4	2·6		6·4	4·4	3·8
1926	0·8	5·4	1·1	8·0		2·1	2·9		7·1	3·0	1·9
1927	1·1	5·9		3·9		2·2	2·9		5·5	1·8	3·9
1928	0·6	4·8		3·8	1·7	1·6	2·4		6·1	1·7	4·3
1929	0·8	4·1		5·9	2·5	1·7	2·4	0·4	5·9	2·9	3·1
1930	2·2	3·6	2·1	9·5	4·3	2·3	3·3	0·7	9·3	9·1	8·7
1931	6·8	4·8		13·9	5·8	4·3	4·8	1·2	12·6	11·6	15·8
1932	11·9	8·7		17·2	5·9	8·3	6·8	2·8	13·1	17·6	23·5
1933	10·6	8·3		14·8	5·6	9·7	7·3	3·5	11·7	19·3	24·7
1934	11·8	6·8		8·3		9·8	6·4	3·3	9·9	14·5	21·6
1935	11·1	6·2		6·5		11·2	6·2	4·2	9·2	14·2	20·0
1936	8·4	6·3	4·2	4·8	5·0	11·9	5·3	4·7	7·9	12·8	16·8
1937	7·2	7·5		2·7		10·5	5·1	3·6	6·7	9·1	14·2
1938	8·7	7·5	3·6	1·3	4·6	9·9	5·1	3·3	8·1	11·4	18·9
1950	6·3	4·1	1·4	7·2	8·7	2·0	1·7	0·5	2·5	3·6	5·2
1951	5·7	4·5	1·3	6·4	9·2	2·4	1·6	0·2	2·2	2·4	3·2
1952	6·8	5·9	1·3	6·1	9·8	3·5	1·7	0·3	2·9	2·9	2·9
1953	6·8	4·4	1·6	5·5	10·2	2·5	1·9	0·3	2·6	2·9	2·8
1954	6·2	3·8	1·6	5·2	8·7	1·8	1·8	0·2	2·3	4·5	5·3
1955	4·7	4·7	1·5	3·8	7·5	1·3	1·8	0·1	2·1	4·3	4·2
1956	4·0	5·3	1·2	3·1	9·3	1·0	1·6	0·2	2·2	3·3	4·0
1957	3·2	5·0	1·0	2·7	8·1	1·2	1·7	0·1	2·4	4·5	4·2
1958	5·0	4·7	1·1	2·7	6·4	2·3	2·0	0·2	3·0	6·9	6·6
1959	5·5	3·0	1·3	1·9	5·4	1·8	1·8	0·1	3·1	5·9	5·3
1960	4·4	2·1	1·3	0·9	4·0	1·1	1·6	0·1	2·5	6·9	5·4

include temporary unemployment. 1913–29 movements in unemployment rates from Galenson; his 1920–29 figures are registrations, and the 1913–20 link is from trade union figures. For 1950–60, we have raised the registration figures by 1 per cent because they do not cover all categories of unemployed and the discrepancy from the 1951 census was of this size.

Canada
The figures are adjusted to a labor force sample survey basis through-the period 1920–60. The 1920–31 figures were supplied by Professor M. C. Urquhart and will appear in *Historical Statistics of Canada*. The 1931–38 figures are from the *Canadian Statistical Review*, 1950–60 from I.L.O. The 1913 rate is assumed to have been the same as in the census year 1910, cf. Firestone, *op. cit.*, p. 58.

United States
The figures are adjusted to a labor force sample survey basis throughout the period 1913–60. 1913–38 figures from *Historical Statistics of the U.S.*, 1960 edition, p. 73. 1950–60 figures are the revised series from *Business Statistics*, 1961 edition, U.S. Dept. of Commerce, May 1961, p. 61. The figures are expressed as a proportion of the total labor force, and therefore differ from the percentages of the *civilian* labor force generally quoted in the United States. In a minor respect, the 1913–38 figures are not comparable with those for 1950–60 in that they exclude certain people who are waiting to take up jobs. The 1913–29 percentages differ from those of *Historical Statistics*, partly because the implicit figure of the civilian labor force seems slightly different in that source.

TABLE E–2
COVERAGE OF UNEMPLOYMENT STATISTICS IN 1960

	Per Cent of Labor Force Covered by Regular Unemployment Statistics	Wage and Salary Earners as Per Cent of Total Labor Force
Denmark	32·9	73·8[a]
France		66·8
Germany (F.R.)	79·9	76·6
Italy	100·0	60·8
Netherlands	79·8	78·7
Norway	69·0	71·4
Sweden	41·0	71·9[a]
United Kingdom	90·8	92·5
Canada	100·0	81·2
United States	100·0	83·7

[a] The figures for Denmark and Sweden are for 1955 and 1950 respectively. As the proportion has been increasing in nearly all countries, the 1960 figure was probably about 75 per cent in these two countries.
Source: The coverage of unemployment statistics is given in the I.L.O. *Yearbook* and was simply divided by our labor force figure. The proportion of wage and salary earners is taken from O.E.C.D., *Manpower Statistics*.

TABLE E–3
DIFFERENCE BETWEEN UNEMPLOYMENT RECORDING IN CENSUS
AND REGULAR SERIES

Unit: 000s and Percentages

| | | *Labor* | *Unemployment as Recorded by* | | *Per Cent Unemployed* | |
	Year	*Force*	*Census*	*Regular Series*	*Census*	*Regular Series*
Belgium	1947	3,481	92	97	2·65	2·80
France	1954	19,151	327	206	1·71	1·08
Germany	1960	25,482	130	122	0·51	0·48
Sweden	1961	3,707	50	12·7	1·35	0·34
Switzerland	1950	2,156	9	6·2	0·42	0·29
United Kingdom	1951	23,214	516	281	2·22	1·21
Canada	1951	5,326	92	83	1·73	1·56
United States	1950	64,749	2,832	3,530	4·62[a]	5·45

[a] See note on United States.

Sources:

Belgium: Census of December 31, 1947, *Annuaire Statistique de la Belgique*, 1949. Registered unemployed is a daily average for December from the same source. Labor force from the census.

France: Census of May 10, 1954, *Annuaire Statistique de la France*, 1959. Registrations for May 1st from same source. Labor force from the census.

Germany: Micro-census of October 23–29, 1960, *Wirtschaft und Statistik*, September 1961. Registered unemployed for October from I.L.O. *Yearbook*, 1961. Labor force from the census.

Sweden: The figure of 50,000 is from the average of the May and August 1961 sample survey, *Arbetsmarknadsinformation*, M 7/1961, p. 3. Registered insured unemployed average of May and August 1961 from *Kommersiella Meddelanden*. Labor force from the sample survey.

Switzerland: Census of December 1, 1950, *Annuaire Statistique de la Suisse*, 1958. Registered unemployed for November 30th from the same source. Labor force from the census.

United Kingdom: Census of April 8–9, 1951, *Annual Abstract of Statistics*, 1958. Registered unemployed for April 16th from the same source. Labor force from the census.

Canada: Census of June 2, 1951, Vol. IV and V of *Census of Canada*, 1951. Survey figures for June 2nd from *Canadian Statistical Review*. Labor force from the survey.

United States: Census of April 1, 1950, *Employment and Unemployment*, Hearings, Sub-Committee on Economic Statistics, Joint Economic Committee of U.S. Congress, 77726, p. 237. Survey figures (adjusted) from same source. Labor force from O.E.C.D., *Manpower Statistics*. As the census records a lower figure than the sample survey for both the labor force and unemployment, we have quoted the census rate of unemployment on the basis of the census labor force figure, i.e. 61·3 million instead of 64·7 million.

APPENDIX F

EMPLOYMENT

The employment index was derived by adjusting labor force figures (Table D–2) by the unemployment ratios (Table E–1) for all countries except Norway.

For Norway, the figures for 1913–29 employment are taken from Odd Aukrust and Juul Bjerke, 'Real Capital in Norway 1900–56', p. 42, paper presented to International Association for Research in Income and Wealth, August 1957. Figures for 1938 and 1950–56 are from *Statistical Survey*, 1958, Central Bureau of Statistics, Oslo, 1959, and 1956–60 figures are from the *National Budget of Norway*, 1962, p. 55, Royal Norwegian Ministry of Finance, Oslo, 1961. The figure for 1938 in the source cited has been adjusted upwards by 3 per cent in line with the adjusted figures quoted in the third source.

The figures for Norway are throughout in terms of man-years, i.e. the figures for some industries are adjusted for part-time activity. The same is true of the Dutch figures for 1950–60.

TABLE F–1
EMPLOYMENT (1913 = 100)

	Belgium	Denmark	France	Germany (F.R.)	Italy	Netherlands	Norway	Sweden	Switzerland	United Kingdom	Canada	United States
1870	63·3	63·9	92·3	59·4ª	77·2	59·3	72·0ª	74·0	67·5	62·6	40·8	37·9ª
1880	67·1	69·7	93·2	63·9	83·0	64·7	80·1	82·6	71·5	69·3	50·2	47·6
1890	74·7	74·4	95·6	69·7	87·3	72·4	79·6	82·9	75·4	76·4	58·4	61·8
1900	84·1	84·5	97·7	80·0	91·1	82·0	89·0	88·9	84·4	87·5	66·9	75·7
1913	100·0	100·0	100·0	100·0	100·0	100·0	100·0	100·0	100·0	100·0	100·0	100·0
1929	107·7	115·6	95·7	110·1	105·2	129·7	110·9	120·9	104·8	105·8	131·4	129·0
1938	98·2	135·1	87·0	122·5	105·9	136·0	127·9	121·3	104·2	110·2	138·9	120·1
1950	97·5	148·5	89·2	126·8	105·6	162·0	139·0	131·5	116·9	119·0	166·9	165·4
1951	101·0	149·0	89·5	130·2		162·9	139·1	132·2	118·7	120·7	171·6	172·2
1952	99·3	148·0	89·7	132·6		162·6	139·8	132·6	120·0	120·2	174·5	174·2
1953	99·1	151·5	89·7	135·8		166·1	139·8	132·9	121·5	121·0	177·3	176·4
1954	100·0	153·7	90·0	139·4	114·0	170·7	141·5	133·5	122·8	122·9	177·7	172·9
1955	101·4	153·5	90·2	144·8		174·1	141·9	134·0	124·0	124·4	182·0	177·8
1956	102·1	153·7	90·9	148·4		177·5	142·1	135·2	125·6	125·2	189·3	182·0
1957	103·1	155·4	91·7	151·7		179·5	142·1	136·1	128·0	125·4	194·0	182·7
1958	101·1	157·1	92·0	153·0		178·1	140·8	136·6	129·9	124·0	193·0	179·5
1959	100·4	161·2	92·2	154·9		179·7	140·8	137·8	131·7	124·3	198·1	183·5
1960	101·4	164·0	92·6	157·8	125·5	182·7	142·1	139·1	132·6	126·5	201·4	185·5

ª 1871.

APPENDIX G

WORKING HOURS

WEEKLY WORKING HOURS

For early years the available figures on working hours are mostly based on guesses by writers on social conditions, or on small samples made by such writers. A number of these writers are cited by Colin Clark in *Conditions of Economic Progress*, 3rd edition, Macmillan, London, 1957; for example, on p. 135, he cites a figure of 66 hours per week for Germany in 1885 from Jean's *England's Supremacy*; on p. 159 a figure of seventy-six hours per week for Italy in 1885 from the same source; on p. 146 a figure of 55 hours per week for the United Kingdom in 1886 from Giffen, who thought hours had been 66 per week fifty years earlier. For the United States, more systematic attempts have been made to measure long-term trends in working hours than in Europe, but these also show considerable variations. The latest of these is by John W. Kendrick, *Productivity Trends in the United States*, National Bureau of Economic Research, New York, 1961, p. 310. He gives a figure of 53·7 hours a week in 1869 compared with 52 in 1909. This is quite a different movement from that shown earlier by J. Frederic Dewhurst, *America's Needs and Resources*, Twentieth Century Fund, New York, 1955, p. 1073, who gives a figure of 65·4 hours a week in 1870 and 55·1 in 1910. The difference between Dewhurst and Kendrick arises almost entirely from widely differing figures for agriculture, Kendrick giving a figure of 45·9 for 1869, and Dewhurst a figure of 70 for 1870. For non-agriculture, the discrepancy is much smaller but in the opposite direction—Dewhurst shows 60 hours in 1870 and Kendrick 62·7. Both figures for agriculture are based on rough estimates rather than surveys. Because of the uncertainty surrounding these rather arbitrary figures, we have assumed that the movement in working hours from 1870 to 1913 was the same in all our countries. This is probably a reasonable assumption, for in the period for which our information is better, i.e. from 1929 to 1960, the long-run movements in many of our countries have been rather similar. For 1870 we have assumed that working hours were 63 per week, and for 1913 53·8 per week. The latter figure is

P

derived from the extensive *Hours and Earnings Inquiry* (published between 1909 and 1913) carried out by the Board of Trade in the United Kingdom. The figure refers to weekly hours in manufacturing (exclusive of mealtimes and overtime) in September 1906. The figures in Table G–2 for years between 1870 and 1913 are interpolations.

Most of the evidence on working hours refers to industrial workers. Data on other sections of the labor force are seldom available except for the United States. For the purposes of measuring long-term movements, these manufacturing figures provide a reasonable approximation. But their cyclical amplitude is probably wider than in the economy as a whole. Hence the drop in U.S. working hours to 35·6 in 1938 should be treated with reserve in making productivity measures.

Belgium
No data available. Movement assumed to be parallel to that in the Netherlands.

Denmark
Movement from 1913 to 1938 derived from K. Bjerke, *op. cit.*, p. 128. 1950–60 figures on annual working hours derived from *Statistiske Efterretninger* and supplements; these figures include an allowance for holidays. The figures in Table G–2 are adjusted to exclude the effect of the holiday changes.

France
All figures from I.L.O. *Yearbooks*. 1929 assumed to be same as 1930, and is for industry excluding building; the 1938–60 figures cover industry, building, commerce, transport and services.

Germany
1929 (industry including building) and 1938 (industry excluding building), figures from I.L.O. *Yearbook* 1945–46. 1950–60 (manufacturing), figures from I.L.O. *Yearbooks*.

Italy
1929 and 1938 (industry) from I.L.O. *Yearbook* 1945–46, p. 86, midpoint of range cited. 1950–60 (manufacturing) from I.L.O. *Yearbooks*, figure for daily hours multiplied by 5·25.

Netherlands
All figures (manufacturing) from I.L.O. *Yearbooks*. The post-war figures are for adult males and they have been reduced by the ratio of adult male to total working hours which prevailed in 1938. The 1929 figure is an estimate based on the movement in the I.L.O. figure for 'normal' hours between 1929 and 1938.

Norway
1929 assumed to be the same as Sweden. 1938–60 (manufacturing) from I.L.O. *Yearbooks*. 1957–60 is a weighted average of figures for males and females.

Sweden
All figures from I.L.O. *Yearbooks*. 1929 figure is for industry. 1938–60 (manufacturing) monthly figures linked to previous weekly figures at 1938.

United Kingdom
1913 figure as cited above. 1929 is an average of the figure for 1924 (October) and 1935 (October) from Board of Trade inquiries. 1938 from *Annual Abstract of Statistics* 1952, p. 124. 1950–60 average of April and October figures for industry, transport and services, *Ministry of Labour Gazette*, September 1958, p. 331, and *Statistics on Incomes, Prices, Employment and Production*, No. 1, April 1962, p. 68.

Canada
1929 hours for the 'business' sector from W. C. Hood and A. Scott, *Output, Labour and Capital in the Canadian Economy*, Ottawa, 1957, p. 202. 1938–60 for manufacturing from I.L.O. *Yearbooks*.

United States
1929–60, the U.S. Bureau of Labor Statistics series for manufacturing from I.L.O. *Yearbooks*. A more comprehensive figure including agriculture is available for the post-war years in the monthly reports on the labor force, but we preferred the manufacturing series as it is similar to the figures used for other countries. In any case, the more comprehensive series shows a very similar movement from 1950 to 1960.

HOLIDAYS

There is very little historical information available on holidays except for the United Kingdom. The results of the Board of Trade enquiries on hours and holidays are summarized in A. Maddison, 'Output, Employment and Productivity in British Manufacturing in the Last Half Century', *Bulletin of the Oxford University Institute of Statistics*, No. 4, 1955. In 1906 the average number of holidays in British manufacturing was 11·2 days, including public holidays; in 1948 it was about 15 days and in 1957 about 18 days. For recent years, cf. 'L'Evolution des Charges Sociales et des Coûts de Main-d'Oeuvre', *Etudes et Conjoncture*, I.N.S.E.E., Paris, August

TABLE G-1

NUMBER OF WORKING WEEKS PER YEAR

	Belgium	Denmark	France	Germany (F.R.)	Italy	Netherlands	Norway	Sweden	Switzerland	United Kingdom	Canada	United States
1870	51·0	50·3	50·3	50·3	49·3	51·0	50·3	50·2	51·0	51·0	50·7	50·7
1913	50·0	49·3	49·3	49·3	48·3	50·0	49·3	49·2	50·0	50·0	49·7	49·7
1929	49·7	48·8	48·8	49·1	48·1	49·7	48·8	48·7	49·7	49·7	49·3	49·3
1938	49·5	48·3	48·3	48·8	47·8	49·5	48·3	48·2	49·5	49·5	48·9	48·9
1950	49·2	47·8	47·8	48·6	47·6	49·2	47·8	47·7	49·2	49·2	48·5	48·5
1960	48·8	47·2	47·2	48·2	47·2	48·8	47·2	47·0	48·8	48·8	48·0	48·0

TABLE G-2

WEEKLY WORKING HOURS

	Denmark	France	Germany (F.R.)	Italy	Netherlands	Norway	Sweden	Switzerland	United Kingdom	Canada	United States
1870	63·0	63·0	63·0	63·0	63·0	63·0	63·0	63·0	63·0	63·0	63·0
1880	60·6	60·6	60·6	60·6	60·6	60·6	60·6	60·6	60·6	60·6	60·6
1890	58·4	58·4	58·4	58·4	58·4	58·4	58·4	58·4	58·4	58·4	58·4
1900	56·3	56·3	56·3	56·3	56·3	56·3	56·3	56·3	56·3	56·3	56·3
1913	53·8	53·8	53·8	53·8	53·8	53·8	53·8	53·8	53·8	53·8	53·8
1929	47·6	48·0	46·0	47·5	46·9	47·7	47·7	48·0	46·9	49·8	44·2
1938	47·6	38·7	48·5	41·3	46·8	44·7	46·3	46·3	46·5	46·7	35·6
1950	46·6	45·0	48·2	41·8	48·2	44·4	46·3	47·5	45·9	42·3	40·5
1951	46·0	45·2	47·4	42·4	47·9	44·3	46·0	47·8	45·2	41·8	40·7
1952	46·0	44·9	47·5	42·4	48·0	44·0	46·0	47·7	45·9	41·5	40·7
1953	45·8	44·8	48·0	42·5	48·3	44·8	45·5	47·7	45·9	41·3	40·5
1954	46·0	45·2	48·7	42·5	48·3	44·0	45·8	47·7	46·3	40·7	39·7
1955	46·0	45·7	48·8	42·6	48·5	(43·8)	45·0	47·7	46·9	41·0	40·7
1956	45·7	46·0	47·8	42·1	48·4	(43·7)	45·0	47·7	46·7	41·0	40·4
1957	45·6	45·6	46·4	42·2	48·1	43·5	45·0	47·4	46·5	40·4	39·8
1958	45·4	45·5	45·5	42·1	48·0	43·9	44·2	46·8	46·1	40·2	39·2
1959	44·8	45·9	45·6	42·3	48·3	42·5	43·4	46·6	46·5	40·7	40·3
1960	44·4		45·6	42·4		42·0	43·4	46·1	46·1	40·4	39·7

8, 1957, p. 863, which provides a guide to the situation in most European countries. The situation was as follows for 1957: Belgium 18 days (annual vacation 12, public holidays 6), Denmark 28 days (18 plus 10), France 28 days (18 plus 10), Germany 22 days (12 plus 10), Italy 28 days (12 plus 16), Netherlands 18 days (12 plus 6), Norway 28 days (18 plus 10), Sweden 29 days (18 plus 11), Switzerland 18 days (12 plus 6), United Kingdom 18 days (12 plus 6). Estimates for Canada and the United States for 1957 were derived from *Canada Yearbook*, 1959, p. 749, and *Statistical Abstract of the United States*, 1959, p. 232. For both these countries the 1957 figure appears to have been 23 days (15 plus 8). It has been assumed that there were no annual vacations in 1870, but that the number of public holidays has been constant over the whole period. For 1913 it was assumed that workers had one week's vacation. This fits in well with what we know of the United Kingdom, i.e. it implies 12 days in 1913 as compared with the British survey figure of 11·2 in 1906. It was assumed that a quarter of the increase in annual vacations was obtained from 1913 to 1929, another quarter from 1929 to 1938, a quarter from 1938 to 1950, and another quarter from 1950 to 1957. It was assumed that holidays increased by one day between 1957 and 1960 in all countries.

APPENDIX H

PRODUCTIVITY

The table on output per man (H–1) is derived by dividing the output series (Table A–2) by the employment figures (Table F–1). The first table on output per man-hour (H–2) is derived by adjusting Table H–1 for changes in annual working hours per man (i.e. the product of Tables G–1 and G–2).

The alternative table on output per man-hour (H–3) is based on the assumption that the labor force moved in the same way as the population of working age. Table D–2 is adjusted by the unemployment ratios of Table E–1 to provide the estimate of employment. This is then adjusted for changes in working hours and divided into the output index (Table A–2).

The significance of these productivity indices is described in Chapter I.

TABLE H–1
OUTPUT PER MAN (1913 = 100)

	Belgium	Denmark	France	Germany (F.R.)	Italy	Netherlands	Norway	Sweden	Switzerland	United Kingdom	Canada	United States
1870	50·2	40·4	55·4	50·5[a]	71·0		56·8[a]	38·5		62·5	49·5	44·6[a]
1880		47·9	61·7	60·6	72·5			45·2		65·1	59·0	
1890		60·6	75·5	73·6	71·7			54·3	76·9	90·4	65·1	67·2
1900		74·2	90·0	85·5	77·3	91·5	80·9	70·1		98·1	74·6	79·8
1913	100·0	100·0	100·0	100·0	100·0	100·0	100·0	100·0	100·0	100·0	100·0	100·0
1929	118·7	116·0	136·5	96·5	126·3	130·1	140·8	101·6	147·4	121·6	111·6	126·7
1938	124·2	118·8	125·7	122·4	145·2	125·2	158·7	127·5	156·0	143·6	103·5	136·0
1950	149·7	145·5	146·1	124·1	153·2	133·8	191·3	171·1	175·4	159·4	167·0	177·1
1951	152·9	144·8	154·4	133·5		136·8	197·5	169·4	183·6	162·6	172·2	181·6
1952	154·1	147·7	158·0	142·0		139·9	204·1	173·7	185·7	162·9	182·9	187·1
1953	160·6	153·3	162·8	149·0		149·0	212·2	179·5	194·0	168·6	187·0	192·4
1954	166·5	149·8	170·1	156·0		155·2	219·1	190·3	207·2	172·5	181·0	193·2
1955	169·3	150·2	179·6	167·5	189·6	164·0	223·5	196·6	217·9	175·9	192·0	203·0
1956	174·3	159·5	187·1	174·7		167·3	234·0	201·0	226·9	179·4	200·6	202·0
1957	177·0	166·6	196·6	180·1		169·5	239·0	207·4	231·1	181·8	198·2	205·3
1958	177·3	169·0	199·3	184·4		171·7	240·6	208·6	232·3	183·3	201·8	205·7
1959	185·2	173·9	203·7	194·3		180·4	250·1	216·8	240·3	188·5	202·4	214·7
1960	191·0	182·1	215·8	207·5	229·4	192·0	263·0	223·6	254·4	193·1	203·0	217·3

[a] 1871.

TABLE H-2
OUTPUT PER MAN-HOUR (1913 = 100)

	Belgium	Denmark	France	Germany (F.R.)	Italy	Netherlands	Norway	Sweden	Switzerland	United Kingdom	Canada	United States
1870	42·1	33·8	46·3	42·3[a]	59·4		47·6[a]	32·2		52·3	41·5	37·3[a]
1880		41·9	53·9	52·9	63·4			39·5		56·9	51·6	61·2
1890		55·3	68·8	67·1	65·3			49·5	70·1	82·5	59·3	75·8
1900		70·4	85·4	81·2	73·4	86·9	76·8	66·6		93·2	70·9	
1913	100·0	100·0	100·0	100·0	100·0	100·0	100·0	100·0	100·0	100·0	100·0	100·0
1929	137·0	132·5	154·6	113·2	143·7	150·2	160·4	115·7	166·3	140·3	121·5	155·5
1938	144·2	137·1	178·5	137·1	191·1	145·4	194·8	151·1	183·1	167·9	121·2	208·8
1950	169·8	173·3	180·2	140·4	200·0	151·8	239·0	205·1	201·9	189·9	217·6	241·2
1951	174·7	174·9	189·8	153·8		156·3	247·6	204·8	210·1	192·6	227·3	246·2
1952	175·9	178·6	195·7	163·5		159·6	257·9	210·1	213·2	194·4	243·5	254·0
1953	182·4	186·4	202·2	169·8		169·1	263·6	219·8	223·0	199·6	250·4	262·7
1954	189·0	181·5	210·0	175·4		176·2	277·6	232·0	238·2	203·1	246·2	269·4
1955	191·6	182·3	221·0	188·1	243·9	185·7	284·8	241·4	250·9	205·8	259·5	276·3
1956	198·0	195·2	228·9	200·5		189·8	299·3	250·0	261·5	211·1	271·5	277·2
1957	202·3	204·5	239·4	213·1		193·8	307·4	258·3	268·2	214·9	272·5	286·5
1958	203·3	208·6	244·9	222·7		196·9	307·1	265·1	273·0	218·8	279·0	291·6
1959	211·0	217·8	251·4	234·2		205·7	330·1	281·1	284·1	223·4	276·6	296·5
1960	218·1	230·5	264·3	250·3	297·7	219·1	351·6	290·1	304·1	230·9	279·8	304·9

a 1871.

TABLE H–3
ALTERNATIVE INDEX OF OUTPUT PER MAN-HOUR (1913 = 100)[a]

	Belgium	Denmark	France	Germany (F.R.)	Italy	Netherlands	Sweden	Switzerland	United Kingdom	Canada	United States
1913	100·0	100·0	100·0	100·0	100·0	100·0	100·0	100·0	100·0	100·0	100·0
1929	128·3	123·8	146·4	111·3	133·3	147·0	120·4	155·7	137·8	121·6	154·4
1938	129·0	139·9	161·6	136·4	169·8	141·8	148·9	166·8	165·2	109·5	209·1
1950	144·6	176·4	161·1	129·6	162·6	143·1	198·6	184·9	186·5	211·9	252·2
1951	152·9	178·6	169·8	142·7		147·3	198·1	193·0	191·0	222·5	260·4
1952	152·7	183·2	175·4	152·5		150·9	203·1	196·0	193·5	237·9	268·7
1953	157·6	191·8	181·6	159·1		160·6	213·1	205·5	199·2	243·6	279·3
1954	163·9	187·2	188·5	165·4		169·3	225·0	220·3	205·0	238·8	286·2
1955	165·9	188·6	198·5	178·6		179·2	233·9	232·3	210·0	252·5	296·3
1956	171·3	202·5	206·4	190·4		184·5	242·4	242·6	217·0	267·1	301·1
1957	175·5	213·1	216·4	204·3		188·9	251·2	249·4	221·8	270·4	309·2
1958	176·1	217·3	221·2	213·2		190·3	256·8	254·6	223·9	276·6	313·7
1959	182·6	226·0	226·5	223·6		197·2	271·9	265·3	227·9	273·0	317·7
1960	188·2	223·5	237·9	239·5	255·7	209·6	280·2	284·9	237·4	278·3	328·8

[a] For the years 1870–1913, the estimates do not differ from Table H–2.

APPENDIX I

INVESTMENT

We have attempted to give figures on investment which are as comparable between countries as possible. Thanks to the O.E.E.C., the post-war estimates are available in a standardized form, although there are still some differences in accounting practice which have led us to adjust the figures for Norway and the United States. The two major areas of ambiguity are the treatment of repairs and maintenance, and the distinction between consumption and investment in purchases of motor vehicles. The cases we have adjusted happened to be extremes; there may well be minor discrepancies in other cases which have passed unnoticed.

Repairs and Maintenance

In Scandinavian national accounting practice, repairs and maintenance are treated as capital formation, and the O.E.E.C. deducts this in order to conform with the standardized system. The deductions for Denmark and Sweden are about a third of capital formation, whereas for Norway the deduction is only about a quarter.[1] These are the adjustments suggested by the authorities of the countries concerned. It could be that the ratio of repair and maintenance in Norway is, in fact, lower than in the other two countries in view of the higher level of total investment,[2] but it is more likely to represent a different interpretation of the standardized system which allows for the inclusion of work on major alterations. It is likely that some allowance has been made for these in Norway but not in the other two countries. In the U.K. national accounts, all repair and maintenance work is excluded, and only new construction is treated as capital formation. In earlier years, the United Kingdom treated repairs to buildings and works as capital formation (but not machinery repairs), and at that time these construction repairs

---

[1] It appears from *Statistics of National Product and Expenditure*, No. 2, O.E.E.C., 1957, that the Danish allowance for machinery and equipment is about a quarter, and for construction it is over 40 per cent. In Norway, all investment is reduced by a quarter.

[2] Investment in construction is, however, as high in Sweden as in Norway, and it is this part of the Norwegian estimates which we are querying.

amounted to about 29 per cent of total fixed capital formation and about 47 per cent of total construction expenditures (cf. *National Income and Expenditure of the United Kingdom, 1946 to 1950*, Cmd. 8203, H.M.S.O., London, April 1951, p. 15). In the United States, additions and alterations to non-farm dwellings are treated as capital formation (cf. *National Income*, 1954 edition, Dept. of Commerce, Washington, 1954, p. 125), which raises the investment ratio for the United States *vis-à-vis* the United Kingdom. We have not attempted to adjust for this as we are not primarily interested in residential construction, but alterations and additions have usually been 10 per cent or more of U.S. residential investment, and in the early 1930s were as much as 30 per cent.

Motor Vehicles

The allocation of motor vehicle purchases between investment and consumption must always be pretty arbitrary, the practice will depend to some extent on tax regulations. In the United Kingdom, 30 per cent of passenger cars are assumed to go to investment, and U.S. practice appears to be similar. For other countries we have no information on the conventions used, but it is possible that there are wide variations. Some check on these possibilities can be derived by considering the ratio of transport equipment to total machinery and equipment investment. From the U.N. *Yearbook of National Accounts Statistics*, 1960, it appears that in 1959 this was 29·3 per cent in Austria, 26·2 per cent in Denmark, 29·2 per cent in Italy, 36·3 per cent in the Netherlands, 60·6 per cent in Norway, 37·8 per cent in Sweden, 31·9 per cent in the United Kingdom, and 26·8 per cent in Canada. The high ratio in Norway is largely due to purchases of ships and boats, but the figures suggest that Sweden and the Netherlands may include more cars as investment than other countries.

We have attempted to break down capital formation into inventories, residential construction, other construction, and machinery and equipment. This was possible for most countries for 1950–60, but for pre-war years the country coverage is more limited. For 1950–60 the information is derived from the O.E.C.D. bulletin, *General Statistics*, September 1962. For 1938 data are from *Statistics of National Product and Expenditure, 1938, and 1947 to 1955*, O.E.E.C., Paris, 1957. Our figures show gross investment as a ratio of G.N.P. at market prices. Inventory changes are the value of the physical change and exclude value changes in the existing level of stocks. All figures are in current prices.

Denmark

1870–1938, derived from K. Bjerke and N. Ussing, *op. cit.*,

pp. 146-7 and 150-1. The figures show investment as a proportion of G.N.P. at market prices. Bjerke and Ussing give figures
separately for construction and for machinery and transport equipment. The figures refer to the O.E.E.C. standardized concept, i.e.,
excluding repair and maintenance expenditures. No figures are given
for inventories which are included with consumption. We have
assumed that the ratio of inventories to output in pre-war years was
the same as for 1950-60, i.e., 48·5 per cent of G.N.P.

Germany
1925-38, derived from Ferdinand Grünig, 'Die Anfänge der
Volkswirtschaftlichen Gesamtrechnung in Deutschland', *Beiträge
zur empirischen Konjunkturforschung*, Duncker and Humblot,
Berlin, 1950, pp. 76, 79, 80 and 95. Grünig reproduces the estimates
of the German Statistical Office for residential and other types of
investment by industry for 1924-34. The figures for inventories
include valuation changes in existing stocks as well as the value of
physical changes, so that they are not suitable for our purpose. For
1935-37 his figures are given only for total fixed investment (p. 80);
data on residential investment 1935-40 are given in *Statistisches
Handbuch von Deutschland*, Länderrat des Amerikanischen Besat-
zungsgebiets, München, 1949, p. 606. Our ratios show investment
as a proportion of G.N.P. at current market prices. Grünig gives
figures for national income at factor cost (p. 76) for 1925-41, and we
have assumed that the ratio of this to G.N.P. at market prices was
the same as in 1936 (ratio of 1·255 : 1). We have assumed that the
ratio of inventories to output in pre-war years was the same as for
1950-60, i.e., 35·5 per cent of G.N.P.

Italy
1870-1938, derived from *Annali di Statistica, op. cit.*, pp. 264-5.
A breakdown is given for residential construction, public works,
inventories and other investment. The figures are the same in
coverage as in the O.E.E.C. standardized system. Our figures show
gross investment as a ratio of G.N.P. at market prices.

Norway
1900-1938, derived from *National Accounts 1900-1929*, Norges
Offisielle Statistikk, XI. 143, Central Bureau of Statistics, Oslo,
1953, p. 106. The original estimates of total fixed investment have
been adjusted downwards by a third to eliminate repair and maintenance expenditures. A breakdown is given for construction, ships and
boats, other equipment and inventories. Our figures show gross
investment as a ratio of G.N.P. at market prices. 1950-60, O.E.C.D.
figures for construction, which are adjusted downwards by about a
quarter, were further adjusted to bring the total correction for

repairs and maintenance to 45 per cent of gross expenditures on construction, in line with practice elsewhere in Scandinavia and in the United Kingdom.

Sweden

1870–1938, derived from *Sveriges Nationalprodukt, 1861–1951*, Konjunkturinstitutet, Stockholm, 1956, pp. 45–52. Swedish figures include repair and maintenance which we have eliminated by a downward adjustment of 30 per cent. A breakdown is given for construction and other investment. No figures are available on inventories. It is suggested that the data on construction prior to 1896 are very unreliable (*op. cit.*, pp. 37 and 41). They certainly seem to be too low, as the ratio of all fixed investment to G.N.P. is only 5·5 per cent for 1870–79, 6·5 per cent for 1880–89, and 8·2 per cent for 1890–99. In view of this, the earlier data are not used here. Our figures show the ratio of gross investment to G.D.P. at market prices. We have assumed that the ratio of inventories to output in pre-war years was the same as for 1950–60, i.e., 33·3 per cent of G.N.P.

United Kingdom

Fixed investment ratios for 1870–1949 taken from P. Deane and W. A. Cole, *British Economic Growth 1688–1959*, Cambridge University Press, 1962, pp. 332–3. The figures of Deane and Cole are derived from the estimates of C. Feinstein, who has kindly supplied me with figures for residential investment which we have used for the period 1870–1913. Jefferys and Walters, *op. cit.*, is used for inventories; these were calculated simply by taking 40 per cent of the first difference in the year-to-year change in national income.

For 1925–38, our estimates of residential construction are derived from Phelps Brown and Bernard Weber, 'Accumulation, Productivity and Distribution in the British Economy, 1870–1938', *Economic Journal*, June 1953. We have used the Phelps Brown index of building costs (p. 287) and figures on residential building from Svennilson, *op. cit.*, p. 242, to construct an estimate of the value of residential construction, which we linked to the 1913 figures of A. K. Cairncross, *Home and Foreign Investment 1870–1913*, Cambridge University Press, 1953. Investment in machinery and equipment is taken from Phelps Brown and Weber, *op. cit.* Non-residential construction is derived as a residual. All of these figures appear to exclude both repairs *and renewals* (cf. Cairncross, *op. cit.*, p. 121). This is also true of the U.K. estimates for 1950–60. It is therefore likely that U.K. investment may be understated relative to other countries. However, this understatement is likely to be small, i.e., less than 0·5 per cent of G.N.P. and is offset by the fact that U.K. construction investment costs are raised by rather high stamp duties.

Canada

Firestone, *op. cit.*, pp. 100 and 114, gives figures for fixed investment and inventories (both excluding public investment) for 1870, 1890, 1900. The figures are: fixed investment, 11·8 per cent, 13·9 per cent and 12·2 per cent of G.N.P. at market prices; and inventories, 3·1 per cent, 1·6 per cent and 1·3 per cent, respectively. Our 1900–13 average is derived from K. Buckley, *Capital Formation in Canada*, 1896–1930, p. 135, who gives a ratio of (private) investment (including inventories) of 22·7 per cent for 1901–05, 27·0 per cent for 1906–10, and 26·9 per cent for 1911–15. Our 1920 figure is from Firestone. 1926–38, ratios relative to G.N.P. are derived from *National Accounts, Income and Expenditure 1926–56*, D.B.S., Ottawa, pp. 98, 32 and 60; these figures include government fixed investment (government inventories not included).

United States

Gross fixed investment, minus military construction and munitions, from Simon Kuznets, *Capital in the American Economy*, National Bureau of Economic Research, 1961, pp. 490, 494. For the years before the first world war, Kuznets' estimates are available in Kendrick, *op. cit.*, pp. 296–7. These are expressed as a ratio of G.N.P. at market prices (Dept. of Commerce concept with an upward adjustment for depreciation on government property from Goldsmith, *op. cit.*, pp. 993, 1023, 1045 and 1063). Figures on private residential investment for 1889–1913 are from Goldsmith, *op. cit.*, pp. 619 and 623, and for 1920–38 the figures on private non-farm residential construction are from *Historical Statistics of the U.S.* (1960 edition), p. 379. Figures on farm and public residential construction are available only for 1929–38 (cf. *National Income*, 1954 Edition, Dept. of Commerce, 1954, pp. 208–9). We have not included this in residential construction as figures are not available on a comparable basis for earlier years, but it was generally only about 5 per cent of non-farm residential construction. Figures on inventories are from Kendrick for 1889–1929, and Dept. of Commerce for 1929–38. They refer only to business inventories and exclude government stock formation. For 1938–60 O.E.C.D. figures on investment have been used. The O.E.C.D. has adjusted the Dept. of Commerce figures to include government non-war construction and government inventories, and includes farm and public residential construction in the residential sector. However, the O.E.C.D. figures do not include government equipment purchases and we have adjusted them to include this. We have Kuznets' figures up to 1955, and for 1956–60, we have assumed that government equipment purchases amounted to $5 billion a year.

TABLE I–1
GROSS DOMESTIC INVESTMENT AS A PROPORTION OF G.N.P. AT CURRENT PRICES, 1870–1924

	Total Fixed Investment						Inventories			Residential Construction		
	Denmark	Italy	Norway	Sweden	United Kingdom	United States	Italy	Norway	United States	Italy	United Kingdom	United States
1870–79ᵃ		8·2			8·0	20·0	0·5		2·0	1·7		4·0
1880–89ᵃ		11·3			6·1	18·8	0·4		2·3	2·6		1·8
1890–99ᵃ		8·9			6·9	18·2	−3·3		3·2	2·0		2·3
1900	14·5	10·0	13·0	11·2	9·4	20·1	3·3	−0·7	1·8	2·5	1·6	2·8
1901	12·7	10·1	12·4	10·5	9·1	19·1	6·0	−0·6	1·9	2·6	1·6	3·3
1902	14·1	10·2	11·9	10·6	9·4	18·3	1·6	−0·4	0·9	2·7	1·7	3·2
1903	13·4	10·0	11·3	11·1	9·2	18·7	2·7	−0·6	2·1	2·7	1·6	3·6
1904	13·3	10·6	12·0	12·1	8·8	19·7	2·1	−0·4	2·9	3·0	1·4	3·7
1905	12·2	12·4	11·3	10·9	8·1	20·4	0·0	−0·3	1·5	2·9	1·3	3·6
1906	15·0	14·1	12·6	10·8	7·5	18·6	−0·9	−0·4	−1·0	2·9	1·3	3·6
1907	15·2	15·6	13·8	12·7	6·6	18·5	4·7	−0·4	3·1	2·7	1·2	3·6
1908	13·4	17·5	13·8	11·3	5·4	18·8	−0·6	−0·5	1·9	2·5	1·0	3·6
1909	12·6	16·9	12·4	10·4	5·4	16·9	3·0	−0·1	1·4	2·6	1·0	3·3
1910	12·0	16·6	13·1	11·2	5·3	17·6	−2·3	−0·1	2·3	1·7	0·8	3·3
1911	11·7	14·9	15·1	10·9	5·0	18·5	2·6	−0·2	2·2	1·9	0·7	3·2
1912	12·3	14·9	15·6	10·4	5·2		2·2	−0·2		1·9	0·5	
1913	12·6	14·1	15·1	11·4	6·0		3·5	−0·3			0·5	
1920		13·0	21·1	13·6	9·1	14·0	1·2	2·3	8·3	0·9		2·3
1921	10·1	11·6	18·1	11·1	9·1	13·5	−1·9	−1·2	0·1	1·1		2·8
1922	10·4	13·4	13·4	9·2	8·7	16·2	0·0	0·7	0·7	1·5		4·5
1923	10·5	14·6	13·6	11·4	8·0	17·9	2·5	0·4	3·5	2·8		5·1
1924	10·7	17·9	13·3	11·8	8·3	18·3	1·3	−0·2	−1·1	2·2	1·4	5·8

ᵃ average.

TABLE I–2

TOTAL GROSS DOMESTIC FIXED ASSET FORMATION AS A PROPORTION OF G.N.P. AT CURRENT PRICES, 1925–60

	Belgium	Denmark	France	Germany (F.R.)	Italy	Netherlands	Norway	Sweden	United Kingdom	Canada	United States
1925		10·1		13·7	18·9		13·4	11·4	9·1		19·3
1926		9·6		13·6	19·2		12·8	11·8	8·4	15·7	19·2
1927		9·4		14·6	17·5		11·6	11·6	8·7	17·4	18·8
1928		9·6		14·5	16·7		13·6	12·4	8·9	19·2	18·4
1929		10·7		12·7	17·2		14·3	12·7	8·8	21·9	17·6
1930		13·6		11·8	17·6		15·2	13·4	8·9	20·1	15·9
1931		13·6		8·9	15·8		14·5	14·3	8·5	17·1	13·0
1932		10·3		7·5	13·3		11·8	12·1	7·3	11·6	9·3
1933		11·5		8·7	14·4		12·0	11·0	7·2	9·1	8·8
1934		12·6		12·3	15·6		12·9	13·8	8·6	10·1	10·5
1935		12·3		15·1	17·1		14·3	16·2	9·1	11·4	11·3
1936		11·9		16·7	18·5		15·6	16·5	9·9	12·3	14·5
1937		12·0		17·0	16·9		17·9	18·7	10·6	15·4	14·8
1938		12·2			15·9		17·8	18·9	11·5	14·3	14·0
1950	16·5	15·0	15·9	18·8	17·4	20·1	24·1	18·9	12·8	21·5	19·0
1951	13·8	15·5	16·9	18·9	18·3	19·3	21·4	18·3	12·8	21·6	17·8
1952	14·4	16·3	16·8	19·1	19·5	18·6	23·0	18·9	13·3	21·6	17·2
1953	14·9	16·3	16·1	20·1	19·1	20·8	25·8	20·7	13·9	22·9	17·4
1954	15·8	16·9	16·4	21·0	19·5	21·0	26·2	20·9	14·2	22·5	17·4
1955	15·5	15·4	17·5	23·0	19·9	22·5	26·5	19·9	14·6	22·5	18·0
1956	16·6	15·9	17·9	22·9	20·5	24·9	24·4	20·0	14·9	25·7	18·2
1957	17·2	16·3	18·9	21·8	21·5	25·6	25·2	19·9	15·4	26·9	18·7
1958	16·3	16·8	18·4	22·0	20·3	22·4	28·7	20·9	15·2	25·2	18·4
1959	17·2	18·0	17·8	23·0	20·7	23·2	26·5	21·7	15·5	23·9	17·3
1960	17·5	19·1	17·4	24·0	22·3	23·4	24·9	21·9	16·2	22·7	17·6

TABLE I–3
VALUE OF PHYSICAL CHANGE IN INVENTORIES AS A PROPORTION OF G.N.P. AT CURRENT PRICES, 1925–60

	Belgium	Denmark	France	Germany (F.R.)	Italy	Netherlands	Norway	Sweden	United Kingdom	Canada	United States
1925					1·8		0·1				1·9
1926					−1·0		0·3			2·6	1·5
1927					−2·5		0·1			4·6	0·4
1928					3·6		0·0			2·6	−0·4
1929					1·8		−0·2			0·9	1·6
1930					−2·7		2·1			1·3	−0·4
1931					−1·8		−0·8			−2·0	−1·7
1932					1·0		0·4			−2·6	−4·4
1933					−0·9		0·2			−2·6	−2·8
1934					−1·3		1·0			0·8	−1·7
1935					2·1		1·5			0·9	1·2
1936					−1·9		0·9			−1·6	1·2
1937					2·7		1·0			0·2	2·4
1938					1·5		1·0			1·1	−1·0
1950	0·0	4·4	3·4	3·8	1·4	6·3	1·8	−0·6	−1·6	2·6	2·2
1951	1·4	0·6	2·0	3·3	2·2	5·0	4·9	3·2	3·9	3·8	3·6
1952	0·9	−0·1	1·7	4·2	−0·1	−1·4	2·7	2·8	0·3	2·1	1·3
1953	0·4	1·8	0·8	1·4	0·3	−0·8	−0·3	−1·6	0·7	2·0	1·2
1954	0·7	1·4	1·4	2·2	0·3	3·7	0·9	0·1	0·3	−0·9	0·1
1955	−0·1	0·0	1·0	3·4	1·4	2·1	0·4	2·3	1·6	0·9	1·8
1956	0·8	1·5	2·1	2·2	0·7	2·2	2·3	1·5	1·3	3·4	1·0
1957	1·2	2·2	1·8	2·5	0·5	2·6	1·0	2·3	1·0	0·7	0·2
1958	0·1	−0·4	2·3	1·7	0·6	0·2	−1·0	−0·1	0·4	−0·9	−0·1
1959	−0·2	2·6	0·9	1·8	0·8	0·7	−1·3	−0·5	0·7	1·2	1·4
1960	0·6	3·3	2·0	2·8	1·5	3·3	1·3	2·4	2·3	0·9	0·8

TABLE I-4
GROSS RESIDENTIAL INVESTMENT AS A PROPORTION OF G.N.P. AT CURRENT PRICES, 1925–60

	Belgium	Denmark	France	Germany (F.R.)	Italy	Netherlands	Norway	Sweden	United Kingdom[a]	Canada	United States[b]
1925				2·3	2·7				1·7		6·0
1926				2·5	2·4				2·2	3·9	5·7
1927				3·0	2·0				2·3	3·7	5·3
1928				3·0	2·0				1·7	3·6	4·8
1929				3·0	2·9				1·9	3·7	3·4
1930				2·8	3·4				1·7	3·3	2·3
1931				1·7	3·3				2·0	3·4	2·0
1932				1·3	2·6				2·0	2·4	1·1
1933				1·5	2·4				2·5	2·1	0·8
1934				2·0	3·0				2·8	2·3	0·9
1935				2·1	3·9				2·9	2·5	1·4
1936				2·7	3·6				2·9	2·8	1·9
1937				2·3	2·4				2·9	3·1	2·0
1938				2·1	1·9				2·8	2·8	2·3
1950	5·0	2·8	2·3	4·5	2·6	3·9	3·4	4·9	2·5	4·9	5·3
1951	3·4	2·8	2·9	4·5	3·0	3·6	3·2	4·5	2·6	4·2	4·2
1952	3·6	2·9	3·5	4·6	3·6	3·8	3·6	4·4	3·1	3·9	4·1
1953	3·8	3·0	3·5	5·1	3·9	4·3	4·1	5·0	3·7	4·7	4·1
1954	4·6	3·3	4·0	5·3	4·6	4·0	3·9	5·3	3·6	4·9	4·5
1955	3·8	2·7	4·4	5·2	5·2	3·7	3·7	5·2	3·2	5·1	4·9
1956	4·1	2·5	4·3	5·1	5·6	4·6	2·9	5·3	3·0	5·0	4·4
1957	5·2	2·9	4·6	4·9	6·1	5·2	3·3	5·1	2·8	4·4	4·1
1958	4·4	2·6	4·5	4·9	5·8	4·9	3·2	5·3	2·6	5·4	4·4
1959	4·8	3·0	4·3	5·4	5·8	4·7	2·9	5·2	2·7	5·0	5·0
1960	5·0	3·0	4·1	5·4	5·5	4·3	2·9	5·0	3·0	4·0	4·5

a Figures for 1950–60 exclude legal fees and stamp duties.
b For 1938 and previous years excludes farm and public residential construction.

INDEX

GEORGE ALLEN & UNWIN LTD
London: 40 Museum Street, WC1

Auckland: 24 Wyndham Street
Bombay: 15 Graham Road, Ballard Estate, Bombay 1
Bridgetown: PO Box 222
Buenos Aires: Escritorio 454–459, Florida 165
Calcutta: 17 Chittaranjan Avenue, Calcutta 13
Cape Town: 109 Long Street
Hong Kong: 44 Mody Road, Kowloon
Ibadan: PO Box 62
Karachi: Karachi Chambers, McLeod Road
Madras: Mohan Mansions, 38c Mount Road, Madras 6
Mexico: Villalongin 32–10, Piso, Mexico 5, DF
Nairobi: PO Box 4536
New Delhi: 13–14 Asaf Ali Road, New Delhi 1
São Paulo: Avenida 9 de Julho 1138-Ap. 51
Singapore: 36c Prinsep Street, Singapore 7
Sydney, NSW: Bradbury House, 55 York Street
Tokyo: 10 Kanda-Ogawamachi, 3-Chome, Chiyoda-Ku
Toronto: 91 Wellington Street West, Toronto 1

F. S. BROOMAN

MACROECONOMICS

Because of its relevance for public policy and the actions of Government, the theory of income and employment appears to many students to be the most interesting branch of economics. This book is an introduction to that theory. It begins by giving the essential definitions of National Income and Product, and sets out the analysis of income-determination in plain words without diagrams or algebra: this part of the book could be offered to complete beginners, though the remainder is intended for second-year students. Further chapters examine the relationship between output and employment; the factors determining consumption and investment; the connection between National Income and foreign trade, and the means by which the government can influence the level of economic activity. In these chapters, diagrams and algebraic symbols are used, but the mathematical methods are of the simplest. Prices, interest, inflation and other aspects of monetary theory are dealt with in a long penultimate chapter, and the book concludes with a survey of growth and cycle theories.
Demy 8vo   *Cloth 35s net. Paper 22s 6d net*

Edited by P. N. ROSENSTEIN-RODEN

CAPITAL FORMATION AND ECONOMIC DEVELOPMENT

STUDIES IN THE ECONOMIC DEVELOPMENT OF INDIA

This valuable series of studies arose out of the work of the India team of the Centre for International Studies of the Massachusetts Institute of Technology under Professor Rosenstein-Rodan. The authors are Professor Rosenstein-Rodan himself, Dr S. Chakravarty (the major contributor), Professors R. S. Eckaus and Louis Lefeber.

They represent a major contribution to method in planning for development which will be of importance to all those working in this field, irrespective of country. At the same time there is here the framework of the Indian Third Five Year Plan, and some of the papers which underlay it and are now released for publication.
Demy 8vo   *About 30s net*

GEORGE ALLEN AND UNWIN LTD